**From a happy childhood in the he
North East, David Hodgson becar
enigmatic footballers produced b**

Loved by teammates, but sometimes eyed
he walked the fine line between being a bi
influence - though it was all good clean fun to him.

He played under great managers, such as Jack Charlton and Bob Paisley,
uncompromising coaches, and starred alongside some of the giants of the
game including Kenny Dalglish and Graeme Souness.

With his eye for fast cars and stylish clothes, he cut the definitive image of
the 1980's soccer star, before developing a career as an agent.

His wild days behind him, he is now settled with a lovely family, and idyllic
life - save for one demon, a love affair with Darlington Football Club.

Now in his third spell as manager, this is the story of his battles with
colourful club owners, in his quest to bring glory to a struggling lower
league club.

Throughout his footballing life one quality has shone out: passion.

Instilled in him as a child, his fiery desire for success has burned throughout
his 44 years - a light that glows as brightly as ever as he continues to chase
dreams.

DAVID HODGSON
THREE TIMES A QUAKER

by David Hodgson

Speakeasy Publishing Ltd

First Edition
First published in November 2004 by Speakeasy Publishing Ltd, Haven Farm,
Lamb Lane, Firbeck, Sheffield S81 8DQ

Picture credits
Pictures taken from The Northern Echo and Evening Gazette archives
with additional pictures provided by Ted Blair, Andrew Wilkinson and
the Hodgson family

A CIP catalogue record for this book is available from the British Library

ISBN 0-9549015-0-9

Printed by Digiset Limited
William Street, Felling,
Gateshead upon Tyne

Contents

Foreword by Mark Proctor.

Acknowledgements

OVER the last three years I have lost count of the number of times people have asked me about all the issues that have taken place at Darlington FC.

In the nine years I have been involved with the club, I only wish I had ignored everyone!

But the desire to put it in writing was too strong to ignore.

I would like to say a huge "thank-you" to Ray Simpson of Radio Cleveland and Andrew Wilkinson of the Evening Gazette, for drinking me out of house and home while preparing this book for the last 10 months – they deserve every drop.

To Martin Gray, for every ounce of effort he put in during seven months of hell last season. He was magnificent, and now Darlo's future is in safe hands.

Mark Proctor has eventually arrived and I am delighted that it took only nine years to get him.

My father for taking so much time to teach me the values of life, and the hours upon hours of playing football with me.

My sister, because she left home at 16, then allowed me her double bed, and the biggest bedroom. And because she was everything you would want a sister to be.

I owe everything to my wife, Beverley, for giving me two beautiful, kind, caring little girls, Brogan and Alessia, and for making my life as perfect as it could get from October 88 to this current date. I know that nothing will change over all the years to come.

Thanks also to everybody else who helped with this book, especially Richard Simpson for his design skills, former Darlo star Norman Lees at printers Digiset, and Alan Wilkinson for proof reading.

Those who have helped and supported me throughout my career, both here at Darlington and previous clubs, are too numerous to mention, but my thanks extend to all of them.

Foreword by Mark Proctor

Hodgy is a one-off. We've been very firm friends since our days together as teenagers at Middlesbrough, and I have yet to come across someone who is so passionate, and yet has such a mischievous sense of humour.

It's no surprise to me that he has achieved so much in the game, but maybe it takes a certain determination after the occasion he dyed his hair blond and went to stay in a gay hotel!

Hodgy works hard and plays hard. Darlington fans already have an insight of his character from his three spells in charge, and if he thinks something isn't right, then he'll let you know.

I've always looked up to Hodgy, ever since he consoled me after I'd had a hard time from the fans one day at Ayresome Park. I could relate to him then, and still do now. We're very much on the same wavelength.

But he has a lighter side, which is demonstrated in this book. You'll realise why he was the "entertainments manager" at some of his clubs!

1

Early days;
"Why don't you
keep pigeons?"

I grew up in Gateshead, the heart of the Toon Army, with a slight disadvantage – I was a Sunderland supporter.

Not the recommended passion in that part of the world, just over the Tyne Bridge from St James' Park, the home of Newcastle United.

The luckiest day of my life was August 6th 1960 – it was the day that I was born at Queen Elizabeth Hospital, the son of James and Audrey Hodgson and the younger brother of Pauline, who is two years older than me. Since that day I have had 44 years of sheer happiness – well nearly 44.

When I was six years old, my parents moved the family five or six miles, which at the time seemed a world away, across town to the High Fell Social Club. There was a bungalow attached to the social club that probably gave the impression I was one of the rich kids, plus it was surrounded by acres and acres of woodlands, which I assume people thought belonged to my parents, but we were only tenants.

And next to this wooded area, which was a bird nester's paradise called the Dell, was a school that had two really good areas for playing football. The school field, directly behind the club land, was fenced in, but all we had to do was remove a couple of planks, and we had the perfect environment in which to play football, as good as you would get.

The Dell was like an adventure playground, there were ropes hanging from trees everywhere. I carved something on every tree – some had my initials on them, others had hearts with girls' initials as well.

Directly behind my pigeon loft was a nunnery, a huge old mansion. It had a sense of the unknown about it, because if ever one of we kids went into the grounds, the nuns would make every effort to catch us, and the story was that if you were ever caught, you would be thrown into one of their dungeons.

There was also a tunnel under the nunnery, and one of the big dares was to walk through the tunnel in the middle of the night.

I had a carefree childhood, but I had plenty of respect for my parents, who spent long hours running the club to make it a success.

The social club was the centre of the local community, although there were quite a few other clubs nearby. What was best about my parents' social club was that the car park had lights. Nothing special, just bright enough for youngsters to kick a ball around and have a game of two or three a side, or even just for me to practise on my own.

Bobby and Jackie Charlton were renowned for playing football against the back wall of their house in Ashington at all hours; I did it as well in Gateshead. I loved the game, and couldn't get enough of it, unless I was looking after my pigeons.

The social club was probably in one of the most exclusive areas of Gateshead, without doubt one of the silliest places to put a workingmen's club. One mile either side was the real working class areas, and just on the outskirts was probably one of the roughest parts of Gateshead, Hendon Road.

I was fortunate in that I got on well with both sets of lads in the neighbourhood. The lads from Hendon Road tended to be Newcastle fans, and on the other side of the High Fell was Sherriffs Hill, and the lads from there were mainly Sunderland fans.

I was a free spirit when I was a lad. I loved the outdoor life, and couldn't really stomach the discipline of school. What was the point of going to school and putting up with boring subjects like maths when I could be playing football with my friends?

I think I set a record for skipping school, although I'm not proud of it today, and I certainly wouldn't encourage my daughters, Brogan and Alessia, to do it because education is so important. In one school year I missed 45 – yes 45 – days. That was nine school weeks, which is quite a chunk.

I couldn't see the benefits of school then, because I was too busy wanting to be a footballer, preferably one who played in the red and white stripes of Sunderland. My ball skills improved immensely, though, and sometimes I still kick a ball against a wall. I miss the wall a bit more now.

I skipped school one day, and instead I was hanging around in the Sherriff Hill estate. My dad found out; presumably somebody had tipped him off. With my parents running a social club, they knew an enormous number of people, so obviously word had got around. Alex Ferguson's spies had nothing on Knocker Hodgson.

Anyway, my dad chased me, and I thought I was getting away from him by jumping over a fence. Unfortunately, my faithful red and white Sunderland scarf, which I always wore, caught on a fence post and dad collared me. He gave me a right hiding – but I still continued to skip school, and that cost me a place in one of the County football squads. I was unhappy about that at the time, but I couldn't seriously expect the school to put me forward if I wasn't there, could I?

There were three more lads, about my age, who also supported Sunderland in the middle of Magpie territory, Ted Cummings, Tom Hutchinson and Steve Nutter. But we had plenty of other good pals, like Sasa Little, Brian Corrigan, George Spriggs, Stephen Oakes, and the Leighton brothers, Brian and Stuart, most of whom supported Newcastle.

There was some real banter when it came to derby day at St James' Park. There was just as much passion, if not more, in those days than there is now. The build up to those games was fantastic, and there was so much anticipation in the air.

Sunderland and Newcastle fans worked each other at the schools I went to, Carr Hill Juniors up to the age of eleven, Beacon Hill until I was fourteen, and Elgin Senior High until I left just before my sixteenth birthday.

But our so-called friends from our gang did the dirty on us once. In theory they were schoolmates and we all stuck up for each other in school, but they pointed us out to the Newcastle fans when we were standing in the Gallowgate end one derby day. It's fair to say that we didn't exchange autographs when we clashed outside the ground, but I managed to get away without much problem.

I liked to keep myself fit. I didn't eat much, so I didn't carry much weight. I ran everywhere, because I had an enormous amount of energy. I didn't have a bike, because I didn't need one. I just loved running.

My sister was also a runner, so forgive the pun; I guess it ran in the family. She looked after me, just like all big sisters do, not just verbally, but physically as well sometimes.

My parents let me have plenty of freedom. They knew it was difficult trying to control a tearaway like me, so they imposed a 10.30 pm curfew, closing time for the club. If I was home by then, great, if I wasn't, then I was locked out. I quickly learned how to sprint, so you can understand how I won a few athletics medals later in life.

Living in a social club had its advantages. At the age of ten, I earned a few bob helping out behind the bar, pulling pints and keeping the place tidy.

I wasn't running the place on my own or anything like that, but my parents let me look after the snug, where a dozen or so regulars would go every night. I became quite good at pulling pints, and even now I can tell a good pint from a bad pint by the technique used by the person behind the bar. Ironically, I don't go into bars now; if I'm honest a restaurant is as good as it gets these days.

I knew which drinks people wanted, so as soon as they came into the snug, I had their drink ready for them, whether it was a pint, a short or a double. I never had a drink, though, and I suppose I never became a real drinker, despite living in a club!

I used to think I was Tarzan when I played in the Dell. It wasn't called the Dell after the old Southampton ground, but because lots of woods were called dells at the time. Tarzan was one of my heroes, because the black and white adventure films were shown regularly on television then. Johnny Weismuller was the star. He had a great Tarzan cry and could swing through the trees like a chimp, which after all was why he was called "Tarzan of the Apes". Here I was in a similar environment, able to act out all the drama I saw on the television.

I never found any apes in the wood, that's for sure. I would rig up rope swings by using ropes pinched from the back of the dray wagons, and sometimes I got a little too adventurous. I managed to break my arm three times by the time I left school just by falling from my homemade rope swings. We had competitions between ourselves, using rope swings to stick knives into the hearts we had cut into the trees.

Of course, being the fierce competitor I am, not wanting to lose at anything, I had to try to be the best, even against lads two or three years older and taller than me. I managed to win sometimes, but other attempts ended with a trip to the local hospital, and a shake of the head from my parents. I impressed the girls, though.

I admit I wasn't an angel when I was a lad, far from it. I was into all sorts, and if it wasn't for my dad's good relationship with the local police, then I could have ended up in court. There was many a time when the police came round late at night to have a chat and a late pint with my dad, on and off duty.

Some of my moneymaking schemes were quite legitimate. For example, I collected Littlewoods Pools round the nearby estates, and made a few quid every week especially with some of the syndicate coupons. I was on twelve and a half per cent of everything collected. I went tattie (potato) picking, but that was back breaking work. I got a few bob for it, and even now I get a twinge when I see people working in the fields.

I also sold a few bottles of beer which sort of fell from the dray wagon. Whenever there was a delivery, the driver would roll the barrels off the back of the lorry into our social club, and after he'd finished, he would always go into the bar for a pint. While he was enjoying his beer, I would loosen the strappings from around his lorry, pinch a bottle or two of Brown Ale, and then replace the crates.

I would sell the bottles at half price, and presto! there was some money to buy a ticket for the next Sunderland match.

That healthy relationship between dad and the police got me off the hook several times. When I was thirteen, I bought an air rifle and took it to the Dell one day. Another lad took his, and we had a shootout, just like idiots. We started firing at each other, and I actually hit him and he fell to the ground.

But instead of backing off, ruthlessly I kept on firing at him. I hit him another three or four times in the legs, and there was blood everywhere. I ran off, trying to avoid the repercussions that would surely come.

I was in Hendon Road when my dad found out from his spy ring. He got out of his car, whacked me around the ear, pushed me over a wall, dragged me back over again, and finally bundled me into the car. He drove me straight home, where the riot act was read out to me, both by the local sergeant and my dad.

There was talk of it going to court, but dad's relationship with the local constabulary got me off the hook, as long as I apologised to my friend, who was by now an ex-friend. I hid my air rifle, and believe it or not, I've still got it to this day, although I would never use it. It's on top of a unit in the utility room.

I knew how to rob the one-armed bandits by tilting them; I could empty the money boxes in telephone kiosks with a lollipop stick. I knew every trick in the book.

I sailed close to the wind on a few occasions. Bottles of spirits and beer went missing from the social club, and my dad sacked some of his staff, because he suspected them of pilfering.

But then word got around that I was selling bottles of beer and spirits, and of course my dad found out yet again. He took me round the side of our house, and asked me in a whisper; "Have you been stealing?" "Yes," I replied. "How long?" he asked. "A few months," I replied, apprehensively.

He didn't go ballistic, but he grounded me for a few weeks. I couldn't even go to football, which hurt me.

To give my dad credit, he re-instated everybody that had been sacked, and admitted to them that he was wrong. He made sure they knew I'd done it.

I suppose I was on the borderline between a troublemaker and a mischief-maker, and it was at that point when my dad found me a hobby to use up more of my time and keep me out of trouble – he hoped. And I'm really pleased he did.

"Why don't you take up pigeon-racing?" he said at the end of an exasperating day.

Pigeon racing was a traditional north east pastime followed by plenty of people who came into the club from the nearby estates.

It was a good suggestion. It gave me an interest outside of football and all the other activities – and in theory it would keep me out of trouble and calm me down. Well, nearly.

Dad bought me twelve pigeons, and we raced them in the Federation competitions. The Federation was the organisation you had to join if you wanted to race pigeons in organised races, and there were loads of members from all over Gateshead.

I wanted to add to my pigeons, so I went looking for skemmies – baby pigeons – down by the Quayside in Newcastle. Pigeons can't fly in the dark, so then it's easy enough to catch them.

I knew that the skemmies perched on girders under the Tyne Bridge at night. For those who haven't been down by the Quayside, you can actually walk underneath the Tyne Bridge, so Ted Cummings and I started climbing up the bridge girders to catch a good bird. I actually climbed all the way from the river level up to the road level on the Tyne Bridge – my head was actually touching the girder under the road – when suddenly a voice shouted; "David, get down from there!"

My dad appeared. How he knew I was there, I don't know, but I suppose word had got around again from his mates. I got another clip round the ear, but at least I hadn't fallen like I had from the swings in the Dell. If I had fallen, I wouldn't be writing this book now!

Pigeons were really time-consuming, and I took to them straight away, from six in the morning till late at night. I watched them feeding, mating and laying eggs, and I built up my knowledge of them in no time.

I skipped school as well. There were times when my dad and I were up at five in the morning to drive down to Boroughbridge in order to release the birds. My dad didn't mind me missing school in those circumstances.

My greatest moment as a pigeon fancier was when one bird, a chequered hen, ring number NE5533 – honestly, I didn't have a name for her – was fourth in a race from Beauvais in France.

When you consider that there were nearly four thousand birds taking part, it wasn't a bad achievement. In order to get a good finish, she had to return to the loft from France by 10.30 on the day of the race.

I waited in the loft for the bird to come. Ten o'clock came and went, so did quarter past, and I was just about to lock up for the night when the bloke from the next allotment pointed along the street, and here was NE5533 following the street lights back to the loft! What a great feeling it was when she got back into the loft and I just managed to clock her in before 10.30. I really felt I'd made it as a pigeon fancier, but I was devastated when we lost that bird, on a simple training session. The chances were that she'd hit an electricity cable, a fate that unfortunately wipes out a lot of pigeons.

My interest in pigeon fancying grew, and my parents even arranged a holiday in the Isle of Wight for us to go and visit a breeder down there.

We, or rather my dad, paid quite a bit of money for six birds – one of them had only one eye but believe me, its breeding pedigree was exceptional – but when you buy pigeons, obviously you have to make sure that they stay in their new loft until they get used to it. This usually takes four to six weeks. So we brought them home in a basket, and my dad built a new loft for them. He told me to finish it off by putting the roof on while he went and worked in the social club. He handed me a hammer and a box of nails.

A simple enough job for him, but it wasn't for me. I didn't use enough nails to hold the roof down, and long before the birds had settled in, a strong wind came along and blew the roof clean off. The birds escaped, and never came back, at least not to our loft, nor to their old loft in the Isle of Wight, or so the chap said. Maybe he had made double money on them!

My dad wasn't happy – you couldn't blame him really – and it was at that point when we both knew that I wasn't going to be a joiner. He was good with his hands, and was very skilful in woodwork and metalwork, that sort of thing. I was absolutely hopeless, and to be honest, I still am. I'm sure my wife, Beverley, will agree.

When I was eight or nine years old, I started collecting birds' eggs, something you can't really do nowadays. There were perfect surroundings around my own home, and my favourite area was Hawkswood (the Metro Centre is now built on it) although I even collected from villages as far away as Beamish and Kibblesworth. I had hundreds of eggs, and not just sparrows and blackbirds. I had partridges, wrens, skylarks, kestrels, and my dad gave me an ostrich egg, although I don't know for certain how he got it, maybe it could have been during his army days.

I was careful how I got the eggs from the nests. I tried not to disturb the nest – because if you do, the bird abandons it – and I used a straw to suck up the smallest of eggs (usually from a wren or a blue tit) and then pop it in my pocket. I only ever took one from the clutch, and would blow the egg myself.

I used my legs on other occasions to get away from the biggest eggs – those belonging to swans. The swans' nests were on an island in the middle of a boating lake in Saltwell Park. I used to hire a boat, row around the opposite side of the island out of the park warden's view, and then gamble that I could pinch an egg from the nest before the swan could see me.

Unfortunately, I took my collection to school, and I let somebody borrow it and I never got it back. Every egg was labelled and carefully packed in sawdust and cotton wool – I was heartbroken when the collection went missing.

My football career progressed nicely, although I still wasn't getting noticed by any football club. A chap called Seppy Thirlaway, who was going out with Ted Cummings' auntie, kept nagging me to go and join a club called Redheugh Boys Club, but it was well outside the boundary of safety, no more than a stone's throw from the side of the River Tyne.

My point was that because I wasn't from the Redheugh area, I was risking a good hiding from the lads in the area, but Seppy said that there were already two or three lads going there – one of them was Peter Harrison, who went on to become a professional and then an agent – and nothing had happened to them. To this day, Peter is a very good friend of mine.

Finally, I agreed, which was just as well, because if I hadn't gone to Redheugh, I can assure you that I would never have become a professional footballer.

Redheugh was a feeder club for Middlesbrough and several other pro clubs, and had all the facilities, presumably paid for by all these other clubs.

I was fourteen then, and I was thrust into a league for sixteen year olds, against clubs such as Dunston and Whickham, who challenged Redheugh for cups and titles. Peter made a point of looking out for me.

We trained every weekday night. The facilities were top quality, and the outlook under the likes of Evan Bryson, Seppy and another chap called old Tom, was very professional.

We trained indoors and outdoors. There were floodlit training pitches in a big schoolyard. We would warm up properly before training, and warm down afterwards. And if the weather was bad, there was circuit training inside the centre, which just about killed everybody.

Plenty of hard work, yes, but well worth it. Redheugh moulded me into a proper footballer, capable of playing at Football League level.

I was also playing more for my school, Beacon Hill. Everybody was scared of a technical drawing teacher there, Bill Newton, who would think nothing of clouting you if you fell foul of him. He was a no-nonsense disciplinarian.

He became our football teacher, and we all groaned. We thought he wouldn't have a clue.

But how wrong we were. He was just what I needed to push me along and encourage me to keep improving. He knew I had talent, and he made a point of helping me.

With a weaker teacher I may not have turned up for football, but because I was scared of him and what he might do if I didn't show up one day, I benefited from his

15

tuition. We won the inter schools' cup under Bill, which wasn't a bad performance at all. He wrote to me when I became manager of Darlington for the first time. It was great to hear from him again – and I made sure I replied!

Overall, I was a prolific scorer. I had plenty of pace, I was powerful, I had a good shot on me, and maybe a chip on the shoulder as well. I even gave a running commentary when I was playing.

Football was my life. I was in the company of some good players at school. One lad, Micky Williamson, who I still keep in touch with, was a class act. We followed each other through school. He was a centre back, and particularly a sweeper, a position that was unheard of in the late sixties and early seventies. The only sweepers in the game at the time were on the Continent, in Italy and Spain. We had nothing like it in the English game. Micky was very quick, very comfortable and had a few trials at clubs. But his problem was that despite his class, he seemed to have a bad game whenever there was a scout watching him.

I played for two teams at school. In the A team I was a striker, and I was goalkeeper for the B team, although as my schoolboy career progressed, I concentrated on my outfield game.

I can only remember one injury, a knee injury against a team on the other side of town. Instead of running like I usually did, I had to hobble three or four miles home. I was in a lot of pain, but did I get any sympathy when I arrived home? No, none at all. My dad didn't bat an eyelid.

Why should he? He played football in the old North Eastern League and in the Northern League for teams like Bishop Auckland, Shildon, Whitley Bay and Spennymoor. There was no sympathy in those tough days when he picked up injuries, so why should he show any to me?

Despite playing for various teams on Saturday mornings, I still managed to watch Sunderland regularly. A bloke called Tommy Brown, who has now passed away, ran a grocery shop a mile or so away from us.

We youngsters didn't realise at the time, but he was a ticket tout. He would get tickets from the players, and pass them on to his customers. If he had some tickets spare, he would pass them on to me, Ted and Tommy.

Some days I would go in his shop, and Sunderland players like Martin Harvey, Dick Malone, Colin Todd or Charlie Hurley would be in there, which I thought was fantastic.

Come match day, Tommy would always have tickets for my mates and me. He would give us a lift to the ground in his Ford Zephyr, driving the ten miles or so in the middle of the carriageway. Nothing could, or would, pass us. Mind you, there was one day when he suddenly suffered cramp, and he nearly ran the car into a brick wall!

I started watching Sunderland in 1966, when I was just six years old. I can't remember when exactly, but it was a friendly against Hearts.

In those days, the ground staff covered pitches with straw to protect the pitch from the frost – they're not allowed to now for health reasons in case the straw is contaminated with chemicals that get into cuts – and before the match, it was piled around the side of the pitch. I sat and watched the match on one of these bales of straw, and thought it was great, being so close to the players. I also admired the orange ball. I was hooked on Sunderland from that moment.

My dad accompanied me to matches until I was thirteen, when he was sure that I could look after myself.

I had plenty of heroes from that era. Jimmy Montgomery, later to join me at Darlington as goalkeeping coach, George Mulhall, George Herd, Billy Hughes, Joe Baker, Bobby Kerr were all heroes to me. My childhood idol was Colin Todd, because he reminded me of my mate, Micky Williamson. He was quick, composed and strong, just like Micky was.

And I must admit I was secretly delighted when I came up against Toddy as a manager, when Darlington played Bolton in the first round of the Coca Cola Cup in August 1999.

Another of my heroes was Charlie Hurley. I was at a presentation when I was a youngster, and Bobby Moncur, who was Newcastle skipper at the time, presented me with a trophy – and I asked why Charlie Hurley couldn't have presented it! When I told Bobby the story a few years later in a show on Century Radio, I'm sure he took the hump.

The year 1973, as all Sunderland fans will tell you, was probably one of the greatest in the club's history. A struggling Second Division team was transformed by the late Bob Stokoe, and started an amazing cup run that will live long in the memory of all their supporters. We beat Manchester City in a fifth round replay, and there was a phenomenal amount of interest when we drew Luton at home in the next round.

We were told that the tickets were going to be on sale at Roker Park a few days beforehand. The lads and I had the right vouchers which entitled us to buy tickets, and decided that we would miss school, and we told our teachers that we weren't turning up the following day.

They instructed us to be there, but of course we ignored them, went to Roker, and got our tickets.

I couldn't help taking my ticket to school to show it off, but the headmaster confiscated it as punishment for not turning up at school. He told me that I could only have it back if I promised, in return, to represent the school at athletics. At first I thought; no problem. Then he reeled off the events he wanted me to enter; the 100 metres, the 200, 400, 800 and 1500, plus the long jump and high jump. I agreed, got my ticket back, and later in the summer I won all the track events except the 800 metres in which I came second, and I was also placed second in both the jumping events.

As for Sunderland, we beat Luton 2-0 to reach the semi finals of the Cup. I saw the semi final win over Arsenal at Hillsborough, and it was Wembley here we come!

But I was destined not to go to the game. I managed to get a ticket for the final against Leeds at Wembley, but my mate Ted couldn't. I asked all over for another ticket, went to see Tommy Brown, rang the club, but I couldn't get another ticket at all, which wasn't surprising really given the amazing demand. I felt guilty about going without Ted, who'd seen all the games with me, so I sold my ticket, and made a few bob that eased the pain.

I watched the game on television instead, and in a town almost full of Magpies, there were only a few of us celebrating that night following the 1-0 win. Little did I know that the next time Sunderland got to Wembley I would be part of the team.

After Sunderland won the Cup, we were on holiday in Majorca and the Sunderland players flew out there as well for one of those end of season breaks. We saw them at the airport, but they were all looking bedraggled and half asleep, and I remember being a little disappointed that they weren't all happy and waving. It wasn't the image I expected, but when I was older I realised why – after all, they'd just won the Cup and had some celebrating to do!

Being a red and white fanatic, I wanted to sign for Sunderland, but the chance never came along, at least not in my early teens. I was really envious of a lad called Stephen Oakes, who was a striker two years older than me and was invited along for a trial. He did all right and they invited him back, but he drifted away from football and wanted to be involved in other things in life. I thought if only it was me. I know I would have been different if I was offered the chance, but I waited in vain for a call or a visit.

When I was about to leave school in the summer of 1976, my mates and I walked around the Team Valley estate, visiting companies, looking for jobs. I just went with them to give them moral support, because I wasn't interested in getting a job; I wanted to play football for a living. I never gave anything else a second thought.

The school entered me in six O levels, but I wasn't really interested in exams – and revising was definitely out of the question!

I liked RE (Religious Education), but I was useless at technical drawing, maths and woodwork. To be fair to my parents, who had seen my school reports, they never tried to persuade me to do anything apart from football. Maybe they knew they were wasting their time, maybe they were hoping that I would just fall out of love with football. I could have joined them in the pub trade, helping them to run the social club, but it was football for me.

You might laugh now, but I was a skinhead in my schooldays. The pop group Slade was very popular, because of their skinhead background, so everybody wore Doc Martens boots and shaved their hair off. Noddy Holder was my hero when the group first started, and I followed the trend. I went to the all night movies, 10pm through to 4am, and one night, while I was asleep in the cinema, somebody slashed my shirt with a razor blade. I knew it was only for a laugh, because if they had meant it, I would have woken up in hospital.

I had plenty of girlfriends at that time, and I was so besotted with one of them, that I nearly stopped playing football. The girl in question was Dawn Ritchie and her grandparents ran The Brown Jug, which was a real hard pub at the top of Hendon Road. We had a lot in common, because we both came from the same environment.

I knew that on the nights when I went to see Dawn at the Brown Jug, the bell rang at around 10.20 for last orders, and I had around ten minutes to get home. On the occasions when I didn't reach home before the last bell there, I had to climb in through the window, but I usually made it.

Several clubs watched me playing for Redheugh. Bolton Wanderers manager Alan Greaves offered me a four-year deal, two years as an apprentice, and another two as a professional, which was unheard of in those days.

Bobby Robson, who was at Ipswich at the time, wanted me to sign for them.

So I decided to have a look at Ipswich, who took quite a few lads of my age from the north east. In fact, this area was a real breeding ground for them.

Eight of us went down near Christmas for a fortnight's trial, which meant staying in a hotel down there and missing the festivities back home.

But youngsters being youngsters away from home, we missed all the home comforts, even though the hotel we were staying in was quite good. Maybe we were homesick, maybe we were missing our mates, I don't know. But we all decided that we would like to spend Christmas at home.

So just to speed the process up a bit, I decided to put some silver paper in the fusebox – I never was much good at DIY remember – and blew the hotel lights. They had no option but to send us home then! I held my hands up later, and Ipswich decided to wash their hands of me. Too much trouble, they said.

When Middlesbrough heard that I was possibly going to Bolton or Ipswich, they took more of an interest in me. Chief scout Jack Watson, who later joined me at Darlington, heard that I was maybe leaving the north east.

When I knew Boro were watching me in a game, I tried even harder than usual, and I must have done well, because Jack went back to Ayresome Park and told Harold Shepherdson, the assistant manager, about me.

Boro came back with a two-year apprenticeship offer, and I accepted it, even though Bolton had a four-year deal on the table. My dad thought I was mad, but I told him that I didn't like Bolton, it wasn't quite right for me. The other young lads at Bolton ran the club down when I was there, and whether that was deliberate or not to put me off, I don't know. It worked though! Ian Greaves tried to persuade me that the other lads would never make it in the game, whereas I had every chance.

So on my 16th birthday, August 6th 1976, my dad drove me down the A19, past Sunderland on the left, the club that I wanted to play for. A few miles further down the road I could see the coastline stretching into the distance. I could see the ICI chimneys at Billingham and wondered if I was doing the right thing. I would have to live away from home for the first time in my life, in a new environment that seemed a million miles away from Gateshead. That wasn't the first time in my career I would almost change my mind on the motorway.

Starting out;
"Hello, I'm from
Littlewoods Pools."

The trip to Middlesbrough to start my apprenticeship seemed to take ages. I'd been down there twice before to look around Ayresome Park with Geoff Woof and Redheugh Boys Club, but the journey had passed quickly with all the excitement. I honestly didn't know that Middlesbrough was just 45 miles down the road from Gateshead. The journey with my dad seemed to take forever.

When I said goodbye to my girlfriend, I told her I might not see her for a couple of years. It felt like I was leaving home for good, and it never crossed my mind that I would be back to Gateshead many times.

I asked my father what advice he could give me, but it was straight and simple just like it always was. "If I advise you which club to sign for, and it goes wrong, you will always feel that I gave you the wrong advice and possibly not forgive me. As simple as that." I'm sure he wanted me to go to Bolton because of the four-year offer. He was just like any parent seeing their son leaving home at sixteen, he wanted what he thought was best.

But I was made welcome at Boro straight away – unlike Bolton – so that was it. My decision was the right one.

I quickly met and got to know and like my new teammates, living in a hostel environment, and that made the settling in a lot easier.

Looking back, it was a great environment in the Medhurst Hotel. Harold Shepherdson, who was England trainer in the 1966 World Cup and later became the chief executive at Middlesbrough, was way ahead of his time in his thinking on youth policies.

The Medhurst was huge. There were 21 bedrooms in it – although there was no number thirteen – and was ideally situated in a beautiful leafy suburb in Linthorpe Road, only ten minutes walk or a couple of minutes drive from Ayresome Park.

Among the players in the Medhurst were Stan Cummins, Peter Johnson, Alan Willey, Tony McAndrew and Billy Woof. All of these players came through the youth system and into first team football, which made me all the more certain that I'd made the right decision. Other players were local and still lived at home.

Little Stan went out of his way to help me settle in, probably due to the fact that he was Sunderland through and through, just like me. Billy was also a massive help. Coming from my hometown of Gateshead, I liked him even more when he gave me several pairs of boots to start my football career with.

I took to Stan in particular, though Alan Willey was great too, and he gave me a couple of pairs of boots when he had finished with them.

Like every household in which there are twenty young lads, there were one or two nutcases. The two that spring to mind are Alan Ramage and Gary Briggs. They were at their worst when everybody else was asleep. They used to sneak into rooms late at night, pulling blankets and pillows over you and then giving you a good old thumping before disappearing.

Those kinds of incidents usually took place in the early hours of a Wednesday morning after a reserve game when they arrived home. Obviously, getting back at that time to the hotel through the fire escape indicated they didn't have much pulling power with the girls. But even though they had shortcomings and were real arseholes, they were both really good lads.

The club later sold the Medhurst, which I feel was a backward step.

It was run by Mrs P, an elderly lady with steely grey hair, a nursing background, and a nasty streak if anybody crossed her. She was the lady who was going to take care of my early football career.

Mrs P positively terrified us. She ruled with an iron fist, and anybody who stepped out of line was always reported to Shep.

She had her own private room, and you were very rarely allowed in. At weekends after our Saturday morning youth game, a lot of the lads would go home until Monday morning. If you couldn't afford to go and were left on your own, Mrs P would make you a cup of tea, but she never really chatted in depth.

Taking into consideration that when I was living with my parents I was able to return home at 10.30pm, that arrangement totally disintegrated under Mrs P. Doors were locked at 10pm sharp, no keys were handed out unless you were a pro and over eighteen, and even that was done reluctantly and begrudgingly.

She had such power, that even the older players didn't have the balls to get a key cut and hand it on. They probably knew best, having had two or three years' experience of the Medhurst!

Jean and Moira were two ladies who made sure that the Medhurst was kept in tip top condition. Having to clean and look after all those rooms, which were regularly trashed by young players, was no easy task. On top of that, they were first class chefs – or maybe that should be cooks. Cheese on toast with beans wasn't a particularly difficult task to do for lunchtimes, but believe me it was the only dish the players wanted!

Weekends in the Medhurst were for those who had blown their money during the week on darts or pool. It was a bit like Home Alone for me, but the problem was you had to share the weekend with Mrs P.

On exactly the same day as me, a little ginger-haired left sided player called Billy Askew arrived at Boro. I had already met Billy, who came from Fencehouses, once before in a practice game, but didn't really know him.

We hit it off straight away, as we both came from the same background. Both of us had aggressive attitudes, were streetwise, and had a big desire to make it in the pro game. But there was one big difference – he was a Magpie through and through –and whereas the Boro grew on me the longer I stayed and my passion towards Sunderland waned, Billy remained a staunch Newcastle supporter.

There was no red blood in his body, and whenever he wasn't involved in a youth game or the first team was away, he was in the middle of the Leazes End at Newcastle.

So deep was his love for Newcastle, that Billy found himself in the worst possible scenario when Middlesbrough faced Newcastle at Ayresome Park in season 1976-77 in the old First Division.

At that time, Newcastle had an air of nastiness about them (which has now thankfully disappeared) and on this day, a group of thirty or forty Newcastle "fans" managed to get into the Holgate End, and eventually fighting broke out.

The fighting was clearly visible from the main stand, and after a ten or fifteen minute brawl, the police managed to gain control and pulled out the Newcastle fans individually.

From where I sat in the main stand, looking towards the right hand corner flag, there was a gate through which you could get into the Holgate End.

And through that gate, came Billy wearing Newcastle scarves on both wrists, and another tied around his forehead, escorted by two policemen. He'd been arrested for fighting!

Unfortunately, he had the biggest mop of red hair possible, and there was no escaping the fact that it was him. And there was no escaping the glares he got from the Boro dugout either when he was frogmarched past.

Shep went ballistic. Billy went through the grinder, and if it wasn't for his great talent, then he would have been sacked. Shep, naturally, was never going to tolerate conduct like that, and he was severely reprimanded.

When you have twenty sportsmen together, then their competitive nature is always going to come out. Every night we competed at pools, darts, snooker and card games. It always turned nasty and yours truly usually won because I knew all the tricks from my days at the social club. It was second nature for me, so I was on to a winner every time.

I was the richest kid in the Medhurst, taking money for fun, not just from the other apprentices, but first team players as well. At least that was how I remember it.

Although there were days when I was more than happy to lose at cards. On those occasions, the loser had to go down the local sweet shop with a list of twenty orders, which was a huge memory task, depending on which greedy so and so wanted what.

But a harder task was trying to remember everything while chatting up the most gorgeous looking girl behind the counter. Everybody tried to lose, even when it was raining, and the trip to the shop was always a delight.

But clearly she wasn't impressed by any of us, because as far as I can recall, she didn't go out with anybody from the Medhurst.

Sweets were sugar, and sugar was energy, so they did us no harm. But generally we had a good diet. We were always given a healthy breakfast, and always returned to the Medhurst for lunch. The last job before lunch was to put all the kit in the laundry room. We would then run home to the Medhurst, have lunch, and run back.

There was always one ordeal that every apprentice had to go through – the initiation. A new apprentice was always initiated at the ground, an ordeal that was much worse than a late night beating.

We were pinned down, stripped, and covered with boot polish from head to toe. And I mean covered. It was a hell of a job getting it off, and you would be trying for days. You couldn't reach your back, so you had to rely on your mates to clean you up. We were also whipped with wet towels, which was very painful, especially when you had no clothes on and were pinned down on the ground.

If you were very lucky, one of the professionals who had a car would give you a lift to and from the Medhurst, but more often than not, you had to walk.

With so much tomfoolery going on, walking between the Medhurst and the ground was always a dangerous thing to do. It wasn't safety in numbers, it was quite the opposite.

There was a 400-yard built up area at the top of Linthorpe Road down to Ray's café that was good for ambushes. There was many a time when a player was suddenly jumped on by his mates, stripped completely naked, and left standing in the middle of a busy shopping street. It was impossible to stop five or more lads from jumping on you and leaving you stark bollock naked in front of a crowd of shoppers.

It only happened to me on one occasion in my first year. Some apprentices would keep on walking starkers to the ground when it happened to them, but instead I quickly backtracked towards the Medhurst, climbed over a fence, and pinched a towel off a washing line to cover myself. I never returned the towel!

When we returned in the afternoon to the ground after morning training there were all sorts of mundane jobs to do. Among them were forking the pitch, sweeping the terracing, and painting the seats. So I had to learn to be a jack-of-all-trades.

This was the side of the apprenticeship that the public and your friends didn't see. The pros' kit had to be collected up, put in the correct baskets and taken to the laundry room.

Boots had to be cleaned, polished and made to look as good as new for training the following day.

The changing rooms had to be immaculate with the bathrooms spotless. It used to take ages to clean the terracing and the stands, and sometimes they had to be done twice a week if there had been a midweek home game.

All this was carried out under the eye of the head apprentice who would earn the title having been the best first year apprentice.

Having the title meant that you had a different job to the others, but if you didn't rule with an iron fist and jobs weren't done properly, then the responsibility fell on your shoulders, and you would be bollocked by coach John Coddington. Plus, you had to be physically strong to get all the work done.

So I made sure that I won the title during my first year, at all costs.

And some of the lessons we learned were harsh. The hardest task of all was at the end of the season when the pitch had to be prepared for the following season.

The summer of 1977 was a hot and sunny one, and Billy has got the scars to prove it. Suncream didn't really exist in those days, and certainly wasn't handed out for free by the club. With his shirt off and the sun beating down on him, Billy suffered badly with the worst burns on his shoulder and back that I have ever seen.

The club physio advised him to soak himself in a vinegar-soaked towel that would ease some of the pain.

But when we went home on the X1 bus that weekend, I made sure that I sat a good dozen seats away from Billy. The smell was very unpleasant, and he got plenty of strange looks from the other passengers as well!

Once our tasks were finished for the day, out came the ball and all the apprentices, first and second year, played on the small concrete car park between the main stand and the Holgate end.

Two turnstile doors became a goal at one end, and huge wooden gates were the goal at the other. My team was more than capable of looking after itself when the games got rough, which was usually every day. The team usually consisted of me, Billy, Australian Craig Johnston, Welshman Andrew Johns, Graham Normanton from Hartlepool and another lad called Alistair, who quite simply loved himself. Alistair was more concerned about keeping his good looks, rather than getting stuck into the second year pros, who consisted of Charlie Bell, Peter Johnson, Davey Frame and the one and only Gary Briggs.

Gary usually had great pleasure of smashing you into the wall, or pushing you into the turnstile gates. It was usually Craig who suffered most.

Craig arrived at the Medhurst one night completely unannounced, direct from Australia, and was a sight none of us had ever seen before.

Mrs P introduced him as a young kid from Australia. He had a Rolf Harris type accent right out of the bush, and hair to match Bob Marley's. He had blond streaks running through every twinklet of hair, and carried a skateboard underneath his arm. He didn't look like a footballer, or appear as if he had any sort of potential to be a footballer. Big Jack Charlton said: "He'll never make a footballer as long as I've got a hole in my arse."

We took the piss out of him something terrible, but if ever there was a player who had such determination to become a pro, then it was Craig.

To start with, he'd paid his own airfare from Australia, and had only been playing for a couple of years – the rest of us had been playing since the age of six. Instead, he'd spent most of his time surfing.

But he had plenty of talent underneath, and he worked harder than anybody I'd ever seen, before or since. After the working day and the game under the stand had finished, then Craig would spend hours on his own kicking the ball against a wall, and he would only just manage to get back to the Medhurst before the 10pm deadline.

One day, a foot of snow had fallen overnight, and we thought there would be no way that we would be able to train at Hutton Road. We even had problems getting to the training ground because of all the snow.

But when we got there, we found the training area all compacted, because Craig had got up at 6am, gone straight there for training, and virtually flattened the snow. The pros and the apprentices were gobsmacked. He was clearly determined to make the grade as a pro, and he succeeded. He got into the first team, and a couple of years later was transferred to Liverpool. He's now working for Adidas, living in Southern Ireland, and is responsible for the Predator boot.

After long sessions of training, the only real escape was to the local cinema. Billy Woof and I must have gone to the pictures more than a dozen times in the afternoon and evening to see Saturday Night Fever, a film which was all the rage in the late seventies, especially in the discos. I loved that film, and fancied myself as John Travolta. Billy and I knew all the dance routines to a T, resulting in one of the funniest ever scenes at the Medhurst, and believe me, there were quite a few.

We moved all the furniture in the big lounge back against the wall, pulled the curtains along, put the music on and started giving fifteen of the players a crash course in the dance routines, all the spins, the hands in the air, the walks, the lot. In that unlikely line up was David Shearer, Tony McAndrew, Billy Woof, Alan Ramage, and Twinkle Toes himself, Gary Briggs.

There were arms and legs everywhere in the effort to dance to the music. And we spent so much time on the routine, that we nearly forgot about a training session that afternoon. Fifteen John Travoltas walked down to Ayresome Park that day. There were some strange looks from passers-by, and from the rest of the players when we walked into the ground!

In 1977, Mrs P announced that she was leaving the Medhurst after ten years, and in her place Walter and Violet Frost took over. They had a son, David, who was the same age as most of us. What a daunting prospect he must have faced moving into the hotel with his parents.

But because there were no restrictions on his social life, he integrated very well, and even at one point joined the Briggs and Ramage crew.

Walter and Violet were a quiet couple, rather strict, but more understanding than Mrs P, probably down to the fact that they'd brought a son up who was no angel.

The hotel was just the same with Jean and Moira doing their jobs, and Violet doing the menial tasks. Walter didn't seem to have any role at all, apart from taking players to the ground if they were late or had slept in.

Mind you, Walter deliberately took his time, and on many occasions it would have been quicker to run than wait for Walter. He had a mustard coloured Morris Marina, which if you were lucky, would go over 20 mph.

I got on really well with Walter and Violet. They were good to talk to, and they would listen if you had a problem. I did, however, upset them on one occasion.

One Saturday afternoon, I managed to get hold of Walter's copy coupon for his football pools, and worked out exactly which games he was hoping would finish as draws.

In those days, the only way to find out football results was by watching Grandstand on BBC or World of Sport on ITV, or listening to the radio. There was no teletext or Internet then.

At around six o'clock, I phoned their private number from the phone in the lobby, and put on a Scouse accent.

"Good evening, I'm from Littlewoods Pools and I would like to congratulate you on winning the pools," and reeled off their numbers as score draws.

Walter and Violet ran into the room where the players were, announced that they were leaving, and shouted; "We've done it! We've done it!"

Because they were so excited, I couldn't bring myself to tell them immediately that it was a wind up. It was only at about ten in the evening, when Match of the Day was starting, that the rest of the lads forced me to tell them.

And even then, it took ten minutes to convince Walter that he hadn't won, because he'd been so taken in by the call from "the bloke at Littlewoods Pools."

But that was innocent fun compared with another escapade that nearly cost me my career.

I assumed that Walter and Violet had forgiven me, but I still had to make sure that they didn't have the opportunity to get their revenge. But for me, the entertainments manager, it was impossible.

By this time, I was more settled than ever into life at the Medhurst. There was an election in the autumn of 1977 and naturally from my background on Tyneside, I was a strong Labour supporter.

Charlie Bell and Peter Johnson were Conservatives, especially Peter, coming from Harrogate. After a long and heated discussion one night, I decided to trash their rooms. I went into the kitchen, found a bottle of liquid gunge, and sprayed it on their beds and furniture. I must have caused hundreds of pounds worth of damage.

But this was payback time for Walter and Violet, the moment they'd been waiting for. In no time at all, Shep was at the front door and ordered us all into the main room.

No one admitted it, so Shep said that it would be sorted out in the morning at the ground. As a group that had bonded well together, I didn't think anybody would let on.

Shep called us all into a meeting in the changing room in which there was a pair of Adidas boots on the table. The numbers on the boots were taped over and nobody knew whose they were – though I had a feeling they were mine, even though everybody wore Adidas boots.

Shep asked again who had done the damage, but nobody came forward to admit it. He told us how the club had bought the Medhurst and that we must respect it.

Then suddenly he walked over to the table, picked up the boots and hurled them at me. Everybody went quiet, and I can still hear Shep shout; "Remove the tape from the back of those boots now!" Sure enough they were mine, number 27. He cleared everybody else out of the room and gave me a horrendous rollicking, far worse than the one I'd received from the police officer years before.

He told me that if I didn't put in the best performance of my life at Everton in the forthcoming FA Youth Cup tie, I would be sacked. I was right on the borderline.

We lost at Everton but I ran my socks off from the first minute to the last. Everton had a big centre half who was with the England youth set up, but he couldn't get near me.

Afterwards Shep pulled me aside and told me I had saved my bacon. I went on being the prankster, but ditched the materials.

By the time I was seventeen I was head apprentice so I kept things tidy. I remember looking after Tony McAndrew's room while he was away in America.

He was immaculate. Every T-shirt was beautifully folded and in its place.

You wouldn't dare look in one of his drawers because he would have known when he got back.

In my first year, I looked after the senior players such as Graeme Souness, Stuart Boam, Jim Platt, Pat Cuff, Peter Brine, John Hickton and Alan Foggon, and in my second year, I looked after the coaches and the physio, Jimmy Headridge. Jimmy always wore white – top, shirt, shorts – and every item of clothing had to be in pristine condition.

He left the Boro to become chief physio at Manchester United, and sadly lost his life to a heart attack. He was a real hard taskmaster, and I made sure I never crossed him.

Billy Askew looked after the other lads. In those days only the shirts were numbered, so it was always a free for all between myself and Billy to make sure we got the best shorts and socks available to keep in the good books of 'our players'.

The best way to do that was for me to get to the ground a bit earlier than Billy. The trouble was that he also knew the best bet was to get there before me. We ended up both arriving at about 7.30 and clambering over the wall to get in. It was a race, and there was often a fight over the kit.

But it was no bad thing, because it was a reflection of our enthusiasm to do the best job we possibly could. They were the standards we set. We wanted to impress. Besides, the better the job you did for your pros, the better chance there was of a bonus at Christmas.

But while it was important to keep in the good books of the senior players, it was even more necessary to impress the coaches. I respected Shep enormously. As England coach I knew about him before I joined the club. To work with the man who had coached the England World Cup winning team of 1966 was quite something. In

27

a way I was in awe of him before I had even met him.

In the case of John Coddington, I grew to respect him. Mind you, I had an early lesson. I was a Sunderland fan, and while I was later to love the Boro, that was a gradual thing, and in my youth Sunderland was the only team for me.

One afternoon when Boro had lost, I heard that Sunderland had won. "Yes" I shouted in the corridor outside the dressing room. Codd pinned me against the wall and, and with his face in mine, threatened to break my nose, saying: "If I hear you utter any words of support for Sunderland again, your life won't be worth living."

Fair warning. I made sure he never heard me do it again.

But Boro gradually took over my life, and I often supported the lads from the Holgate End when I was not playing. Even when I was with Liverpool, I once went in the Boro end to cheer them on.

However, I was not only a young prankster, but also a footballer in the making, and playing the game was my first love. But I had a problem in my first year as an apprentice, because my body changed, as it does at that age.

It affected my play because I was picking up various injuries, and even if it was painful I kept it to myself, which was a mistake. I remember playing badly in a cup-tie at Hull, because of it. We got away with a replay, but Bobby Murdoch, the youth team manager, lost the plot with us and was fuming.

We won the replay, but I was still not at my best. Hull had two huge twins playing at the time, both nutcases. One of them in particular gave me a hard time, and I thumped him in the tunnel at the end of the game.

Bobby heard about the incident, but didn't know who had done it. He pulled us all in. I admitted it. Bobby said I was lucky the referee hadn't seen it. He praised me for being honest enough to own up, and I suspect that he admired me, for having the nerve to do that to a hulking great brute of an opponent.

Muscular strains, particularly my hamstring, became more and more regular, because I was playing reserve games and junior games. I went through "Deep Heat" by the bucketful – I rubbed it on every night, and then stretched regularly in my room at the Medhurst to try and cure the problem. Fortunately Jimmy the physio heard about my injury, and because of his excellent rehabilitation programme I was able to fully recover and put it behind me.

Players didn't want to admit they had problems because there were some tough games in the Northern Intermediate League, and playing through the pain barrier was commonplace. There were some tough lads around. Two in particular played for Barnsley, David Speedie and Mick McCarthy, and went on to become household names. I'm not surprised they did so well. They had a fantastic attitude and you always knew you had been in a game when you came off the pitch having played them.

We had been brought up to give as good as we got. On Thursday nights I trained with George Wardle, who was Durham Schools coach, an incredible man who had the ability to balance anything on his head, shoulders and feet. He was an advanced

Football Association coach and realised the value of good balance. He had mastered it, and it enabled him to do all his tricks.

We had training sessions in the car park, usually after dark with the lights on. He used to whack players with a stick if they didn't do things the way he demanded. You could never get away with that these days, but it was typical of the times, and we accepted it without any complaints.

We would play statues to improve our balance. You had to stop the second he shouted, and remain motionless. Sometimes he would shout "stand", other times "sit". If he barked out the order to sit just as you were passing a puddle, you had to sit right in it. If he saw you ease to one side to avoid the water, out came the stick. You then got a whack and still had to sit in the puddle. I guess the idea was to make a man of you. I got the impression he wanted lads to stand up to him.

It was something I always remembered. Many years later when I was Darlington manager we had an excellent youth team coach, Stuart Gibson. If he had a fault, however, it was that he was too soft with the young lads. He was extremely understanding and treated each of his players individually. The young players respected Stuart enormously, so I made a decision that the third year apprentices and first year pros would work with former Sunderland keeper Jimmy Montgomery.

Jimmy is older than me and probably had an even tougher football upbringing. He gave the young Darlington lads a hard time, but one or two, like Mark Kilty and Graham Liddle, did stand up to him. There was something of George Wardle in Jimmy. As a manager you need different sorts of characters on the coaching staff, because different people instil different qualities in impressionable young players. I have taken something from many of the coaches I have worked with and under, and George and Jimmy definitely had qualities that came in useful – not that you appreciated that as a teenager with a wet backside in an exposed car park on a chilly night.

In my first year at Boro I struggled to settle in and do myself justice. I was still very much in my old world and perhaps didn't fully appreciate what I had around me.

Take the players for example. I was with a club that had players of the stature of Graeme Souness, David Mills, David Armstrong and John Hickton. Names that rolled off the tongue for every Boro fan.

But being a Sunderland fan, the likes of Billy Hughes and Dennis Tueart were my heroes. One of my worst youth games for Boro was against Sunderland. My concentration on that day was very, very poor, and I realised that concentration was one of the qualities required in order to be successful. A lot of stick came my way, especially I recall from Alan Ramage, after that game.

In that first year I couldn't stay out of trouble, had injuries, and could not come to terms with being in a professional environment. If I had taken the earlier option of joining Bolton I think it would have been curtains. My career would have been over before it started.

But Middlesbrough was closer to home and I was surrounded by people who were keen to help me. I remember one training session, when I couldn't cross the ball properly from a wide area. With one attempt, I even hit a greenhouse on some adjoining land to the Hutton Road ground where we trained.

Codd lost the plot big style. He marched some distance towards me, gradually getting closer and closer, and shouted; "It will be easier for you to pack the game in and get your P45."

He made me look like a fool. I trudged away to do as he said by leaving the training ground, but my teammate Michael Scannell ran after me and stopped me in my tracks.

"Hodgy, don't listen to what he's saying. He was a centre half for Huddersfield Town, he couldn't even put a cross on Spot the Ball, never mind cross the ball from a wide area. Walk off the pitch now, and you'll be giving in to his bullying." Michael was right, it was a case of knuckling down and concentrating on a little bit of extra care and thought on the deliveries. It was as simple as that – all I had to do was concentrate.

Michael was a supremely talented Irish teenager, who looked set to be the next George Best. Sadly he was badly injured in a car crash and never fully recovered the talent he had.

We had a big Irish contingent at that time. There was Jim Platt of course, and Alex McGarrity, a big Northern Ireland centre half, who our manager Jack Charlton adored. Unfortunately, big strong player though he was, Alex could not come to terms with the problems in his homeland.

Once, at the height of the IRA conflict, the Medhurst phone rang, and when Mrs P called Alex and said it was for him, he froze, because he thought there had been a family disaster such as a bombing or shooting.

Having a big Irish contingent at the Medhurst made it easy for us to understand that a member of someone's family back in Ireland could be caught up in a bombing or a shooting. We knew that life was difficult for the Irish lads due to the problems back in their homeland and we respected that, never taking the opportunity to wind them up with phone calls or anything of that kind.

Alex couldn't keep the problems back home out of his mind, so after discussions with Jack, the club agreed to terminate his contract on condition that he could go back to Ireland, but couldn't return to England as a professional, unless it was with Boro. He went back to Ireland where he went into the roofing business. It was a great shame, because I could tell that all the coaching staff really rated him. But I guess unless you are brought up in that environment of division and hatred, whether it's over religion or anything else, you can never really understand.

Of course we had other excellent players who never made it for one reason or another. It's a precarious business and talent alone is not enough. Never was, never will be. There is more to being a footballer than that. Lots of lads came and went. Some simply weren't good enough, and others you could have put your house on making the grade.

I remember a Richmond lad, Colin Blackburn. He scored the winner when we beat Manchester United 1-0 in the FA Youth Cup. I think he played only one first team game. As I recall every club in the country wanted to sign him. He was a top all round sportsman, a very good cricketer in particular. But he was another who fell by the wayside.

I could have quite easily been another who dropped out. I was homesick, and was advised not to go back to Gateshead every weekend. It was good advice. One of the things I have learned about the north east is that it doesn't change. Whether you go back to your roots a week later or after an absence of several years it doesn't really change. It's all there, so why rush back?

Billy Woof helped me a lot at that time, as did Stan Cummins. Stan might have been knee high to a grasshopper, but what a talent. And not just as a footballer. He was a great pool player – if only just big enough to see over the side of the table. He was one of these people that just seem to ooze technical ability whatever they turn their hand to. But what made him special was he was such a nice lad. No over-confidence, no arrogance. Just a down to earth, pleasant helpful lad, who was a good listener. It may be wayward, brash players who make the news, but fortunately there are people like Stan in the game as well.

I came through it all somehow, and the following season, 1977/78, my second year, my career began to take off.

I was older, wiser, and what helped me most was that I was quicker and stronger. I was excellent in the pre-season cross-country runs, and at the sprinting. Everybody wanted me to be in their team pre-season, especially for the running competitions. The young lads, myself included, were closer as a group, and some of us were on the fringe of the first team squad.

But we weren't all mates, laughing and joking together. A young powerful striker called Dave Shearer came down from Inverness. And he never spoke to anybody in the Medhurst for weeks. He was as hard as nails. Not the best looking lad in the world, but the way to win a woman's heart is through laughter, and it couldn't be any other way for Dave.

In his first game, which was against Chelsea, on April 4th 1978, he scored two goals – and that's when he became a human being.

One evening we went to a nightclub, called the Black Cat in Stockton. A lot of the older pros were there, but even they were amazed when Dave downed around twelve whiskies. When we left, Stan offered me a lift in his brand new Ford Escort Mark 3, which had a golden eagle painted on the bonnet. We were just setting off when Dave walked across from the club doorway and shouted for Stan to pull over. It was about the first time I had ever heard Dave speak. As Stan stopped Dave punched the bonnet so hard he buckled it.

Stan was only around 5ft 2in and Dave was a giant, but Stan was determined to get out of the car and scrap it out, but couldn't as Dave had his hand firmly across the door. When we saw the car in the training ground car park in full daylight next day, the extent of the damage was obvious. It must have been some punch to do that damage.

The club slapped an alcohol ban on Dave, but he deteriorated as a player. He lost weight, his body strength went, and he couldn't cope. So the club lifted the ban, and after that he always had a bottle of whisky in his room, but his football improved again.

By that time Walter and Violet were running the Medhurst, and one day Walter went up to Dave's room to ask – or tell – him to switch his music down. I don't know what tone of voice Walter used, but I vividly recall him tearing back downstairs, with Dave, whisky bottle in hand, chasing him.

Dave later became mates with Terry Cochrane. The two of them loved a drink, and became a pretty bad double act. Dave would bet on anything, even two flies crawling up a wall. He was always on the scrounge for money – and you could hardly refuse him. But whenever he won, which was quite often, he always paid you back.

When we were down in London to play QPR on their notorious plastic pitch, manager Bobby Murdoch allowed us to go out. Dave went to the greyhound racing at White City and won a fortune. He came back with a wad of notes, and straight away paid off all his debts, including the £100 he owed me.

A lot of the lads had a drink that night, and although it was not the ideal preparation for the game, we drew 1-1 and Dave scored.

There were a few eye openers for me, but I was learning, and one thing that helped was being made head apprentice by Bobby in my second year. I took that role seriously and was either nasty, or good at it, depending on your point of view.

I was forever laying the law down to Mark Proctor and Steve Bell, making absolutely sure they carried out their tasks. If, for example, one of them had to wash the floor, and it wasn't done to my satisfaction, I would sling the bucket of dirty water on the floor and make them do it again. "Get some clean water," I'd say. "How can you wash the floor when the water is that filthy."

I came to the end of the second year of my apprenticeship when I turned eighteen – a nervous time for any young football player hoping to be offered a professional contract.

Five of us were coming out of our apprenticeships, and we were all confident little Billy was the favourite to be signed on professional forms because he'd already been involved with the first team.

I was a regular in the reserves, more than holding my own, but looking back there were five or six senior pros in front of me, all strikers. Being as close to Bobby as I was, I took it upon myself to ask him if he could give me a little nod or a wink as to whether or not I'd be staying on as a pro.

Bobby replied; "Are you prepared to stay on as head apprentice, even if you're a pro?" It was a strange and cryptic thing to say, but when I sat down and took stock of what he had said, he was quite simply saying that I was turning pro.

Obviously the answer to his question was no, and all the young lads were delighted when I declined.

If driving the other apprentices was a bit harsh and arrogant of me, there was still another side to me. That of the stupid kid, who did things without thinking. It was all borne out of enthusiasm, but daft nonetheless.

One snowy day Billy Askew and I stayed back at Ayresome Park after finishing all our tasks.

There was snow two or three inches deep on the pitch, and the reflection from it provided enough light for us to see. So we took a ball out there, set two goals up and played for two hours, flattening all the snow in a wide area across the centre of the pitch. It froze overnight. The scheduled first team game had to be called off, and Shep, not surprisingly, went mad.

Looking back on it, you can see that it was obvious what might happen, but it never crossed our minds because we were happy to play football. However sometimes there was no way of guessing what would happen next.

When Bobby was coach and Big Jack was manager, Jack asked Bobby one day which two players could afford to miss training. "Hodgy and Gary Briggs," said Bobby. "They are fit enough to have a day off without doing any harm."

Jack called us over and stuck us in the back of his Landrover with two Labradors, which jumped all over us. The vehicle stank. We didn't have a clue where we were going. An hour or so later – at least it seemed that long with those dogs – we stopped high in the Cleveland Hills.

We got out and were handed big sticks. Jack got his gun out, and sent us off pheasant beating! We whacked a bush and up shot the pheasant. Jack was hopeless. He only got two, even though we must have sent dozens up.

He told us to give the brace to Violet as a treat, so at least the day provided one major talking point – the generosity of Jack Charlton, something very rarely witnessed. He was known for being tight. And it was true.

Big Jack once asked me to run him a bath. He said that if it were the best bath he had ever had he would pick me as a substitute for John Hickton's testimonial match. I ran him a bath of the perfect temperature, arranged the soap, got a towel warmed and ready and generally pulled out all the stops.

Jack had his bath, then commended me on it and said I had earned my place on the bench.

Unfortunately, it was a promise he didn't keep.

Another job I remember being given, I think by Jimmy Greenhalgh, was in an orchard in Great Ayton, where I had to shake all the apple trees to get the ripe fruit. I stripped the whole orchard and was given £5.

It may not have been the sort of task young footballers were normally asked to carry out, but it was all part of your education. An education that I thoroughly enjoyed.

Off the mark;
"Funky, Funky."

I was very soon on the fringe of the Boro first team, although I knew that I would have to be patient for my big break.

I longed for the day when I was in the first team and playing the game could take centre stage. As luck would have it my first game as a member of the squad was at Newcastle in January 1978, while I was in my second year as an apprentice. We stayed at the Five Bridges Hotel in Gateshead, right by where I used to live. It was the spot where I used to look after the wagons to earn some pocket money.

It hit me how far I had come since those early days, and I felt like a king as I jumped off the team bus. I wished that everybody I had known in my early years could have been there to see me. I even looked across to the bankies, where the pigeon lofts were, and wondered if my dad would be there.

Even though I didn't play, we won 4-2 to crown a fantastic trip.

I finally made it onto the pitch as a first teamer in September 1978. I came on as a substitute in a 2-2 draw at Nottingham Forest, David Mills and David Armstrong scoring for us.

Forest had tough duo Larry Lloyd and Kenny Burns at the centre of the defence, but I had no respect for reputations, and was fearless of so-called hard men. I went right through Burns in a 50-50 tackle, and set up one of the goals.

John Neal, who was manager by then, told the media that the game changed in our favour when I came on. I was so proud that I lived on adrenalin for days.

My full debut came in a 0-0 draw with Bristol City at Ayresome Park on November 4, 1978. I remember David (Spike) Armstrong, sometimes known to the lads as Einstein because he had an answer to every question, telling me that if I was to make my mark, I had to win over the "Chicken Run".

Coach Jimmy Greenhalgh told me I was up against former England defender Norman Hunter, and must not be intimidated.

I decided that in my first challenge I would smack the first opponent with my elbow whoever it was. It turned out to be Norman. I flattened him, knocking him out. One of his teammates, Gerry Gow, came up to me and said: "You had better make sure that for the next 85 minutes you can either run, or jump, because if I get near you, I will kill you." In no uncertain terms, I told him to "go and get f....d."

I had incredible enthusiasm, and ran non-stop all match. I even ran into one of our strikers, Micky Burns, at one point. "What the hell are you doing?" he demanded to know. I believe I won the respect of the Chicken Run.

Late in the season we played the return game at Ashton Gate. Norman remembered the earlier incident, and as he came up to me before the match I feared a severe warning to stay clear of him. But he said: "Let's strike a deal. If you don't run all over the pitch, I won't boot you up in the air."

I apologised, and he told me not to worry, because during my career I would often face that situation with central defenders. But he said that as the season was petering out, he didn't want to get the runaround.

I tried to make the most of every opportunity that came my way. In February 1979, we played at Arsenal, and Billy Ashcroft, who was a heavy smoker, had problems breathing – some of us thought he was having a heart attack.

As he was being stretchered off, Arsenal full back John Hollins ran over to him and repeated the words from a smoking advert, "Smoking can damage your health" which raised a laugh or two. But what had John Neal been thinking of, expecting Billy to man mark Liam Brady, one of the best midfield players in the country at the time?

With Billy off the field, it was left to me as substitute to mark Liam, who was technically very gifted. This was an opportunity I wasn't going to cock up. I followed Liam everywhere around the field, and although I was slightly embarrassed to say it, Liam didn't get a kick. I had the slight advantage of being quicker than him. That wasn't difficult, but that was the advantage I had. It was obvious by the reports the following day that I'd done everything asked of me in a goalless draw.

All the reports read well, but what did concern me deep down was that I might give the impression of being a defensive midfield player. That didn't concern John.

After the game, we went to Southend for a few days' break, and stayed in a hotel that was a little different – gay people ran it.

Whenever they got in the lift, we got out. Whenever they entered a room, we walked out. It just shows how ignorant you can be. By this time, Proc and I had been to the hairdressers' and had silver streaks put in our hair, so god knows what signals we were sending to the gay lads in the hotel.

It wasn't until the last night of our stay that all the players sat in the company of the hotel lads and everyone exchanged opinions. It was all quite interesting, and they were amazed that whenever we entered a lift, a room or a bedroom we all escaped. They made it very clear that they weren't interested in us, that they knew how gay people integrated and they had no intention of even trying to hit it off with us. From then on there was no embarrassment, although they did make a lovely comment about the blond streaks!

At first, Proc and I didn't play in many games at all together, but suddenly we became virtual regulars. It happened when Terry Cochrane fell ill. Proc had been booed off the previous week, even though he'd started the season well and scored a few goals. I left the stand immediately and went down to the changing rooms to have a chat with him. Probably because I'd been the head apprentice, I felt that I had the experience to explain that sometimes things don't go well on certain days, which in this instance was what had happened to Proc in front of goal. From that moment Proc and I hit it off, and when Terry went down with illness, it was our chance to make the most of it.

The game went well – I think it was at home to Everton – and we played quite a few games together over the rest of that season.

We both played in the next game and for around ten after that. It was from March 10 to April 17, 1979. We went unbeaten, staved off relegation, and it was put down to our arrival as a duo. Proc scored a lot of goals – five I think in that run. The lads called him 'Johnny on the spot' because he always seemed to be there to pop them in.

Proc was a local lad from a big family, and had more aunts and uncles than I care to remember. Everybody from Cargo Fleet to Ormesby knew who the Proctors were. No surprise then that every presentation that was done for a couple of seasons in the Middlesbrough area was done by Proc and me. From visiting sick fans in hospital, to speaking at boys' clubs, workingmen's clubs and social clubs, you name it, we did it. We didn't mind, and didn't refuse anybody.

From then on, I was Boro through and through, and my love for Sunderland slowly diminished. The following season, 1979-80, we became regulars together. David Mills moved on to West Brom, which opened the door for me, and I played all but two games that season, missing the games at Derby and Manchester City. Proc only missed four.

I made the decision near the end of the 1978-79 season to move out of the Medhurst, and move in with my girlfriend Debbie Soppitt. She lived in a two up, two down terraced house near Ayresome Park, but it was a bit unfortunate as her parents were in the same house.

Her parents moved another single bed into Debbie's room, on the understanding that we would sleep in separate beds. Were they joking or what?

It was also during this time that I became extremely lethargic, and lost my sharpness and sparkle on the training ground. The club called in Lennie Hepple, a balance expert, to see if he could help me regain my sharpness and sparkle.

Lenny had followed me closely on an end of season trip to Spain, and was amazed at my enthusiasm to do everything at a hundred miles per hour. It didn't take him long to work out where the enthusiasm had gone, or so he thought.

He gave me some simple instructions. After training every day, I had to walk the length of Linthorpe Road, going up to people as if I was walking into them, and then suddenly move quickly to one side or the other. It was Lenny's way of getting the movement into my body by moving left and right with quick feet. Not surprisingly, that didn't go down too well with a lot of people.

It worked, but the answer was simpler than that. Bomb Debbie out and leave her house!

Next stop, the Proctor household. I mentioned my problems to Proc, and he suggested that I move in with his family and be part of a family lifestyle. That was an understatement. Already in the house were Marty and Micky, his parents, Geraldine, his older sister, then Proc, Patricia, Martin and Anne-Marie. They all lived in a three-bedroomed dormer style house on Ormesby Beck. The lads lived in one room, the girls in another, with Marty and Micky in their own room.

Just after I moved in with the Proctors, I lost my mum when I was eighteen. She'd been ill for a while, although I never asked what was wrong with her. I'd seen her several times in the fortnight before she passed away.

I was at home with my dad and the rest of the family. The phone rang at 5.45 one afternoon, and before my dad answered it, he said: "This is the call to tell us that your mum's died." Sure enough it was. "We'll be there in ten minutes," he replied.

I'd just bought a Rover 3.5, having just broken into the Boro first team, and on my way to the hospital, it suffered two punctures. So I didn't get there at the same time as my dad, and I never saw my mother again.

She never came to watch me play, but she always supported me in other ways. She once opened a bank account in my name and put £100 into it, which thirty years ago was a lot of money. She knew a tremendous number of people, and it was standing room only at her funeral. There was a massive turn out.

My first goal came at Queen's Park Rangers in its pre-Astroturf days on January 20th 1979. I came on as a sub when we had a corner. Not knowing where the hell to go, I took up a spot just outside the eighteen-yard box, mainly to keep out of the way.

Somehow from the corner the ball found itself at my right foot, so I slightly moved it to the right and with so many defenders between me and the goal, I had no option other than to bend it up and over the oncoming defenders. Within seconds the ball was nestling nicely in the queen's eye, the top right corner, giving keeper Phil Parkes no chance at all.

I turned with my finger in the air and ran back down the pitch shouting "funky, funky." I don't know why. I think it was the in saying at the time. I can clearly conjure up that goal in my mind anytime I want.

After that I thought I could do it all the time, and was forever doing it in training, until John Coddington said: "For Christ's sake will you quit that and join in with what we are meant to be doing." However, it was better to get a bollocking for that than for hitting the greenhouse as had happened some time earlier.

I was never a great goalscorer, and thought of myself more as an all-round forward, full of running, quite good in the air considering I had no great height, a good passer of the ball, but mainly a thorn in the side of defenders, never giving them a chance to dwell on the ball.

But I suppose even strikers who are not instinctive goal getters, have their day. Mine came with the hat trick I scored against Spurs at Ayresome, one with my left foot, one with my right, and the other with my head. Two were in front of the Holgate fans. I've still got the match ball, signed by all the team.

Spurs had a good side too, with the likes of Graham Roberts, Garth Crooks, Ossie Ardiles, Ricky Villa and Steve Perryman playing that day.

After the game, it was normal practice for any player who had scored a hat trick to meet the press, but in all honesty, it was something I could do without, especially as I wanted to get away from the ground and go out with the lads.

The only pressman I wanted to speak to on that occasion was Jackie Milburn.

The Newcastle legend was a sports writer on the News of the World, and had taken time out a month or so previously to explain to me about showing a little more composure in front of goal.

I managed to get a message to him to meet me in a quiet part of the ground. I thanked him for the good advice he'd given me only a few weeks earlier. I assured him that I had taken everything on board, but somehow I felt that I wasn't going to be the great goalscorer he thought I would be.

He was a lovely man, very helpful, modest about his own success and thoughtful. How could you help but like and respect him?

On that particular day in my career I understood what it felt like to be Jackie Milburn. Everything I touched flew into the net. The difference between us was that it was a one off to me. He seemed to have spent his whole career in that mode. Later on in life, Doug Weatherall, a good friend of Jackie's and a fellow sports writer, gave me a video called "Wor Jackie". He knew of the friendship between Jackie and me, and felt that I should have an exclusive copy. Over a quarter of a century later, I still have it.

I prided myself on being a good winter player. I tended to come into my own in November and play particularly well through to February, although I like to think that I played just as well in the other months. I loved playing on cold nights in particular. When everybody else wore long sleeves I stuck with my short-sleeved shirt. I could run through mud all day because I had such stamina. When I think about it, I got player of the month awards between November and February, and I even got a manager of the month award in December when I was in my second spell at Darlington, so even as a manager, winter suited me.

I once scored twice at Wolves in the heaviest mud imaginable. It was March 1, 1980. You don't see pitches like that these days. One of the goals was a forty-yard lob over the keeper. Reporter Bob Cass caught up with me on the team bus afterwards and said that he had just witnessed the best display ever by a young player.

I scored seven league goals that season, third best in the club behind Micky Burns and Spike Armstrong, and one in the cup, away at Birmingham. That one was a bit special, because it was a good goal, devious, and I had to beat one of my ex-Sunderland heroes, Colin Todd, to score it.

The ball bounced between the two of us, and I lifted it over him with my hand. He stopped, as did the keeper, but the referee missed it and I volleyed the ball in. I always moan about referees these days, but I suppose that was one of the times when

I didn't get a raw deal.

Toddy went ballistic, demanding that the referee should book me, and proceeded to call me all the names under the sun. He was my hero, but there was no way I was going to allow him to give me dog's abuse. I gave him back as much as he gave me, which resulted in us both being lectured by the referee.

The name of the game was getting away with what you could. In the same game Archie Gemmill and Proc were lectured by the referee and booked. Archie, while pretending to pat Proc on the back in a friendly way, was actually pulling his hair. I spotted his little trick and went over to tell the referee what Archie was doing right in front of his goddamned face. Archie was a good player, but a nasty piece of work. If I remember rightly, he was called "the Poisoned Dwarf".

Frank Worthington played that day, and he was known as the king of fashion among footballers. When I saw him in a hotel, he said: "I know who you are. You're the pretender to my throne in the fashion world. But you still have some way to go." I had a good try at beating him!

We finished ninth in the first division that season, one of the best ever by the club. We beat Liverpool and also saw off Arsenal 5-0. We were just two players short of being a top of the table side. We needed another striker – though I don't know whether John Neal would have replaced Billy Ashcroft or me. I believe he tried to sign Argentinean Rene Hausman.

I felt we also needed a really top-drawer centre half. Tony McAndrew, Irving Nattress and Stuart Boam were all very good, but we maybe needed a really commanding player with great presence in that department.

However that Boro team had great strengths. Spike and Proc were excellent passers of the ball, never giving it away. Craig Johnston was full of running and scored his share of goals, while John Craggs and Stuart Boam were consistent defenders.

I could run and create goals, while Terry Cochrane had wizardry. Then we had Bosco Jankovic, who was often troubled by hamstring injuries, but when fit had the sort of skills British players didn't possess. He could protect the ball and drag it away from players in a manner very rarely seen.

Yugoslavs were just beginning to come over to England then, and he was a big part of our team. He had no great pace or aerial ability, but ball control was his forte. He was a lovely man and very intelligent, a lawyer as well as a footballer. And he was smartly dressed too. He always carried a little leather bag under his arm, and held his cigarette in a holder. He and Jim Platt were particularly close. I was very sad when I heard that Bosco had died after returning to his homeland. I assumed he had been killed in the war over there, but later learned that it was a heart attack.

A smashing bloke though he was, he had a hard side to him. When we played in the Tokyo Cup in Japan, one of the Spanish players in the Espanol side we came up against, was giving us a particularly rough ride, as it appeared that he didn't like the British.

Bosco pole axed him, then said to the stricken Spaniard: "I'm not English. Don't mess with me."

Tony McAndrew led by example, laying down the level of commitment that others had to follow. With Jim in goal we had almost everything you could ask of a team.

However there were a few fights on the training ground, often involving Tony. I once cut his eye with my elbow, and it took him a while to get over that. I kept out of his way. We were very different characters, but good teammates, and on Saturday afternoons that was all that mattered.

That trip to Tokyo was amazing. Espanol apart, the other teams we faced were Boca Juniors, and the Japan national side. We won the tournament.

Before the first game in Tokyo, a rather suspicious-looking chap knocked on the door of my and Proc's room, wanting to speak to us. His English was perfect, so we had no problems understanding him when he began to explain his proposition. He was prepared to pay us 100 dollars per man if we won the next game of the tournament by two clear goals.

Proc and I wondered if we could make it happen without telling the others, and pocket the cash ourselves! But we had no choice other than to tell the rest of the players what deal was on offer.

We won the game – I can't remember who it was against – by two clear goals, and as good as his word, the same chap knocked on our door with a briefcase. He was dragged through the doorway without his feet touching the floor!

The poor guy went white, but not as white as Proc and me when he opened the briefcase to reveal a case full of American dollars. He paid fifteen players 100 dollars each.

He then offered an even better deal. If we were to beat Japan by three clear goals, the reward on this occasion would be 250 dollars each.

This was too good to be true. We beat Japan by three clear goals, and after the game, he appeared in our hotel with a slightly heavier briefcase, and sure enough, it was full of American dollars.

The next offer after that was 500 dollars per man to beat Boca Juniors in the final by one goal. This game has stuck in my mind for many years, but not because of the money, for another reason. It was the turning point in my football career.

I damaged my knee ligaments in a bad tackle in the semi-final, and under normal circumstances there was no way I would have played, because injuries like that usually take two or three weeks to overcome.

The backroom staff wanted me to play, and so did John and the club doctor because Boro wanted to win such a prestigious tournament. They convinced me that with the help of injections, I would get through the game without any further damage. There was big money at stake – not the players' potential winnings, but big prize money for the club if we won the competition.

Spike went to great lengths to talk me out of the injections. Who should I listen to – Spike or the gaffer?

In hindsight and with due respect to John, Spike was right. I should never have allowed the gaffer to convince me to take injections, not just one, but four. I had two before the game and two at half time. I was assured that the injections wouldn't do me any more damage than had already been done with this being the last game of the season, and I would return to pre-season training with no problem at all.

I played my part in the final, even though the game went to extra time. I must admit that the pain was excruciating, especially in the latter stages of extra time.

However, we won the game by the one goal that our friend wanted. We couldn't get back to the hotel quickly enough, and everybody piled into our room waiting for the knock on the door.

As good as his word, it wasn't long in coming. He carried the same briefcase, but it was three times its normal size, containing 500 dollars per man, making our earnings 850 dollars each from the trip.

Apart from the bribery, it was an amazing trip. The hotel was fabulous, the massive shopping centres were out of this world for that time (1980), and there were 70,000 Japanese fans at every game. We were treated like pop stars. Girls came to our rooms, the nightlife was phenomenal, the discos unbelievable. At some the entrance charge was $25 but for that you could drink as much as you liked. Dave Shearer was in his element, picking up trays of drinks, but instead of handing them round, he knocked them all back.

He got totally drunk, and the last I can recall he was throwing ice cubes at a huge wooden carved elephant in the centre of the club. On the plane home Sheik, as he was known, won a bet with us that involved us all buying him a whisky. When we got home he came flying down the baggage conveyor belt. What a way to end a fabulous trip.

The following season, on a trip to Morocco, the club paid the players their win bonus for the trip to Tokyo. Put together with our spending money from the club, and there were some big fat wallets.

So fat, in fact, that the pickpockets along the streets of Casablanca found the temptation too big to resist, and had a go at Proc.

One guy asked what we were looking to buy as we browsed around, and we replied "clothes."

He assured us that he knew the best boutique in Casablanca, and told us to follow him. After going down alley after alley, it became obvious that we were being set up. Suddenly, on the ground, right in front of us, was Proc's wallet, how it had got there we didn't know. Unfortunately, Proc had been pickpocketed, but fortunately for us, the guy had dropped it right in front of us. Proc shouted "You f...ing arsehole", and the guy panicked and ran off before we could get to him. How lucky were we? There was nearly 2000 dollars in that wallet.

In my six years at Boro I played under several managers, and all were very different.

Jack Charlton had an aura that came from being a World Cup winner, and playing for Leeds United, an awesome team under the management of Don Revie in the 1970s.

My breakthrough into first team football came under the guidance of John Neal.

He made me feel as if the team couldn't do without me – my right knee was well aware of that! He always said positive things to me, both during the week and immediately before games. "Come on my son, you're the boy," he would say, treating me as if I was special. He told the other lads to give me the ball and I would destroy the opposition. With encouragement like that I was bound to feel good.

I was heartbroken when he went to Chelsea. When Boro sacked him, the players were told not to tell anybody. As I drove away from the ground with Proc, we heard a banging in the boot. It was Bob Cass, who had been tipped off about the story. Being naive kids we confirmed it. It was Bob who told us that Bobby Murdoch was taking over.

Bobby was the biggest influence on me in my last year as an apprentice, because if he had not been youth and reserve team coach I may not have developed. He had trust in me at an early stage, and bestowed the role of head apprentice upon me.

He was a superb coach, who had the full respect of all the players. He didn't tell you what to do, he showed you. I owe Bobby everything professional football has given me.

When I went to Liverpool, Kenny Dalglish took me under his wing and told me that if there was anything he could help me with, inside or outside football, I only had to ask him. It was only much later I learned that Bobby had phoned Kenny and asked him to look after me. Bobby was promoted to Boro manager before he was ready, which was a great shame, as he had so much to offer as a coach.

He had tremendous vision, and after games would sit you down and go through everything that had happened on the pitch. He was open and honest, and I learned so much from him. To this day, when I leave a player out of the side, I tell him exactly why, sometimes spending twenty minutes with him. That's something I learned from Bobby.

When he died I spoke to Proc about whether we should go to the funeral but we were advised that it would be pointless. Bobby had so much respect in football, none more so than in his home city of Glasgow, where he was a legend, having won so many honours with Celtic.

I watched the cortege on the television news that night, and it was obvious the information we had been given was correct. The streets of Glasgow were packed and it seemed that the whole of the city had come to a standstill.

If ever I was to look back at a turning point in the history of Middlesbrough Football Club, it has to be the FA Cup quarter-final defeat at Wolves in season 1980-81. We had beaten them twice already in the league, and were confident of winning at Molineux, even after they had drawn at Ayresome to take us back to the West Midlands.

We had also beaten Spurs shortly before, and they were waiting for us in the semi final if we saw off Wolves. Suddenly, we could sniff Boro's first ever silverware.

Before the home game against Wolves I had to have an abductor muscle strapped up to enable me to play. I trotted out thirty seconds after the rest of the lads, and got the most incredible support, presumably because the crowd had thought I wasn't playing.

I hadn't trained all week, and struggled to get through the game. Andy Gray put Wolves ahead with a header. When Spike went off for stitches in an ankle injury, things did not look good for us.

But no sooner had he come back on, he set up Terry Cochrane to equalise. The game finished 1-1, but we were very optimistic that we would go through in the replay, because we hadn't played at our best.

We had a memorable night afterwards, not just because of the result, but also because it was Geraldine Proctor's 21st birthday.

Micky and Marty had just paid for a beautiful new varnished ceiling in their living room, which was like looking into a mirror. Only thing was, this mirror was then splattered in champagne thanks to my antics early in the morning.

Micky and Marty didn't say anything on the night, although I knew too well that they weren't all that pleased. What made it even more embarrassing was that I was still living with them! There was no escape.

Proc and I went swimming the next day, which wasn't something the club had ordered, but it just seemed to be the logical thing to do after Geraldine's birthday party and the match the day before.

After the swimming session had finished and Proc and I had virtually drowned each other, I was amazed to have a relaxed feeling in my abductor area, so much in fact that it had virtually cleared up. Knowing we had a replay three days later, it was a massive relief knowing that I could go into such an important game injury free.

Overall on that night, Wolves had the upper hand throughout the game. A big Geordie called Norman Bell gave Billy Ashcroft and Irving Nattress a torrid time. We went 1-0 down with a goal by Mel Eves, but we equalised in the second half when yours truly scored with a header right in front of our 7,000 travelling fans.

The pendulum swung our way. Wolves were on the back foot and we had chances, and just before the ninety minute mark Terry Cochrane unfortunately missed a sitter. We were that close to a semi final place, because if we'd scored then, Wolves wouldn't have got back into it.

John Neal addressed us all in the centre circle before extra time started, and said something which surprised me when he told the lads, who were expecting an inspirational word or two; "Just give the ball to Hodgy all the time."

In all due respect, to be paid a nice compliment was very much appreciated, but David Hodgson couldn't beat Wolves on his own that night. I was just as tired as everybody else on the pitch, and I'd put in a good ninety minutes' work.

But in extra time, Norman Bell put them ahead, and then outjumped Billy

Ashcroft to set up John Richards for the third.

At the end I remember going to the Boro fans behind the goal. I have never felt so low, so hurt, and I collapsed. I had gone, physically and mentally. Jim Platt came back out of the tunnel to console me and help me back to the dressing room. Our big chance had gone, and I was devastated. Wolves lost to Spurs, the eventual winners, in the semi final.

I remember we stopped at the services on the way home. Billy had to stay on the bus because the fans, who were just as bitterly disappointed as the players were, blamed him for our defeat. That was the first time I had seen that side of the public. I was close to the fans, and had stood behind the goal on the terraces with them. I said to some of them: "Don't blame Billy. It's over now." But they did.

Going into the 1981-82 season, things looked significantly bleak.

Spike, Bosco, Craig Johnston and Proc all left, while John was sacked. All the stability we had in the club disappeared overnight. Replacing those people was impossible. Full internationals and under 21 players had left, and they weren't cheap to replace. And at a football club with no money, the future looked bleak. It seemed as if I was the best hope of convincing the public that things would work out ok in the end.

I entered into negotiations for a new contract, and they dragged on for weeks. In the end, I got the deal I wanted, and stood my ground. I wasn't prepared to let chairman Charles Amer and co re-sign me on the cheap.

What possibly didn't help my case was that Proc told me exactly what he was on at his new club, Nottingham Forest, and I used that against Boro in my negotiations.

But every day when I went back to Proc's house where I was still living, Marty would tell me that there was something else in Proc's contract that he'd forgotten to tell me about, such as a car and a holiday. So it was back to the Boro for more talks. And eventually the deal was agreed.

On a personal level I was all right financially because I had agreed a long deal. As well as agreeing an £80,000 signing on fee, I had cars and holidays as part of my terms. I was even offered 50 acres of forest out Great Broughton way. It was full of Christmas trees and I didn't know what to do with them.

Another part of the deal was a plot of land at Ormesby. The club said they would build me a house, but I had to go up there and do some of the work myself, to avoid the taxman clamping down.

And then a day after I'd signed the new deal Marty confessed that he'd been winding me up over Proc's contract, and that he'd signed for Forest for £600 per week, and there was no car, and no holiday!

With all the contract talks to one side, and having been given the deal I had stuck out for, I knew I would have to perform even better than I had in the previous two seasons.

But things didn't turn out the way I had planned.

I had a groin injury throughout the summer, which I later found out stemmed from a back problem. I had to be put in plaster from my chest to my knees to try and solve it.

But I couldn't sleep for two of the four weeks that I was in plaster, and the treatment didn't work anyway. I was then sent to the warm climate of Malta to try and get some movement back, but that didn't work either and I have had the same problem ever since. Then I missed most of the pre-season because of an Achilles tendon injury, so I entered a crucial season nowhere near the condition which I expected myself to be in for an important First Division campaign.

Injuries niggled me all season. My abductor and Achilles flared up, and together with a half a dozen cortisone injections you could say it was a tough season. The team struggled because quite simply we never replaced the top players that we'd lost at the end of the previous season.

The discipline and professionalism within the club had also declined. Bobby, who had taken over from John as manager, began to feel the heat, and he lost a little bit of respect from the players. The season turned into a nightmare.

There was an example just after Christmas in the 1981-82 season of the professionalism disappearing from the club. We had the FA Cup game that I mentioned earlier on the Astroturf at QPR, and the night before the game, the players were instructed to be in bed by 10pm, but that wasn't adhered to. At four in the morning, most of the players and coaching staff, Bobby included, were still drinking as if there was no tomorrow. That certainly wouldn't have happened if John Neal, Spike and co had still been at the club.

The sports centre the club built cost more than was expected, then it failed building regulations. The club went into turmoil, becoming messy and unprofessional, culminating in relegation.

I felt very sorry for Bobby, because everything caved in on him. We lost players that were not only very good, but had the club at heart, and weren't replaced properly.

In the summer of 1982, with the club relegated to the Second Division, I signed for Liverpool, so I didn't get a lot of the financial deal that had been agreed.

Ironically my last game for Boro was against Liverpool in an evening game at Ayresome Park. Some of the Liverpool players were half cut, because Graeme Souness took them to the opening of Willie Maddren's sports shop where more than a glass or two of champagne had been drunk.

When they turned up at Ayresome Park, word came through that they were still pissed from the afternoon session.

Surely, we could finish the season on a high, against a team that was half cut? It goes to show how good Liverpool were, or how bad we were, when the game finished 1-1.

I was carried off the field by the fans because there was talk of me leaving and they wanted to make their feelings known. They were singing: "Hodgy, don't go." But the deal had been agreed between the clubs long before I ever knew – some say a year before.

Other clubs had tried to get me before, but Boro were not so badly off financially then. Bobby Robson, when he was at Ipswich, had allegedly offered £1 million plus Alan Brazil for me. There were rumours that there was an offer of that amount for one of our players, and me, Proc and Craig Johnston all wondered if it was one of us. It turned out to be me.

Everton manager Howard Kendall also wanted me, with players, including Gary Stanley, said to be coming the other way. But that didn't happen either.

It was Jim who told me that I was going to Anfield. Apparently he had been tipped off. I still remember the tannoy announcement on a club open day asking me to go to Shep's office. The club had already sold a lot of season tickets, before they told supporters that I was leaving.

Shep told me that Liverpool wanted me, but I didn't want to go. However Shep drove me down to Merseyside and I met Bob Paisley, the Liverpool manager. Liverpool offered me £700 a week. I told them I wanted £1,250, and they were stunned. But Shep told Paisley that it got worse, because I was also owed £50,000, a car and appearance money. I didn't look at what players at other clubs were getting, just at what the Boro lads were on.

Even on the way home I told Shep that my heart was at Boro and I really didn't want to leave.

But the chairman of Boro, Charles Amer, told me I had to go, otherwise the club was bankrupt. I told him straight that if he hadn't built the new gym there was no way he would have had to sell me.

But in the end my father and friends told me that turning down Liverpool would be crazy, because it was far too good an opportunity to miss. So I reluctantly agreed to go, and signed a four-year contract worth around £75,000 a year, rising to £100,000 by the third year. But Liverpool would not provide me with a car as they didn't believe in giving perks.

But even though I agreed to go I couldn't get my head round the fact that I was leaving Boro after so many happy years.

When I drove to Liverpool to sign for them, I pulled over and parked on a flyover above Knotty Ash. I burst into tears, saying to myself over and over: "I don't want to go to Liverpool."

Then I saw in my mind all those people back home saying: "You are joining the champions." I dried my eyes, and plucked up the courage to continue the journey to Anfield and go through with it.

I was no longer a Boro player.

England star
and Walton Jail

On one away trip in 1980 with the Boro, while we stopped at the services, John Neal, the manager, made a telephone call back to Ayresome Park.

When we set off again, he called for Proc and me to go down the bus to see him. He said: "Tweedle-Dum and Tweedle-Dee, congratulations are in order. You have been picked for the England under 21 squad for a game against Norway."

He used to call us Tweedle-Dum and Tweedle-Dee, or sometimes other names that went together. We were inseparable.

The game was a friendly at Anfield – one of my future homes – and Tweedle-Dum (sorry, I mean Proc), Craig Johnston and me all played. The significance of playing for my country went over my head. We won 3-1, but that was the beginning of my pelvic problem. I picked up a knock during the game, and the strength seemed to go out of my lower abdomen.

Looking back it was a great achievement for me to play for my country, no doubt about it, even though it was a friendly, and not even at Wembley.

In total we were to be called up twelve times each, though I missed six of the games with that pelvic trouble. When I didn't play, Proc did, and vice versa. The England bosses obviously didn't want us together!

We stayed at the Post House Hotel, Heathrow before some games. The two of us, and one or two others were the kids from the north. The rest were the London boys, the likes of Vince Hilaire, Terry Fenwick and Mark Dennis. There was a divide, but most of us got on reasonably well.

It's strange that the actual games and squad get-togethers didn't mean all that much to me, yet when we got back to the Boro training ground we felt like kings, different from everybody else, because we had been away on international duty.

Gary Shaw tended to be my room partner with England, and we became firm friends. We still speak now, and it's a shame that he couldn't make it to the fund raising game we had at the Reynolds Arena in January 2004.

Gary was top scorer at Villa, and although I was never prolific, I was in the England side and Gary was left out. That has always struck me as a strange decision.

Once I said to him that I would pretend, during a game, that I had picked up an injury, so then he could come on for his first England cap, but he told me not to, adding that his time would come. I was prepared to do that sort of thing for a good mate.

With his good looks, blond hair, and goalscoring skills, he was the boy on the way up in the Midlands. Sadly his career was cut short by injury.

When I got the job at Darlington in 1995, he was first on the phone to congratulate me. He's now involved in PR and radio work.

As for my England games, I recall one at Portman Road against Sweden where I played particularly well. Even though I said that it didn't mean much to me to wear the white shirt with the three lions badge, it must have gone to my head, because my club boss John Neal watched that particular game and in the warm up I was flicking balls up in the centre of the pitch.

John told me afterwards that it was not like me to do that sort of thing, and that I never did it when I was playing for him at Boro, which was a fair point.

Anyway, I had what I felt was a magnificent game. Afterwards Ipswich manager Bobby Robson came to see me in the changing room – he had previously offered £1 million for me, but Boro had turned his approach down. John shot in straight after him through the open dressing room door to make sure that he wasn't tapping me up.

John was clearly worried, because he said he would drive me straight back north, even though I was not due in for Boro training the next day. But I persuaded him to let me stay, and have a night out.

I was still with the national squad by the time I signed for Liverpool. In one England game against Germany, the European Under 21 championship final, I played with my knee strapped up. I had to come off – to be replaced by Justin Fashanu – and Liverpool went ballistic because I missed a few games while recovering from the injury.

In the second leg in Germany I gave away a penalty, from which they scored, but redeemed myself. I picked up the ball on the halfway line, beat two men, and rolled it past the keeper for Paul Goddard to tap in. That was one of several goals I made for him, and we beat the Germans on aggregate.

I think that was my last away trip with the side. After the game, we went out into the red light district in Bremen. There were six or seven of us, but in one nightclub, Gary and I got separated from the others. We got into a spot of bother because four of the locals surrounded us, clearly looking for trouble.

The two of us lashed out, and because we were athletes somehow got away. These days that sort of incident would have been blown up out of all proportion by the newspapers and make back page headlines.

John Lukic, our keeper, never drank, but one night we forced a glass of champagne down him. We thought that would be the end of his temperance days and he would join the drinking culture, and become one of the lads. No chance. The next morning when we crawled in, he was already up and dressed in his suit. He made us look a right bunch of scallywags.

Justin Fashanu was sometimes my room partner, and I liked him very much too. He was a great lad, though socially he didn't knock around with us much.

After games he used to go missing, off on his own somewhere. At the time we didn't know he was gay. He was discreet, but looking back on it, we had a fair idea where he had gone.

Later when I became an agent I fixed him up with a couple of clubs. By then I was aware of his sexuality, and had to inform the clubs that were signing him. But he never gave them or me any trouble at all.

He trained hard, was a good player, and his behaviour was impeccable. I was shocked when he committed suicide. It was a real tragedy, because he was a smashing bloke though presumably very troubled. But it didn't show when I knew him.

I was twice picked for a select under 23 England side, chosen by Bobby Robson. At the time, that was the step between under 21 and full international, and I played well in both games. But even though I was closer to a full international at that point than at any other time, the full call up from Ron Greenwood, the England manager, never came.

I may well have become a full international, had injuries not prevented it. One summer I was told not to book any holidays, and hand my passport in. The reason was that I was wanted by England. Unfortunately I picked up an injury and never got the nod to join the squad.

But I was runner up in the Professional Football Association team of the year in 1981/82, so that was an indication of the esteem I was held in.

Many things passed me by in those days, but looking back now it would have been a massive honour to play in a full international. Those lads who do should treasure it forever, and I'm sure that most of them do.

After my first season at Liverpool I knew that I would never get the ultimate honour, but on reflection I could have done more to make it happen.

I'm the first to admit that I never scored as many goals as I should have done, but I had enough other qualities. I was good in the air, quick, strong, never backed out of a tackle, could cross balls for fun, and would run through a brick wall.

But maybe there were too many distractions. I didn't gamble or drink much – except on occasions that were down to a bit of stupidity.

So maybe I allowed myself to lower my standards a bit, and even to do that on rare occasions is too much if you want to bridge the gap between being a young international and a full one.

The more the years go by, the more I remember those under 21 games – and the two or three goals I scored – with affection.

I scored against Poland in Warsaw in March 1982, and made a goal for Paul Goddard. There were some star names alongside me in the England team. At around that time Clive Allen was transferred twice for £1million, from Crystal Palace to Arsenal, and then Arsenal to Spurs.

He must have been earning big money, but I was on over £1,000 a week. I had a brand new Porsche Monte Carlo and then a Ferrari, and my cars were as good as anyone else's. Justin Fashanu, with his big Jeep, was the only one who was different.

I don't recall anyone bragging about what they had – not even me – but you were aware of it. There was a certain amount of status involved. However, on the pitch it was all for one and one for all. There was a team spirit pretty much the same as in club football. You wanted to win, and win together.

And it was an honour to play alongside lads such as Sammy Lee, Clive Allen, Terry Fenwick and Paul Goddard. But I was up there with them, and at my best had a lot to offer. If I hadn't there was no way that Liverpool would have come in for me, nor would Bobby Robson have offered £1 million to take me to Ipswich.

Strange, isn't it, that Clive earned more publicity, fame, and probably money than I did, yet while his claim to fame was moving for the magical seven figure sum twice, I can always say that my club turned down that sort of money for me.

However, despite enjoying playing for the England under 21 side, I was not particularly an avid watcher of England internationals. I perhaps didn't have the in-built patriotism that many people have. I was not an England fan, as such.

Gary Bannister, later to play under me at Darlington, where he was one of our best players, played with me at Sheffield United's ground, Bramall Lane, for the England under 21 side.

I remember him as a right oddball. He played for Sheffield Wednesday at the time, so knew the city well. So I asked him where the nightlife was in the city, because I was the entertainment manager of the side.

He took us to a club, and then instead of parking up and joining us, he drove off. The lads were not best pleased.

For me it was a lovely night. I walked into the club empty-handed, and I walked out of it hand-in-hand with a girl called Debbie Smith. On that night, I beat one or two of the big-hitters, Shawsy included, although Shawsy hung on to the death, right up to the car, trying to change Debbie's mind.

Personally, I'd like to think it was a one horse race, but to be honest it might have been the Porsche. What the hell, Shawsy was on the way back to the hotel on his own.

I drove Debbie home, and we sat talking for hours in the car. It turned out that she was going out with Steve Davis, the snooker player.

I gave her what I said was my phone number – but it was actually the number for Walton Jail. To do that was a standing joke in Liverpool.

I bumped into her two years later, when we were heading for an end of season trip to Marbella. She came up to me and said: "You don't remember me." I asked her to give me a clue and she said: "Walton Jail".

I told her that unfortunately that was the done thing to give out the number for Walton Jail. Rather rude, I know, but that was me being arrogant, and she didn't seem to mind, for she was part of a group of girls that went to Marbella at the end of every season.

It turned out that I ended up playing snooker against Steve Davis at Preston

Guildhall in one of Phil Neal's testimonial events. I was a decent player, and at the start of the match made a joke of hitting the ball with the wrong end of the cue.

The referee gave four points to Steve. It was much more serious than I thought. I then took my dicky bow tie off, and Steve had a quiet word with me. "Keep things straight. You won't get away with anything here."

I agreed and promptly made a break of 20, but didn't feel smug for long, because Steve cleared up with an 85. He was world champion after all.

It was a good insight, however, into playing another professional sport at a decent level. The most daunting thing was the silence.

When you play football, there is always crowd noise. But when you look down a snooker cue and can hear a pin drop, the pressure is intense – different from anything I had ever experienced. Ever since then I have had total respect for top snooker players.

Steve was an excellent lad and a great laugh. Suddenly I could see what Debbie saw in him.

John Parrott was just coming on the scene at the time. Sammy Lee, Howard Gayle and Stigger (Steve Foley) knew him, and stitched me up good and proper. We were in a snooker hall in Liverpool, and the lads told me that there was a kid who wanted to play me for £100. To tempt me, he offered me a fifty-point start. I took him on, potted a couple of balls and thought I was in for some easy money.

He then made a break of over a hundred, and long before he had completed it, I knew I'd been done up like a kipper.

However it was worth it, because he gave me my first ever cue, a genuine branded John Parrott cue, complete with a case. We became mates and played together quite a few times. Of the Liverpool stars Bruce Grobelaar and Ian Rush weren't bad players, while Ronnie Whelan was excellent.

As for me, I never became a snooker star – or a full football international footballer. But my under 21 days were happy times during which I made some good mates. And I never deviated far enough from the straight and narrow to see the inside of Walton Jail.

Merseyside magic;
"Put the blue
light out."

I drove through Liverpool towards Anfield in order to sign for one of the biggest clubs in Europe.

Twenty years ago, they were the strongest force in Europe, and regularly won the European Cup, the Football League, the FA Cup and the Milk Cup. That's why their fans are so desperate for success now.

They had top players such as Kenny Dalglish, Ian Rush and Boro old boy Graeme Souness, and I had been in two minds whether to sign for them or not.

After all, if I had gone back to the Boro, then even though the fans would no doubt have welcomed me back, the club was under such intense financial pressure that if they didn't sell me, they would probably go to the wall. Liverpool had paid £450,000 up front for me, so financially it would have been a huge blow for Boro not to receive the money.

I was actually late signing for them because I had spent so much time thinking about whether to turn around and go back to Boro! I just blamed the traffic on the M62 for the delay.

There was hardly anybody else around Anfield, because Bob Paisley and the team were at a pre-season tournament in Malaga, so my old Boro teammate, Craig Johnston, met me at the ground.

There were a few formalities to go through, but not many. I checked the contract, made sure all the details were right –the Liverpool lads were shocked by the £1200 per week I was on, and probably caused one or two wage demands from them – then had a quick medical. Not an exhaustive medical like the ones these days, just a quick check by the doctor, which probably suited the groin and abductor problems I'd picked up at Boro.

Medical over, four-year contract signed and it was off to Craig's for the night before we flew to Spain.

Craig had gone up in the world since he left Boro for Liverpool a year earlier. Everything was white. White house, white sofa, white walls, he even had a white rabbit hutch with white rabbits!

The following day, we flew to Marbella and found the team hotel. Considering it was about nine in the evening, there wasn't a single person from the Liverpool party to be seen. I assumed that they were all in bed early, bearing in mind there was a game the following day. Ultra professional, or so I thought.

Craig and I went to bed at about ten. He never said a word, quite conveniently, about what the club usually did before matches.

At about one in the morning, there was a loud banging at the door. I thought there was an emergency, but no, it was Phil Thompson. "Get dressed," he said. "I'm taking you down to the port."

I told him we had a game the same day, but he insisted.

I really thought it was a wind-up. I expected to be taken to an empty bar somewhere, but no, he led me to a bar called Sinatra's, which just happened to be a place I'd been to with Boro on a close season tour.

What a shock when I went through the door. The place was absolutely heaving, and right in the middle, was the entire Liverpool first team squad. Kenny Dalglish, Alan Hansen, Mark Lawrenson, Ian Rush, Ronnie Whelan – you name them, they were there, surrounded by loads of people.

I was absolutely flabbergasted; I really thought I was dreaming to see all these Liverpool greats knocking the drinks back, within a few hours of a game.

Tommo asked me if I wanted a drink, and I told him I'd have a Coke, and he burst out laughing. He said that he'd heard I was a bit of a lad – the reputation had obviously spread as far as Liverpool then! – and bought me a beer.

We stayed till five in the morning, playing a game called Fizzbuzz, a numbers game in which you tried to avoid saying a multiple of five or seven. If you did, then you had to down a drink.

I don't know who won, I really can't remember, but we were the last ones out of the pub.

At nine o'clock in the morning, Ronnie Moran and Joe Fagan woke everybody up. The routine was that Ronnie opened the curtains, Joe spoke to the player. They always did it that way, the Liverpool way, whether it was a friendly or a Cup final. I can always remember Ronnie looking at me that first morning and saying, "It's taken us a long time to get you!"

At training that morning, I adopted the same attitude as I had at Boro. Whole-hearted and full-blooded, after all, I was trying to impress and not do anything daft in my first training session. That was my first mistake.

I made a couple of tackles, and Joe pulled me to one side. "We don't tackle at Liverpool, we close men down instead." I couldn't believe it, but again, I suppose, it was the way Liverpool had always done it, and there was plenty of silverware to prove that.

The session was a bit of a joke to me. No urgency, no running, it was dead straightforward, just five a sides. I couldn't understand it after Boro's training sessions.

In the evening, we played Real Betis in the tournament, and I went on as a sub in the second half, and scored. Graeme Souness, another former pal from the Boro, was the first person to congratulate me.

The final was against Malaga. Before the game, everybody said how much they were looking forward to having a few drinks after the game in the town, so shall we say that the emphasis was getting the game over with, win or lose.

We were level at the end of the ninety minutes – which from the social point of view was unfortunate – so it was a penalty shootout. Drinking time was slipping away, and when it came to my turn, I couldn't remember whether if I scored we won, or if I missed we lost. I was never much good at penalties – I didn't take them at Boro, remember – and the ball ended up out of the ground.

Game over, and within thirty minutes of the final whistle, we were back in Sinatra's. Bob Paisley gave us his blessing, and he went back to the hotel with his coaching team. Another long session until five in the morning, and now I understood why there was a great team spirit at Liverpool.

The daft thing was, when I got back to Liverpool, the club put me into the George Hotel, and I never saw a Liverpool player for a drink for weeks afterwards!

A week or two later, we played Spurs at Wembley in the Charity Shield. I came on for Kenny Dalglish, and I could have scored a hat trick, but we had to settle for a 1-0 win. It went really well for me in front of a big crowd, but I didn't really think that I would begin the league season the following week in the starting line up, because it just wasn't the Liverpool way. It was the normal practice for a player to spend a few months playing in the reserves, learning the Liverpool style of play and the Liverpool habits before he was even considered for the first team. If he wasn't considered to be educated enough in the Liverpool way or just couldn't grasp it, then it was reserve team football – or a transfer out!

But as the build up for the first game against West Brom at Anfield continued, I had a feeling that I might be included, because some people dropped hints. And on the Wednesday before the game, I was included in the first team in a practice match against the reserves on the Anfield pitch.

Sure enough, maybe against my expectations, I was named in the team for the West Brom game, and I'm led to believe that previously only Kenny, Souey and Lawro had been given their first team debuts immediately after signing.

I couldn't have asked for a better start in front of a big crowd. I had a hand in Sammy Lee's opening goal, and then I won the penalty for the second, which ace penalty taker Phil Neal put away. I chased a ball through, got there before the keeper Mark Grew, who pulled me down. It was a fantastic feeling to do well in front of the Kop and to hear the reception they gave me.

It got better. I scored at Arsenal a week later in a 2-0 win, then a few days later, my close pal Proc came along with Nottingham Forest. Proc had been transferred to Forest the season before from Boro, and there was plenty of friendly banter on the pitch. "Great ball, Mark" I said a couple of times, and got some fierce looks from Souey for saying it. I think Souey forgave me –I scored twice in a 4-3 win.

I also scored in a 4-0 win at Dundalk in a European Cup tie in September.

Even though I scored a few goals, nobody in authority told me that I'd played well. It was another of Liverpool's ways, in which they expect you to be able to stand on your own two feet. In a way that's right, but maybe at the time I needed someone to put an arm around me and tell me. But again, you couldn't knock Liverpool after all the trophies they'd won.

But then things started to go wrong, which I suppose they had to after the great start I had.

I damaged my knee ligaments at Swansea and had to be subbed – Terry MacDermott replaced me and told me that I'd had a nightmare – but I still decided to go and play in John Craggs' testimonial at Ayresome Park. Craggsy was celebrating ten years at the Boro.

I returned to Ayresome Park for the first time since my departure a few months earlier, and got a great ovation. There were some top players on the field, including Kevin Keegan, and I scored a hat trick against my old mate Kelham O'Hanlon.

Kevin Keegan nearly lost his eyesight that night after being accidentally poked in the eye by Darren Wood, which stole my limelight a little. There was speculation that he might have needed an eye operation, but fortunately he recovered – but everybody had forgotten about my hat trick!

I arrived back at Anfield and got a real bollocking from Joe Fagan and Ronnie Moran for playing at Boro with an injury instead of missing the game and receiving treatment. I had certainly dropped a clanger, but in my eyes I was doing a favour for an old teammate of mine at the Boro. And if I hadn't shown up, then Craggsy might have taken my absence as a snub.

And the injuries meant I was out of the side for a few weeks. I was dogged by niggling injuries when I was at Liverpool, and most of the time it was my knee – the same knee in which Spike Armstrong had advised me not to have a cortisone injection a couple of years before.

One thing I learned when I was injured – the Liverpool coaching staff didn't want to know me. I was no use to them, so the stories about Bill Shankly years before were true! That attitude certainly knocked my confidence, because when I was at Boro, people like Bobby Murdoch and John Neal would have put their arms around me and consoled me. I found life hard at times being in and out of the team, unlike my days at Boro, when I felt a real part of it. I wanted to play in every game when I was fit; after all, when I was fit, I played when I was at the Boro.

But I can't really argue against being out of the team, because again, the club's success at that time was well proven. In my first season, we won the League and the Milk Cup, and reached the quarter finals of the European Cup!

I was out of the team for five weeks because of the injury I picked up at Swansea, and was steadily returning to full fitness. One day we were playing Everton in a derby game at Goodison Park, one of the most passionate derbies in football.

I didn't expect to play because I still wasn't 100 per cent fit, so I went for a few drinks with Michael Farrow, an old friend of mine. We were out until five in the morning, and returned home the worse for wear. I think it was fair to say that I was now accustomed to the Liverpool style of drinking!

We had to report to Anfield at ten in the morning, and I dragged myself along as a formality.

On the way into the ground, I bumped into Thommo, who asked if I'd been out. "I'm still out now." I replied.

"You'd best sober up quick, because you're sub!" replied Phil.

I thought Phil was winding me up, but no, there was my name on the team sheet as sub. It hardly registered because of my hangover.

Phil told all the lads, of course, and they did their best to drop me in it with Bob, Joe and Ronnie. They tried to get me to sit next to one of them on the bench so they could smell my breath or look at my eyes, but I managed to squeeze into the smallest place possible away from them, and avert their gaze, or not speak directly to them all match.

This was the game in which Ian Rush scored that memorable four-timer against Everton, a game which is still talked about at great length, at least in the red half of Merseyside. Everton just couldn't deal with Rushy, which wasn't the first or the last time they couldn't get to grips with him. I came on for Kenny and scored with an overhead kick, but unfortunately it was disallowed for a foul by somebody else.

I scored twice in the Milk Cup that season. I scored one of the goals against West Ham in the quarter final when we won 2-1, and another in the first leg of the semi final against Burnley in a 3-0 win. It was after that game that Tom Saunders, the chief scout who was nicknamed Mr Liverpool, pulled me to one side. "I know it's not traditional to say you've done well," he said,"but your performances are more than justifying your inclusion." Praise. I thought I'd made it! It was unusual for him to say that, and I always had time for him, even after I'd left the club.

I know many people have said and written countless times over the years that Bob Paisley was a great man, and so I make no apology for repeating those sentiments now from my own perspective.

He was magnificent at man management. He was a quiet, unassuming, ordinary man with no airs and graces at all. But what a manager. There was nothing about him to suggest that he was one of the most highly regarded men in football.

The players loved him and respected him, because he stood by them.

For example, in a pre-season tournament, the players wanted some complimentary tickets, but the organisers wouldn't give any away. We complained to Bob, who got us all into reception, and in a loud voice told us to pack our bags because we were going home. The organisers thought he was joking until Bob said: "You wanted the best, now you've lost them." Within half an hour, we had fifty tickets!

We once played a game in Tel Aviv, and afterwards, the players had a long drinking session that ended in a brawl in the city square. It was something to do with Rushy and me! We fought anybody and everybody.

We decided to go back to our hotel, but the problem was that they all looked the same. (Well, after a few beers, they probably did!) And in typical Liverpool fashion, some of the more sober lads pretended that they had gone into the wrong hotel, and come back out, when it was really ours.

Finally, after wandering around for ages, we bumped into a Liverpool director, Mr. Moss, and Alan Kennedy, right on cue, collapsed in a drunken stupor in front of him.

"Do you know that you represent one of the biggest clubs in the world?" he shouted.

By this time, I had bent down to pick Alan up, although I was virtually lying on the ground with him.

So I crawled over to Mr. Moss, pulled myself up by his trouser leg and said: "Come on, you old bugger, don't get too upset." He calmed down, although in my own drunken haze I could sense that he was still very annoyed, and he got us back to the hotel.

We wondered what our punishment was going to be. Maybe a fine, sent home in disgrace? We didn't know, but we were worried.

Bob waited for us in reception the next morning, and when each of us arrived, he gestured us over with a quick flick of his finger

Bob told us all to sit down in his soft Geordie accent. He called us clowns because we'd been fighting.

He asked Alan Kennedy, sporting a black eye, "Who hit you?" and then pointed at Rushy, sporting a bruise on his cheek, "Who hit you?"

And then he turned to me and said: "You're a real Geordie, you are, you haven't been hit at all." Which we thought was a strange thing to say.

Bob ordered us all to go upstairs into a private room, and inside, there were Mr. Moss, Joe Fagan, Roy Evans and Ronnie Moran. Bob joined them around a table with a white tablecloth draped over it. Bob made a point of how important playing for the club was, and Mr. Moss said: "I have represented Liverpool for twenty years, and never in my life has anybody addressed me as Mr. Moss, you old bugger!"

Oh no, this is it, I thought.

No sooner had I said that to myself, then Bob pulled the tablecloth off the table, and there was a huge crate of beer – and the cue for another drinking session. I was absolutely amazed, but that was the Liverpool way!

He had a knack of spotting players' strengths. He pulled me in training one day, and commented about the number of chances I sometimes missed in front of goal.

"If you pretended that the goalposts are players, you would never miss," he said. "You've got an ability to put the ball between two players, but when you've got two posts in front of you, then you miss."

The last time I spoke to Bob was after I'd submitted a transfer request when Joe Fagan was manager. Bob, who was then a director, grabbed me by the back of my hair on the way to another reserve game. "Why do you want to leave?" he said in his soft Geordie voice, and walked away.

One of the biggest disappointments on the field as far as I was concerned was our exit from the European Cup in my first season.

We were determined to regain the cup that Liverpool had won thanks to a left foot drive by Alan Kennedy against Bayern Munich in 1981. Liverpool had lost the following season against CSKA Sofia in the quarter finals, Aston Villa eventually winning the trophy.

We beat Dundalk 5-0 over two legs – and in the second round we were drawn away to Helsinki in Finland.

Some Football League grounds can be described as characterless, but Helsinki was much worse than that. There was no atmosphere, the pitch was frozen solid, and there were only 5000 or so fans in the ground. No wonder we lost 1-0, it was just like a training game. We turned it around though in the second leg, beating them 5-0 at Anfield.

In those days, the competition was for league champions only, and so the quarter final wasn't until March, in Widzew Lodz. We lost 2-0 over there, but we were quite confident of turning it around in the second leg at Anfield. However, we conceded an early goal to go 3-0 down on aggregate, and despite a stirring second half in which I scored, we went out 4-3 on aggregate. Their early away goal gave us too much to do. It was a big blow to Liverpool, especially after Nottingham Forest, as well as Villa, had won the competition in previous years. After all, Liverpool thought they were the top English team in Europe.

There was plenty of consolation. We won the league, even though we didn't win any of our last seven matches, and I finished the season with enough league games under my belt to earn a championship medal – one of my most treasured possessions – to go with the Milk Cup winners' medal which I was given as part of the squad which got to Wembley and beat Manchester United 2-1. I wasn't there, because I was suffering from Quincy's disease.

It was strange how medals were handed out at Liverpool. There was no ceremony, no announcements. We came in from training one day and found our medals next to our kit. I held mine and looked at it for ages, while the other lads, who had won a few medals before, just nonchalantly popped them into pockets, as if they were picking up a handkerchief or something.

I played a few games alongside Rushy, who became a Liverpool legend, even more so after he scored those four against Everton in the local derby. He wasn't a great all round player, but he could sure score goals. Outside the box, he got the ball and passed it, and never took more than three or four touches. He wasn't a target man, and didn't dribble.

But he was breathtaking in the area. He had fantastic speed over the first few yards and could easily beat defenders to the ball. And he could read Kenny well, and knew where he was going to put the ball for him.

For training, he would turn up wearing the usual training kit, which consisted of a very heavy woollen jumper, which was a nightmare to wear when it was wet. If you didn't run around on a wet day, it became even worse. On one occasion when we were training on a red gravel surface, Rushy was in his usual mood of standing around in front of goal. Because of the heavy rain, he suffered the worst, and had to be carried off with hypothermia!

However, come Saturday afternoon, he was as fast as lightning again. He scored around eighty goals in my two seasons there. I could have done with somebody like him in my Darlington years, Marco Gabbiadini excepted.

Rushy and I were quite friendly. We travelled together quite a bit, and he drove a Renault Fuego, which by a little stretch of the imagination, looked like a Porsche 924. A friend of mine had a BMW in pristine condition available, so I put Rushy in touch with him. He managed to find the money, because believe it or not, even though he was the top scorer in the league and a huge crowd hero, he wasn't on more than £500 per week. He wouldn't have problems finding a car these days with all the money that's about in the Premiership!

My £450,000 transfer from Boro to Liverpool was the highest transfer that season. I didn't exactly tell the lads that I was on £1200 per week, but they had a fair idea. Mind you, I spent £1300 per week on clothes!

Kenny Dalglish was, and still is, a great friend. I learned a few weeks after I'd joined that he'd got the tip from my old boss at Boro, Bobby Murdoch, that I would need looking after. I knew the two of them were good friends, and of course they were both Celtic and Scotland legends.

Kenny was an enormous help. Not only with sponsorship deals, but also with carpets, kitchens and decorating. Kenny seemed to know everybody.

I bought a new house in the Wirral, south of the River Mersey, for £82,000, a huge amount of money then, and Kenny arranged almost everything.

It was fantastic. It was a white walled house in its own grounds, and there were blue lights shining on it from the lawn, which made it look really nice at night.

I thought nothing about it, but other people did. The chairman, John Smith, approached me after a game one day.

"Hodgy, I've got a problem in the Wirral," he said.

"What's that?" I replied, hoping I could help him with something and gain some brownie points.

"Your house."

"My house?"

"Yes, your house has blue lights. Change them to red, please."

That's how deep passions ran in Merseyside.

The house looked gorgeous in blue, and didn't look quite the same in red.

On another occasion, I must admit I two-timed Amanda, my girlfriend. She was away, and I took another girl, Jill, back to the house. The drive was quite long, and when it was time to go home, I reversed my car out of the drive, and told her just to follow me.

I sat waiting for two or three minutes, but there was no sign of any reversing lights. I drove thirty or forty yards back down the drive, and all I could see was a pair of headlights parked neatly on my front lawn. I'm sure it was a put-up job by the chairman, because she'd ripped out the blue lights shining on the house.

There were tyre marks all over the lawn where she'd tried to drive away and got stuck. There were holes over a foot deep in places. Plus, she told me later, she hadn't passed her driving test.

When Amanda came home and saw the state of the lawn, I blamed Rushy and his new car.

I went with Amanda to the bank, where Jill worked. "You won't be wearing that sweater of yours again, now that somebody else has got one," she said, pointing at Jill. I didn't dare tell her that it was mine!

At the start of season 1983-84, Liverpool bought Michael Robinson from Brighton. He'd been one of Brighton's top players and helped them to the 1983 Cup final, in which they'd beaten us at Anfield in the fifth round and then lost the final in a replay to Manchester United.

He was one of the most polite people I'd ever met, and he roomed with me on away trips. He even helped me write my transfer requests.

I was by now the entertainments manager in the dressing room, with the responsibility of looking after the new players.

Michael went with us a on a pre-season tour to Morocco, and on the first night, he asked reception for an extra pillow. I thought he was just uncomfortable, but he laid it next to him and cuddled it, pretending it was his girlfriend! Needless to say, that incident spread like wildfire, but the rest of the lads really took to him.

Joe was the manager now, because Bob had called it a day and become a director of the club. The lads had a nice touch for Bob, insisting that he led the way up the Wembley steps to receive the Milk Cup the previous season.

Michael was brought to the club as my replacement, but he and I became such great friends. We used to travel together to training, and if we were late, Joe or Ronnie would say, "Fog in the tunnel, again, lads?"

On another trip, to Lucerne in Switzerland, we were staying in a really smart hotel, which was ranked as one of the top hotels in the world. Our room was fantastic, really top class. There were two massive beds, huge sofas, minibars and state of the art televisions, by far the best I'd stayed in.

Michael fancied a drink, so he rang down to reception and asked for a pot of tea and some biscuits for two people.

Ten minutes later, there was a knock at the door and here was a fleet of people with a trolley each. One with a pot of tea for Michael, one for me, a third with a plate of biscuits for Michael, and a fourth for me. It wasn't a wind up. We couldn't believe it.

Some of the lads came in, and told us that their rooms were nowhere near as good as ours. Joe and Ronnie came along, and said that our room was far superior to theirs, and we expected to be swapped. But no, the arrangements were left as they were for the full week. It was another example of how Liverpool wanted the players to be happy and comfortable.

However, I was frustrated at sitting on the bench all the time, and in my second season at the club, I must have been on the bench about twenty times.

Our social life was incredible. After one particular night on the town, an argument broke out between us. It was nothing serious, but more about body shape and who was the thinnest between us. I maintained that I was and that he had a big backside, and some friends managed to get hold of a measuring tape. They must have fixed the result, because they announced that my backside was two inches bigger than his. I walked out of the house in the huff.

Michael never told me that he hadn't passed his driving test, even though he was driving around in a 7 Series BMW. He drove me to training one day, and he was doing a ton when there was a blue flashing light behind us. In a panic, Michael admitted to me that he hadn't passed his test, and had no insurance to go with it. To his relief, the police car passed us, obviously on its way to an emergency. I didn't travel much with Michael after that.

Michael was very upper class. Nobody called him Micky, but he wasn't a patch on Souey.

He was nicknamed Champagne Charlie, and in all due respect to Michael, Souey was a class above everybody else. He wasn't just our leader on the pitch; he had total respect in the changing room, and had a real air of arrogance about him. He was one of the lads right to the nail.

He scored some great goals from long distance, and although he didn't have great pace, you never saw him receiving the ball unless he was in space. He had a football brain on a par with Kenny Dalglish, and could dominate a game from start to finish because he was head and shoulders above everybody on the pitch.

His car was always a top of the range Mercedes, although he nearly conned me into buying a Golf GTI from him once. I'd discovered that he'd bought it for next to nothing, and he was trying to bump me!

Come to think about it, he bumped me several years later, something which he conveniently forgot about on his move to Turkey.

He was a superb leader, and was a real hard man in midfield. He was a ball winner, but he had a really good creative side to him as well. Nobody argued much with him on the field.

We played at Sunderland one day and Sunderland defender Shaun Elliott – who later became a great friend of mine when I moved to Roker Park – made it known that he was going to "kick" me and Rushy.

Souey pulled me to one side, and told me to hold the ball on the touchline when I got the opportunity.

So first chance I got, I did what Souey told me, and Shaun tried to do me from behind.

I saw Souey coming in from an angle, so I backed slightly into Shaun, who was then completely cleaned out by Souey, who won the ball, and put Shaun into the

Sunderland dugout.

On another occasion, we played Forest at Anfield, and playing for Forest was Martin O'Neill who for some reason Souey didn't see eye to eye with.

Martin got the ball just in front of the dugout, and Souey scythed him down from the side. Martin was lifted on to a stretcher, made some sort of adverse comment to Souey, who replied, "You won't be out for the second half, I take it!"

Souey was a magnificent leader of Liverpool during that time. It was because of his leadership and aggression that Liverpool won so many trophies during his time there. He returned to Anfield later as manager, but even though his team won the FA Cup, he never managed to win the league.

I was proud to be part of one of the greatest moments in Liverpool's history in 1984.

The European Cup was a tough competition in those days – some would argue tougher than its successor, the Champions' League – but it was even tougher in 1984 because we had to play Roma in the final on their own ground, the Olympic Stadium!

Talk about having an advantage, but that didn't bother us. Most of the players in the squad had been involved in big European Cup ties before, so we were mentally ready for it.

I dressed for the occasion, in my role as fashion trendsetter. I wore a cream and brown chamois leather suit, with Jesus sandals to match. Told you I liked to spend my money in those days on clothes!

Not surprisingly, there was a hostile atmosphere in the stadium, and our fans were well outnumbered.

While we were in the tunnel waiting to go out on the field – I was one of the subs – I started singing the catchy Chris Rea song at the time "I don't know what it is, but I love it."

Sammy Lee and Craig Johnston joined in, and by the time the Roma team joined us in the tunnel, every single one of the Liverpool players was in full song, mega loud. The Roma players were taken aback; they must have thought it was an English battle song or something.

Other people have taken the credit for starting that song, but I can assure you that it was me.

The match, of course, will be remembered for the penalty shootout win, and Bruce Grobelaar's wobbly knees act. Talk about a cool head, but his trick certainly worked, with the last Italian putting his penalty way over the bar, ready for Alan Kennedy to finish Roma off with a successful spot kick.

The night out afterwards was unforgettable, at least while we were still sober. The trip home the following day was amazing. We had a tour around the city on an open top bus with the three trophies we'd won that season – the European Cup, the Milk Cup and the Football League title. At the time, it didn't all sink in, and there were times later in my career when I wish it had done, because I might not have left.

I wish now that I'd dug in mentally, and scrapped it out for a place in the starting line up. Maybe I shouldn't have allowed certain things to get under my skin, and maybe I should have used my head a little bit more.

Joe Fagan took over from Bob Paisley at the end of my first season in 1983, and there were times when we didn't see eye to eye. We had a big fall out one day before we were due to play Brighton in an evening league game in March 1983 just before the Milk Cup final, when Joe was assistant manager.

We'd flown down there on the morning of the game, and after lunch, we returned to our rooms for three or four hours' sleep.

Around about 5.30, Joe Fagan and Ronnie Moran went through their usual routine of waking the players up, but there was no need to wake me up, because I hadn't slept at all. I was in a terrible state – I was freezing and shivering non-stop.

I told Joe that I couldn't play, and he went ballistic with me, suggesting that I didn't want to play, a touch of psychology maybe.

But I was in no fit state to play, and I was sent to the club doctor, who immediately insisted that I return home, because I had a temperature of 110 degrees.

The doctor gave me some tablets that unfortunately had an adverse effect and made me hallucinate, which caused my girlfriend, Amanda, to panic. She called my usual doctor in Lower Heswall village, and when he came, he immediately told Amanda I had the wrong tablets.

After I went to a specialist, I was told I had Quincy's disease, which affects the mouth and throat, and I lost nearly two stones in weight. Even on the Thursday leading up to the Milk Cup final against Manchester United, I was in a real bad way, but I still insisted on going to the match. I sent Amanda into Liverpool to buy two suits, one to travel in and one for the match, but I didn't manage to wear either suit – because I just wasn't fit enough to go. I would have been at least a sub.

When I was fit again, my first priority was to see Joe, and told him that he owed me an apology, but I was never convinced that he was satisfied.

There was another incident in training one day. Joe felt I wasn't trying hard enough, and he told me; "If you're not going to train properly, then don't train at all," which was a contradiction to my first session a year earlier. I suppose it was his way of making way for the arrival of Michael Robinson from Brighton, although Liverpool were strongly interested in Charlie Nicholas from Celtic as well. I suppose I should have seen it coming earlier.

After we won the European Cup in 1984, we went on a trip to South Africa. Not all the players were keen on going, and some of the star names didn't go.

I thought I played really well in all three games, and we won the tournament, picking up some good prize money in the process.

The winners were always invited back, but no way did the players want to go back the following year – they fancied their old haunt in Malaga.

So we sort of staged an argument with one of the organisers afterwards. I asked the barman for a bucket of ice, which I poured over an organiser's head. I apologised later, but for some reason, can't think why, the club never got invited back.

The players went to Malaga on holiday, and I didn't return for six weeks except to attend the wedding of TV commentator Clive Tyldesley. He was so methodical, that when he married his wife, Pauline, he worked out the route from every guest's home to the venue for the wedding, with descriptions of every landmark along the way – although he didn't do a route for me from Malaga! The next day I flew back out to Spain.

I returned to Liverpool for pre-season training two stones heavier, and shaped like a bottle of Guinness.

By then, Souey had left the club for Italian club Sampdoria. Joe asked to me to pop into the training ground one day. I wondered – bad news or good news? Bad news, I'd be staying, good news, I'd be going. How stupid was I, wanting to leave Liverpool?

After some small talk, I brought into the conversation just what he was expecting of me in the new season.

"Do you fancy playing on the right side of midfield?" he asked.

"You're joking," I replied. "That's Sammy Lee's place."

I realised soon after that Joe didn't want to hear that sort of reaction. At the start of season 1984-85, I was named as sub for Liverpool against Everton in the Charity Shield. The game wasn't going Liverpool's way, and on the bench, I suggested to Joe that he put me on so then I could cause problems for Everton full back John Bailey, who didn't have any pace. But Joe refused, and the following Monday, I told Joe that I wanted to leave.

He asked me where I wanted to go, and I told him "I want to go home". Boro were out of the question because they were struggling, so Sunderland was my choice.

Joe phoned through to reception and asked for Len Ashurst, the Sunderland manager, on the phone. Joe handed me the phone, and said: "If you want to go to Sunderland, you ask their manager if he wants you." I already knew they did through my mate Proc, who was now at Roker Park after moving there from Nottingham Forest. I spoke to Len, and spoke about a move.

Leaving Joe on the phone to discuss the deal, I returned home. Joe said he would call me later in the afternoon if a deal could be reached.

Sure enough, he rang at 4pm, to tell me that a deal had been agreed, and I could talk to Sunderland about terms – but he told me over and over again not to sign until I'd spoken to him. He was playing mind games, but I didn't grasp them.

I went straight up to Sunderland, and because I was carried away by the notion of joining the club I supported as a boy, I signed on the dotted line, even though I was taking a big pay cut. I rang Joe, who went ballistic.

"You're stupid, you've just made the biggest mistake of your life," he blasted.

I thought I wasn't figuring in Joe's plans. Just a few weeks later, it was announced that my mate Kenny, who'd also told me not to be too hasty, was going to become player-manager of Liverpool.

Joe could have rubbed it in if he wanted to, but he didn't. "Hodgy, I never opened your transfer requests, you're still entitled to a cut of the transfer fee." Thanks to Joe, I got £25,000, because it appeared as if I hadn't asked for a transfer.

Joe's prophecy was proved to be correct. It was a stupid thing I'd done – I regretted signing for Sunderland immediately.

Back to the north east;
The train now standing
at Seaburn Station

Initially, it was great to be back in the north east, looking forward to playing for the club I'd supported as a boy from the Fulwell End. I was going to achieve my boyhood ambition and wear the famous red and white stripes.

But it was a move I would live to regret, and the warning signs were there from my first day at the club.

Len Ashurst, the Sunderland manager, quickly made his mark. He said he wanted to introduce me to the press, and that was fine by me. But I wasn't ready for what came next.

A small passageway led from the manager's office to the boardroom where the press were assembled, and as Len and I were walking down this corridor, he suddenly stopped, rammed his finger in my chest and said: "You are at Sunderland now, not Liverpool, and you will do as I tell you," and proceeded to tell me what I had to say and what was expected of me. I didn't take kindly to that. I was by now a senior professional, and I didn't need him to tell me what I had to say to the media, especially in such an aggressive manner.

It didn't help when I entered the press room, and Bob Cass, whom I knew from my Boro days, offended me straight away: "It's not normal for Liverpool to let good players go," he said. He may have meant that they had broken with tradition and that I was one of their good players. But I took it to mean that he thought they had sold me because I had not lived up to their expectations.

Diplomacy was called for. I couldn't harp on about Liverpool, because that would upset Len, and I didn't want to turn on Bob, and create an immediate bad impression with the press.

So I said: "I'm the same player that you wrote about and praised when I was at Boro."

However, deep down I knew he had made a valid point.

I missed the first game of my spell at Roker Park, because I had not signed in time for the first game of the season. We beat Southampton 3-1, Gary Bennett, Barry Venison, and my old mate Proc scoring the goals.

We had Chelsea to look forward to next. I loved the training. I was back home. I was happy, or so I thought.

We travelled to London on the Friday, and on Saturday morning Len came into my room with some kit, and said we were to go training. He took four of us to Hyde

Park, and ran us into the ground. I could not believe it.

A week earlier Len had been prodding me in the chest, and now he was making me run my socks off. When I got back to the hotel room I was dripping wet with sweat – so wet that Proc asked me if it was raining. And he was being serious.

I was a substitute, but went on for Proc. I had fifteen or twenty minutes, and even though we lost 1-0 I felt I did very well, and certainly covered a lot of ground on what was a very hot day.

I went in the bath for a soak, and had my whole body, even my face, under the water. Then through the water I could see Len bending over the bath. I surfaced, and he said: "You're not fit. You need to do a lot of running. If you were one of the fittest lads at Liverpool, then the rest of them can't be very fit."

Once again, he left me shaking my head in disbelief, and I began to wonder what I had let myself in for.

The next game, against Nottingham Forest, I pulled a stomach muscle, and didn't play after that for eight or nine games.

The team went on a good run while I was out – coincidence I hope – while ironically Liverpool struggled. I was asked by Sunderland to tap up Sammy Lee, as he was out of the Liverpool side. He was interested, but in the end nothing came of it.

I also had a fallout with the chairman Tom Cowie over a car. When I signed for Sunderland, I arranged a car deal with Vic Young, a local Nissan dealer, through a pal of mine, George Spriggs.

But then Tom, the owner of the Cowie car group, told me that I had to drive a car from another garage, Bradleys.

I argued that because there was nothing in my contract about having to drive a Bradley car, then I could arrange a deal with whoever I wanted.

The club insisted that I should drive a Bradley car, but I stood my ground. In the end, I agreed to drop my deal with Vic in return for two cars, one for me, and one for my girlfriend. Tom said: "I'm a car magnate, and I've been done over by a player over a car."

While I was out of the side, Len sent me to watch the opposition Sunderland were due to play, and compile reports, which I didn't mind doing. I learned skills that came in very useful later in my career.

The good form of the team continued, and it didn't really surprise me because we had some good players. A lot of us, me included, could best be described as misfits. We had talent, but had not fulfilled our potential.

I remember us beating Manchester United 3-2 at Roker Park. I was back in action by then and Len asked me – or rather told me – to play in a deep role and make sure that by whatever means possible, I got striker Mark Hughes, whom he singled out as the United dangerman, off the pitch.

We went for a ball together and I elbowed him to the ground. The ref missed it, but Bryan Robson didn't. He and other United players influenced the ref by protesting to him, then Hughes jumped up and had a go at me. The ref sent him off, then turned to me and dished out the same punishment.

I got changed and sat in the dugout feeling chuffed with myself. After all, I had done what I was told, and didn't feel bitter because I deserved to be sent off.

When I went back into the dressing room at the end of the match there was an envelope addressed to me. It was a fine of two weeks' wages for being sent off!

I was furious, and knew there and then that I had had enough of Len's style of management.

The schedule he put me through didn't help either. Even after training he would take me to a roundabout at Washington, drop me off, and tell me to run back. But it kept me fit. I could outrun the other lads, even the good ones like Nick Pickering, and he was picked for England. He loved running, and used to train with Olympic runner Steve Cram, a staunch Sunderland fan.

But despite my treatment from the gaffer, the football was enjoyable, some games more than others, and I was delighted when we beat Chelsea, managed by my old mentor John Neal, in the semi final of the Milk Cup, as the League Cup was known in those days.

I went up for a challenge with big Chelsea centre half Joe McLoughlin, elbowed him, and broke his nose. Fortunately, the referee didn't spot it; otherwise it would have been another sending off.

John said afterwards: "Hodgy, that's not you." But he had a selective memory, for he didn't complain when I was at Boro and did something similar to Norman Hunter that time against Bristol City. However, I was disappointed in myself for giving him the chance to say that.

Nevertheless we won 2-0 and had one foot at Wembley, but we had a hostile second leg at Stamford Bridge to negotiate.

For the second leg we got to Chelsea late because the crowds in the street deliberately held up the team bus, so we had to get changed on it. And even after the game started the fans did everything they could to intimidate us.

Being a former Chelsea player, our midfielder Clive Walker had a particularly rough ride. The home fans loudly booed him every time he touched the ball, and one fan even ran on the pitch and tried to kick him. But to be fair some fans cheered him, because he had been a big hero at Chelsea.

I also recall Dave Speedie, ironically a former Darlington hero, deliberately got Shaun Elliott booked, and unfortunately because of that Shaun was suspended and missed the final. It was a huge blow, because he was Sunderland through and through and paid a huge price for allowing himself to be baited.

In a way that cost us the cup, because David Corner came in for the final instead of Shaun, and unfortunately made the mistake that led to Norwich scoring the only goal.

But the Chelsea game was bizarre. There was pandemonium everywhere on and off the pitch, and, honestly, there was actually a police horse galloping across the pitch when the cross came in for Colin West to score our third goal. The ref said he didn't want to stop the game if he could help it.

It was a real hostile night, and it was around that time that the controversial Chelsea chairman, Ken Bates, wanted the authorities to erect electric fences round pitches. That was extreme thinking even for those volatile times, but anyone at that game could be forgiven for thinking that Ken had a point.

Even after the game, things threatened to boil over. Clive went to confront Speedo, and Micky Droy, who was Clive's best friend, lifted Speedo by the collar and dragged him away. But it didn't help when one of our lads offered to send Speedo a cup final programme.

Shortly before the final we beat our Milk Cup final opponents Norwich 3-1 in a league game, a valuable win for us in our relegation fight. I scored one and set Ian Wallace up for another.

I had always played well against Norwich, for Boro and other clubs, and at one point Norwich boss Ken Brown tried to sign me.

Before we travelled to the final, Len picked the team, and we worked together at Roker, but then he changed it on the morning of the final, going round the rooms to tell the players, which naturally didn't go down well.

Before the game Len called me into his room and asked what effect I thought Wembley could have on a young player. I said that it didn't do Richie Pitt any harm when Sunderland won the FA Cup in 1973.

David Corner got the nod, and his mistake cost us when the ball was stolen away from him leading to the only goal. But to be fair to the poor lad, he had been given the shout (not by me!) to let the ball run out of play for a goal kick. He tried to shield it over the line, but it was nicked from him and three touches later, the ball was in the back of our net.

Centre forward Colin West was left out, and Ian Wallace played on his own up front in a formation that we hadn't used before. Against Dave Watson and Steve Bruce he had no chance. I played wide on the right, but the whole balance of the team was upset by the line-up.

Clive missed a penalty (Westy was the usual penalty taker), and early in the game I hit the bar. It was me who won the penalty, when a defender slid in on me and handled the ball as I tried to go round him.

It was a bad day all round. The wives and girlfriends were supposed to have prime seats behind the directors' box, and that was the area the players waved to when we came out thinking that they were there. But instead they had been placed near the tunnel end. And to make matters worse they had been dropped off at the top of Wembley Way and had to walk down to the ground in their best clothes, to wolf whistles and jeers from both sets of fans.

Even on the tour round the streets when we got home, only a few fans showed up. Barry Batey, one of the directors, arranged for the team bus to go around the streets near Roker Park, but it was a complete disaster. Everybody, fans and players, were flat. I'm sure it was different in Norfolk.

However it had been a friendly final, because the Norwich public were, and still are, great people, and the atmosphere in the ground was really good.

It was bitterly disappointing to lose, because earlier in the season we were going through a good spell and even scored the winner at Watford when the ball flew into the net off Nick Pickering's backside!

In the fourth round we drew 0-0 at home to Spurs, and in the away game the manager had us training to use some unlikely tactics. The idea was to deliberately get ourselves caught offside to disrupt the game and knock Spurs out of their stride.

When the ball was played back to the Spurs keeper, we were to close him down so that he had to launch the ball forward rather than set up the play from the back.

We knew that our central defenders Shaun Elliott and Gordon Chisholm would win the header and send the ball forward, leaving our forwards, Howard Gayle on the right and Clive on the left, offside. That would mean a free kick, and Spurs' rhythm was disrupted.

Spurs hardmen Paul Miller and Graham Roberts gave me a hard time in that game, even spitting at me to try and rile me, but I gave as good as I got. And even though Roberts scored with a penalty, we won 2-1, Clive and Chis scoring.

So all the omens looked good, but in the final it wasn't to be.

And from the final it went downhill. We had an awful run of results, winning just once in the last couple of months of the season after Wembley – and that was a dull 1-0 win at Coventry. Len lost the support of the dressing room. Two or three of the lads may have been unprofessional, but he lost us.

To be fair to him, however, he was dedicated to the club, as a player and a manager. Len had played for the club in the sixties, and desperately wanted to do well. He had played with some of the Sunderland all time greats like Charlie Hurley, and wanted to make his mark as a manager at the club for the right reasons.

Now that I'm older I can see what he was trying to achieve, but it slipped away from him.

At the end of the season, the players wanted their FA Cup Final tickets, but Len said he didn't have them. However one of the lads looked into the bin in his room, and there was the envelope. Needless to say, that didn't go down too well either. Normally the players got them, but not this time, and we had to draw lots for a couple which we'd managed to obtain from other people.

Bill Bradshaw of The People newspaper did a big article on Len. I got a phone call from Bill one day when I was sitting in my rented house in Acklam.

He said that some of the other Sunderland players had told him various things about the manager. I told Bill that I wasn't interested. I said that if the manager was to lose his job, I didn't want to be brought into the equation. I stressed that if the other lads wanted to talk, then let them. I wouldn't have any part in it, on or off the record.

I said to my girlfriend, Amanda: "Len is going to get the sack". I had had many a ding-dong with him, but I didn't want him to lose his job.

When the article in the paper came out, it implied that a recent big signing had dished the dirt. That pointed towards me, but I knew who was responsible.

There was a players' dinner the same night, and I went feeling very uncomfortable because I knew that suspicion would fall on me.

The manager was sacked, and in what the club called a huge coup, Lawrie McMenemy returned to his native north east and took over. I was delighted that Frank Burrows stayed on, because I thought the world of him. He was demoted from first team coach to reserve team coach, but at least he was still there, as he had been brilliant to me during the difficult times at the club.

I must admit, I think I would have cracked up if it wasn't for Frank. He was, and still is, a very understanding bloke. He spent a lot of time with me, encouraging me and helping me, plus he also gave me some responsibility with the youth and reserve teams by running training sessions. So some good came out of a really intense situation, and I learned plenty about how to handle players. To this day, I consider him to be a very good friend.

Originally I thought it was brilliant that Lawrie had taken over, owing to the name he had in the game for the success of his Southampton team.

He had even been talked about as a possible England manager, so I was excited about the prospects of him taking over.

I tried very hard to keep myself in shape that summer, so that I could impress in pre-season training. When we reported back the new manager gave a big speech about his huge house in Hampshire, how much money he had, and what he had achieved in his career.

He told us; "Imagine there is a train at Seaburn station, so if you want to be successful, jump on the train with me".

What a load of rubbish. As far as I'm concerned that train has never left the station.

We went to a hotel near London for a training week. It was a normal week, with plenty of hard work. There was a good spirit amongst the players, all of whom were trying to convince the gaffer about what we were capable of doing. Lawrie gave us a day off as he said we had all worked very hard. He told us to get out of the hotel and do our own thing, but having said that, something wasn't ringing right between Lawrie and me.

I went into London with Barry Venison and Dave Swindlehurst. All we had to do was ring in to say whether we would be back for the evening meal.

When we rang, coach Lew Chatterley answered, and told us to get back immediately. When we asked why, he said that we were all going to the pictures. We were happy shopping, but thought we had better do what we were told.

We jumped into a black London cab. It took two hours and cost a fortune, around £140 if I remember correctly.

When we arrived, hardly any of the other lads were there, and the film was rubbish. Lawrie had done it on purpose.

On the way home from the weekend on the coach, a fight broke out between Ian

Wallace and Shaun Elliott. Keeper Seamus McDonagh, a gentle Irish giant, stepped in to break it up. I was at the front of the bus and didn't get involved, but the manager blamed me. I had to go and ask the driver to tell him that I had no part in it, and the driver did.

From there the relationship between me and Lawrie deteriorated 100 per cent. I never hated a manager so much, and even called him Lawrie MyEnemy.

Alan Kennedy came to the club from Liverpool as captain, and great bloke though he was, he was not captain material. Frank Clark, Eric Gates, Frank Gray and George Burley signed for us as well.

I sussed exactly what the manager was doing. He was bringing in experienced players to do the job for him, just as he had done at Southampton, with Peter Shilton, Kevin Keegan, Mick Mills and Alan Ball.

Lawrie's training sessions were terrible. Then his son Chris arrived as coach. One of our best coaches, Ian Hughes, who had won the FA Youth Cup for the club, lost his job. It was a tough decision for Lawrie, to replace a respected coach with his own son.

However, I didn't mind Chris McMenemy – even though I hated his father. Chris won the respect of all the players, young and old. I had an awful lot of time for him.

Because my relationship with Lawrie had deteriorated so much, I was left out of the team, but returned for a League Cup match at Roker.

I stepped up to take a penalty, and heard Lew Chatterley yelling from the touchline to the lads, ordering them not to let me take it. I scored at the Fulwell End and a couple of the players made gestures towards Lew.

I was scoring goals galore for the reserves, but the manager made me train with the kids. I turned up for first team training one day and he made me rush to catch the mini-bus with the juniors. Frank asked what I was doing there, but we both knew that Lawrie was trying to sicken me off.

But I worked even harder, and I remember Eric Gates asking me how I managed to keep my chin up.

I didn't know how I did it, because I was having a bad time. I had split up with Amanda, which was pretty hard as I had been with her for a long time. Even though I had a club car with my name on it, I was back home living with my family, and trying to force my way into the first team picture. It was like starting all over again.

It happened that Lawrie's sister had been working at the Pear Tree pub in Gateshead, but unfortunately she had lost her job before my dad took it over.

Lawrie called me to his office at 1pm one afternoon, and left me waiting outside for three hours. I knew I would be fined if I walked away, so I stood there – like the Coldstream Guard that he used to be.

He knew I was there. I kicked the wall from time to time to ensure that he knew, but he claimed, when he finally saw me, that he had forgotten.

He said he was unhappy with my social life, and proceeded to tell me that he'd seen my car parked outside a pub on Sunderland Road in Felling most nights.

At this point, I was laughing so loud inside, that I could hardly control myself.

He asked me about my social life, and I said, "I don't have one," which at that time was true. He asked if I was calling him a liar. I said, "Yes."

He said he had evidence that I was out every night, but I stood my ground and said that I didn't go drinking in Sunderland Road.

He then asked; "Has your car been parked outside that shitty pub, the Pear Tree, in Sunderland Road every night?"

I admitted it, and he looked smug saying: "I knew it."

I couldn't get the words out quick enough. His face fell when I said: "I live there. Every night I go through the bar, through the back, and up to my room."

He didn't know what to say, and eventually muttered something about my clothes being too flash and the lads didn't like them.

And I replied by saying; "You must have been looking in the mirror yourself when you thought of that one."

It's strange to think that he almost took over at Manchester United during his days at Southampton. If he had, in my opinion, they would have been doomed.

We went seven games without a win at the start of the season, and then I was recalled for the game at Shrewsbury.

We had drawn 1-1 at Leeds the week before and I assumed that the team would be unchanged. When I was picked I was delighted, and was getting changed when Lew came up to me and asked me what I was doing.

"Putting my strapping on," I replied. "I've always done it myself."

But Lew said: "Not while I'm here you don't." That's what he and Lawrie were like. Changing things for the sake of it, and upsetting people along the way.

I was playing really well in the game, but Lawrie pulled me off and put Howard Gayle on. I was far from happy.

Anyway the manager had a top of the range BMW, but could not drive it back from the game, as he had had too much to drink with the directors.

I said I would drive it home, but he said: "No way." However there were no other volunteers, as we had won our first game of the season – Nick Pickering scored twice – and everybody wanted a drink on the bus.

So I got to drive this brand new Series 7 BMW. It did 120 miles per hour, and it's a good job that there were no speed cameras, or I would have got more points than Sunderland!

I had to fill up with petrol on the way back, but as I didn't pick up a receipt, the manager wouldn't reimburse me. But I got my own back. I bided my time, then a few weeks later let his tyres down on a long distance away trip, and he was stranded!

The animosity between us continued. Maybe he had got the impression that Len Ashurst's sacking was down to me, though I swear to this day that it wasn't.

Lawrie even put it in the newspapers that I was only at Liverpool as entertainments manager, which really annoyed me.

For an away game at Carlisle, Clive and I were left out of the squad, so we went off to the Post House hotel at Washington to play snooker. We had a bottle of wine while we listened to the game on the radio.

Two lads came in and beat us at snooker taking £50 each in bets from us. They completely conned us by letting us win the first couple of frames, before suggesting that we played for money, and like fools we fell for it!

Unknown to Lawrie, by now I lived with Dave Swindlehurst, one of our strikers, in a place overlooking Sedgefield racecourse – it was Stan Cummins' old house.

One Thursday, Dave and I had a fight, I can't remember over what, and I put his shoulder out.

After Dave told Lawrie he was injured, I went in for training, and Lawrie said he was picking me rather than Dave for the next game at Boro. He made it sound like he preferred me. He didn't know that I knew Dave was injured.

I had an abductor problem, but I defied it by playing on a rockhard pitch at Boro. We lost 2-0 and Lawrie said I hadn't pulled my weight.

In a game at Oldham when we were 1-0 down, the Sunderland fans turned on the manager. We got a penalty and I snatched the ball, only to hear the familiar cry of Lew Chatterley trying to stop me from taking it. I scored.

To this day I still say that Lawrie was an imposter as a football manager. And one thing is certain. I can hold my head higher in Sunderland than he can.

I later heard – from Jim Smith and Ken Brown – that Lawrie tried to stop Norwich from signing me, as he wanted to offload me to a club in Sweden, IFK Gothenburg, who went on to win the European Cup. I refused to go.

At one point Lawrie tried to convince me to go to Darlington – so I could have arrived here earlier than I did!

Lawrie sounded out Darlo manager Cyril Knowles, and of course he agreed, because Darlo at the time were in the old Third Division.

I immediately told Lawrie that I had no intention of joining Darlington, and I actually drove down to see my old Boro team mate John Craggs, by now the Darlington assistant manager, at Feethams, and told him face to face why I was turning the Quakers down. I told him that I had no intentions of coming to Darlington, and that I was better than the Third Division. John accepted that, so I turned my back on Feethams – not for the last time in my life!

Inevitably, the day came when I was called into Lawrie's office, to be told that because of my injuries he was letting me go, despite the fact that I'd been scoring plenty for the reserves.

And then he had the nerve to tell me that if I couldn't get fixed up with a club, I could go back to him and he would try and sort something out on lesser terms!

Geoff Davidson, the secretary, looked amazed. He knew that it had all been a personal issue, and he was clearly surprised to hear that. There was also the matter of the club writing off a player for nothing who had cost £175,000 from Liverpool just two years before.

In July 1986, a few weeks after I was freed, I was offered a very large sum of money, £25,000 to be exact, by a national Sunday newspaper, to tell my side of the story.

The witch hunt had begun for Lawrie, but my principles were the same as they were with Len. No matter how much the newspaper offered, I wasn't going to be responsible for a man losing his job. In fact, I did the opposite, and did a piece with a different newspaper saying that I thought Lawrie would turn Sunderland around, amongst a few other positive things.

A month later, Lawrie spoke to Ken Brown, the Norwich manager, and asked him to pass on his thanks to me for the article I'd done. My response to Ken was, that it was a shame he couldn't have rung me himself.

Incredibly a few months later, Lawrie wrote a big article himself in one of the nationals, and his attitude was exactly the opposite. He slaughtered me, Proc, Howard Gayle and Clive Walker, blaming us for Sunderland's downfall, which was totally unjustified. Then he took a fortnight's holiday to avoid the backlash. Thanks Lawrie!

Around the world without playing; "Are you injured again?"

The phrase "Have boots will travel" clearly applied to me after I was released by Sunderland, and it became a journey that was to shape my life after I finished playing.

For the first time in my playing career, I was a free agent, under contract to nobody and in a position to negotiate my own wages.

But I had a big obstacle to overcome, the fact that the word had gone around football circles that I was supposed to be a lazy so and so, and a troublemaker, amongst other things.

I had a call from IFK Gothenburg, through an agent called Tom Lawrence junior, who was part of the Strata group based in London. I went for some talks, and I was persuaded to take part in a training session, though to be honest even though IFK Gothenburg went on to win the European Cup, I wasn't overly impressed with the standard. They offered me a deal which included a house, a Volvo car and an £80,000 signature fee, and I almost signed until it broke down on agent's fees.

Jim Smith, the manager at QPR at the time, offered me a better deal, but I didn't fancy moving to London. Willie McFaul, who was then Newcastle manager, was supposed to be interested, but I heard nothing definite. I suppose if I'd signed for them, I would have played for all of the north east's big three, just like Alan Foggon in the seventies! Don't know how it would have gone down with my Sunderland supporting mates back in Gateshead, though.

Coventry City asked me to tour Holland with them, but I didn't fancy Highfield Road.

Ken Brown at Norwich, who had been manager when they beat us in the Milk Cup final, then got in touch. Lawrie had spoken to him and told him, for reasons best known to him, not to take me.

So to prove Lawrie and Ken's original impression wrong, I signed for £500 per week, which was about half the other offers, with no signing on fee. It bothered me that Lawrie had gone out of his way to say those sorts of things about me, and fortunately Ken relied on his own judgement and remembered me from my days in the England Under 21s and at Boro.

I looked upon the move as a great opportunity to re-establish myself in the First Division after being out in the cold at Sunderland.

Just when I thought my career at Carrow Road was starting well, injuries again interfered, much to my frustration. I scored three in a pre-season friendly at Cambridge, but then hurt my ankle wearing a pair of borrowed boots at Colchester, which meant I missed the start of the 1986-87 Football League season.

I managed to come on as a sub a couple of times for Norwich in September 1986, and I got a chance to play in the Littlewoods Cup against Millwall in late October because Wayne Biggins was injured. I couldn't have played better, and scored a hat trick playing alongside Kevin Drinkell in a 4-1 win.

I played the next three games in the First Division, but Wayne recovered, and Ken restored his partnership with Kevin, dropping me to the bench.

The 0-0 draw at home to Manchester United in November was a defining point in my career, as it seemed to spark off a wave of injuries.

Paul McGrath, the United centre half, caught me in the lowest part of my back in a challenge, and I collapsed to the ground unable to move. My back was in total spasm, and I was very conscious that if I moved, I could cripple myself. I had twisted my back, and had to be carried off the pitch after lengthy treatment.

I was in hospital for several days, and out of the first team reckoning for two months, an absence which I couldn't really afford from a personal point of view. Norwich physio Tim Shepherd was a tower of strength with plenty of encouragement– just like a few others during my career!

When I was fit again, it was very tough to get back into the first team. Norwich reserves played every Friday night, and Ken's policy was to pick the best players from the reserve game as subs for the first team the following day. It seemed pointless to me – how could a player be match fit if he'd run flat out the previous night for ninety minutes? I made the subs' bench a few times, but never really made an impact.

Then, out of the blue in March 1987, Middlesbrough asked if they could take me on loan.

I had great misgivings, because I wasn't match fit thanks to the injuries, and I was a few pounds overweight, but the appeal of returning to my first club, and to the north east, was huge.

Boro's chief scout Barrie Geldart had been to watch me in the reserves, and convinced manager Bruce Rioch that I could maybe do them a job. This was Boro's Third Division season, when they were reborn after the crisis in the summer of 1986.

It was great to go back to Ayresome Park, and the fans were really good to me, but I couldn't do the move justice. It was a different era. I'd left five years previously, a long time in football terms, and another group of fans had come along who wouldn't have been there in my previous spell. Nobody saw the old me – they didn't have much chance to!

I played two games for Boro. My debut was a 3-1 defeat at Bournemouth, and my second game was at home to Joe Jordan's Bristol City, one of Boro's main promotion rivals. It was a game to forget as far as I was concerned – and I'm sure I could say that for Bruce as well!

Early in the game, Joe Jordan elbowed defender Colin Cooper – who was then in his teens – and I gave Joe a few verbals for doing it. When City got a corner, Joe tried to elbow me, but missed, which was fortunate, because if he had connected, he would have smashed my face. We had a right ding-dong in the middle of the penalty area.

I must admit, I lost my temper completely after that. When Keith Curle came sliding towards me for the ball, I waited for him out of the corner of my eye, and elbowed him. The linesman saw it, told the referee, who then quite rightly sent me off. Fortunately, Keith and I get on better now, and I keep my elbows down when he approaches.

Bruce was livid, sent me back to Norwich, fined me two weeks' wages, and held on to my registration for the duration of my month's loan, which meant I couldn't even play reserve team football.

My initial impressions of Bruce weren't good, but I got to know him better post-Boro. We always had a nice conversation, and he was a thoughtful man.

The whole Boro episode was a disaster before I went back, when I was there, and when I left. I really wish I'd never done it, and I bet Boro did too!

I went back to Norwich reserves, and scored a total of 27 goals for them that season, enough to help them win their reserve league for the first time in many years. Dave Stringer, the reserve team manager, made the point that the team couldn't have done it without my goals, which was really good of him.

However, Ken decided to release me at the end of the season, saying that he needed to create a financial space to bring in another striker, who eventually turned out to be a Carrow Road hero – Robert Fleck from Chelsea.

And I began to think that maybe I was at the end of the road as a player. I'd suffered a string of injuries, and wasn't enjoying myself because I was hardly playing first team football. In fact, I hated the game.

But Ken came up with a thought-provoking suggestion; "Why don't you play abroad?" he said.

A Dutch side, Twente Entschede, made an enquiry, but my old Boro team mate Billy Ashcroft, warned me off Dutch football. Ken instead suggested using an agent, who took me out to Spain to sign for Cadiz – at least that's what I thought.

I was told that they were a Spanish First Division team, who were building a 25,000-seater stadium (I was to hear that in a different context later in life!) and were sponsored by Tio Pepe sherry.

They showed me all their drawings and plans, and I shook hands on a deal with their president. How naive was that – signing on the basis of a drawing!

I returned to England, only for Jim McLean, the manager of Dundee United, to contact me. They were the club that was challenging Celtic and Rangers in the Scottish Premier League at the time, and he wanted me to sign for them. I told him I wouldn't because I'd already shaken hands on a deal with the Cadiz club president, and I was going to be as good as my word. Pity the Spaniards weren't.

I found out later I was the victim of a con trick. It wasn't Cadiz I signed for, but another team called Jerez Club Deportivo.

I flew out to Spain, and they showed me some apartments that were disgusting – they weren't good enough for a dog kennel. My girlfriend and I both had high expectations, so we rented a house, which was owned by a doctor, on a private estate, overlooking the Atlantic at Puerto Santa Maria. Trouble was, it was outside the radius demanded by the club, who found out some time later and demanded that I move closer, which I did to another house overlooking the grand prix circuit.

The facilities and coaching were terrible. We went away for a fortnight's pre-season preparation, and we came back less fit. Antonia Naya was a former Cadiz player and at that time, head coach. We never broke sweat in pre-season, we played six of our eight games on bumpy gravel pitches, which were completely unsuitable, and it was an utter joke.

I had problems with a club car I'd been promised. I was told to pick it up from Hertz, and the club would sort everything out. I handed over my credit card details in exchange for a Ford Escort, which I expected the club to pay for, the standard practice.

Two months later, the police turned up at the training ground, demanding payment for the car from me! It turned out the responsibility for the car was mine in Spanish law, and so I had to stump up. In turn, I submitted a claim for £3,500 to the club for the car hire, saying that they should pay the bill.

But the club couldn't pay it, and nor could the president because he was under investigation regarding other matters.

I met a chap out there, Pedro Domecq, who was a big help. I met him in a bar, and he spoke with a perfect English accent, which wasn't surprising considering that he was educated at Oxford. He was part of the Domecq sherry empire, and he sorted a few things out for me. I never got the car money back, but Hertz didn't pursue me for any more outstanding money either.

It got to the point where I went on strike and refused to play, because the club had messed me around so much and hadn't paid me for six months. I wasn't even insured, so I could have broken my leg and not been taken care of.

One day, Martin Leach from the News of the World got in touch to do a piece about British players abroad. There had been a few Brits playing in Europe, like Ray Wilkins, Gary Lineker and Gerry Armstrong, but not all that many at the time.

I told him about the problems I was having, so he came out to Spain with a photographer.

I drove them to my rented house from the airport, and after they had admired the view of the Atlantic and the Grand Prix circuit, and sat for a while having a few drinks around the pool, Martin said: "Life's not too bad then!"

Obviously, in terms of the story he wanted to do, that was a dilemma. How could I say that I was having a bad time when I was living in a five-bedroom villa, with a large swimming pool and a magnificent view?

79

The photographer then had a brainwave. On the way into my house, he'd spotted two metal gates with iron bars, so he told me to stand behind them as if I was in prison, and he took a couple of photos.

The headline in the News of the World the following Sunday was "Get me out of this hell", with the picture underneath, and everybody back in England thought I was actually in prison!

One day, I thought I was being invaded, just like one of those old Western films. I looked down my drive, and there was a huge cloud of dust coming towards the house.

It was the rest of the squad, coming for a party and to make a decision – on whether we should throw the relegation battle against Atletico Bilbao, managed then by Howard Kendall, the former Everton manager.

Some unknown person had offered money to throw the game, and somebody else had offered us £1000 per man to beat them. So the decision was win or throw.

After two hours and a few boxes of wine, we decided to go for the win, because it was easier to beat them –which we did.

There were more incidents with the club. They signed a lad called Henrik Larsen (not the one who later made his name for Celtic), but only after he played a couple of games for the club did they realise that he wasn't the player they intended to sign.

He stayed with me in the villa, but then disappeared back to Denmark without paying his accommodation bill. Morally, I paid his share of the rent, because at that point we were well behind with it, having not been paid. The poor doctor who owned the house hadn't been paid by the club for six months!

I stayed in Spain, and stuck it out until I was paid in the summer, although I was still owed money for the car and a few other things.

The first year of my contract finished on September 30th 1988, I negotiated my release and I immediately flew back to England. I had learned a lot about living and playing abroad, an experience that was going to be of immense help later.

When I came back to England, I moved in with my girlfriend in Manchester.

But then fate took a hand, and it was through an old friendship with Bryan Gunn, a delayed train and another old friend, Frank Burrows, that I also got hitched.

When I moved to Norwich, I initially rented a flat which I then went on to buy near Norwich city centre. Gunny had just moved down from Scotland, and was initially put into a hotel by the club. He broke into the side straight away, but he was a poor man's Bruce Grobelaar. He was having an absolute nightmare. So manager Ken Brown obviously felt that Gunny needed some sparkle in his life, and asked if I would allow Gunny to move in with me, and I agreed.

We became very close, to such an extent that I was actually the best man at his wedding, but there was a drawback to that – I had to be a Jock for the day! I had to wear a kilt for the wedding, and to be honest I looked a million dollars in it, even though I say so myself.

Frank knew I was back in England, and wanted me to sign for Cardiff, who were

My mam (second right), and my dad (extreme left), with a group of friends, probably wondering what I'm up to

Early years, but the cheeky grin was already there

Three times a Quaker

My first proper hobby – pigeons

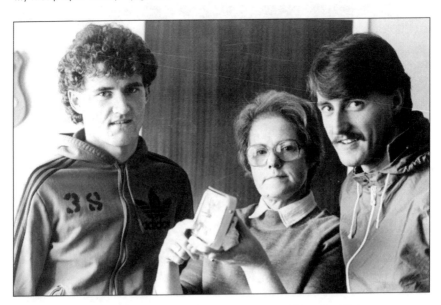

What time is it? At the Proctor household with, Mark and his mum Micky

Proc and Jock! I was proud to be best man for two great mates, Mark Proctor and Bryan Gunn

Three times a Quaker

Crocked in Japan: The building and me!

Plastered in Japan: Not for the first time

Bad hair day: I'm hardly a fashion icon in this pose

Three times a Quaker

On the trophy trail with Boro skipper Stuart Boam

Blond one minute, brunette the next, maybe I should have dyed the 'tache too

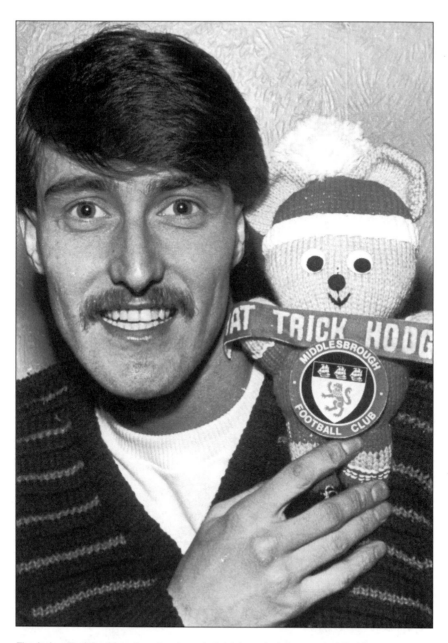

The lads got sick of hearing about my hat-trick against Spurs – but Teddy was impressed

Three times a Quaker

Two legends together! With the great George Best after Jim Platt's testimonial

Graeme Souness, great player and great mate, pictured with a young Boro fan

Head boys: Craig Johnston and I discuss contrasting hairstyles

Golden ball: Boro boss John Neal and top sports writer Bob Cass present me with the Sun newspaper award for my hat-trick against Spurs

Three times a Quaker

Finding the net for Boro!

Measuring up: Boro physio Tommy Johnson checks me out when I return on loan

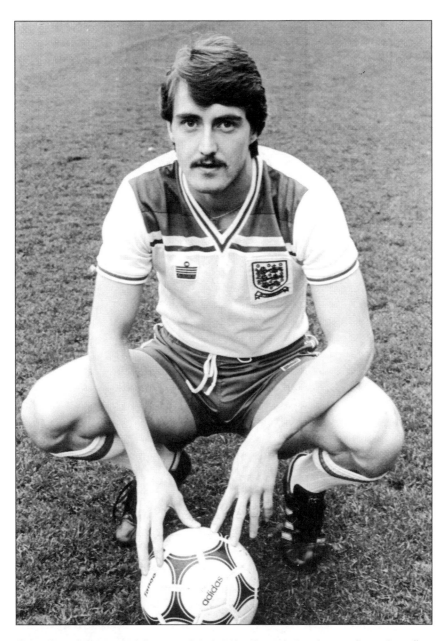

Three Lions: but I never fully appreciated at the time what an honour it was to pull on the England shirt

England manager
Ron Greenwood
looks impressed –
but didn't hand
me a full cap

Get in there:
celebrating a goal
for Liverpool
against Blackburn

then playing in the old Third Division. I had no problems with that, because I had great respect for Frank for the way he'd looked after me at Sunderland when I was out in the cold.

I caught the train from Manchester to Cardiff, but instead of arriving in Cardiff at 4.35 in the afternoon as scheduled, it arrived at 5.25, which was too late for me to sign that day, because the club office and the Football League both closed at 5pm.

So Cardiff put me in a hotel for the night, and Frank instructed the hotel that no calls should be put through to me, except from Gunny, who was registered as my contact with the PFA, which I agreed. Frank was obviously keen to make sure he signed me.

There had been some mysterious calls for me at home on my answerphone, but nobody had left their name. But after spending an hour or so in the hotel, Bryan phoned.

"I know who the mystery club is," he said.

I thought it would be somebody in the bottom two divisions, in which case it would be a no, because I was happy to come to Cardiff just for Frank.

"You're not going to believe this, but it's Sheffield Wednesday. They've been trying to get hold of you."

Wednesday were one of the leading clubs in the old First Division then, but I had promised to go to Cardiff. It was very tempting; another opportunity to play again in the First Division, when I thought the chance had gone.

I phoned Frank, in some trepidation, and told him what had happened. I expected him to go ballistic, but he was quite calm. He knew about Sheffield Wednesday's interest before, when manager Howard Wilkinson had a chance to sign me at Sunderland, but Howard decided not to proceed. So the deal, at the time, died.

However, Howard had revived his interest. To Frank's immense credit, he told me to go to Wednesday, and even paid for a taxi to the station and a train ticket! What sort of man would do that? Even now, I still have the utmost admiration for Frank, both as a person, and as a manager.

So Sheffield Wednesday became my fifth English club, and my old mate Proc made a bit of money on my first day thanks to me.

Howard wanted me to run fifty laps – about ten miles – around the Hillsborough training pitch in a certain time. Some of the Wednesday players, knowing that I'd had a few injuries and what had been said previous, reckoned that I wouldn't do it, but Proc knew better, he knew that injury-free, which I almost was at the time, I could run for fun.

In fact, I failed the medical because of my abductor problem, but because I was costing them nothing in terms of transfer fees, Wednesday still signed me.

Assistant manager Peter Eustace, stood sergeant-major style with a stopwatch. When he shouted for the last lap, I knew I was doing well, and sprinted round the last lap in 70 seconds, not bad going.

But as I ran over the line, he said; "I've made a mistake, two more laps to go!"

I still managed to beat the required time, and I said to him and Howard; "Now do you believe Lawrie McMenemy?"

I was feeling the best I had for a long time, until the injury jinx struck again.

I played in a friendly against Ronnie Glavin's team – maybe it was Frickley or Emley – and I over-stretched going for the ball. Proc said that I looked like John Cleese by the way I was walking, one of his funny walks in Monty Python.

I was in great pain, and my whole structure of running was completely unbalanced.

Despite treatment from Alan Smith – who used to play for Darlington before becoming a physio – I just couldn't recover properly.

Unknown to Alan, teammate Gary Megson, whom I later helped as an agent, took me to a chiropractor on Chesterfield Road who treated my pelvis, my abductor muscle and my hamstring. I got all my strength back, which made Alan think that I had been pulling a fast one!

After a couple of sub appearances for Wednesday – I scored at Charlton – I made my full debut against Everton on November 5th 1988 and played a blinder in a 1-1 draw.

I managed to establish myself in the team, but there were a couple of fallouts with Peter Eustace, who replaced Howard when he had gone to Leeds.

Results picked up, and we got away from relegation trouble temporarily, mainly because Peter introduced new training methods, which went down well with the players.

However, results started to go against us, and Peter re-introduced Howard's old methods, but the players had gone down that road previously with Howard, and they weren't received at all well in the dressing room. They had worked under Howard, but he was a different type of manager to Peter, plus times had changed and Peter should have stuck to his principles.

Peter and I then had a big fall out after the Millwall game in December.

I was suffering from flu, but he asked me to go on the bench, which I reluctantly agreed to. Then, with five minutes left and the score 0-0, he wanted me to go on the field.

I suggested that he shouldn't change things around, and to settle for a point the way we were, because we looked capable of holding on for a draw.

But he insisted that I went on. So I did as I was told. When Millwall won a corner, I tracked back to help the defence. The ball came to me, I tried to play it back to keeper Chris Turner, but Teddy Sheringham nipped in and set up Tony Cascarino for a simple tap in.

In the dressing room afterwards, Peter kicked off big style, and accused me of throwing the game, which was absolute nonsense and an insult. Some of the other lads stuck up for me, but he refused to play me in the side.

I came back to Middlesbrough with Beverley for Christmas, and was stopping at

Crathorne Hall when Peter phoned up on New Year's Day, and asked me to play the following day against Coventry City.

So I had to dash from Crathorne Hall, managed to find an open petrol station near Wetherby to fill the car up, and managed to get to Sheffield by the 5pm deadline.

Guess what? I injured my Achilles, and we lost the game. Peter had a real go at the players in the dressing room afterwards, and broke down in tears. The job was too much for him, and eventually Ron Atkinson replaced him. I'd never got near the level of fitness required for the First Division because of all the injuries, and I think Peter held that against me.

A conversation before a game really struck a chord with me. I was really keyed up to play my old club Liverpool, but when we trained in the morning, the abductor problem in my back played up again, so I had to pull out of the team.

Peter wasn't very pleased, and nor was I. Kenny Dalglish saw me before the game in the tunnel, and asked me: "Are you injured again?" It was so humiliating. Since my Anfield days, I had always seemed to miss playing Liverpool because of injury.

Big Ron was a like a breath of fresh air. He'd tried to sign me when he was at West Brom and I was still at Boro.

He loved to have a laugh. On the first day of training, he started speaking to me in Spanish, because he'd just returned from a spell as manager of Atletico Bilbao! We had a conversation in Spanish for about a minute or so, while the other players just stood, looking completely baffled.

He changed things around. He said he needed some colour in the team, so he signed Carlton Palmer and Dave Bennett!

Ron was as straight as a dye, and he lifted Wednesday to fifteenth in the table.

I didn't play many games because of a knee injury that was calcifying, and I managed to get through to the end of the season without an operation. The last game I played that season was at Arsenal on 21st January – and it turned out to be my last in the English First Division.

Later that season, something happened which affected me, and millions of others, very deeply – the death of 92 Liverpool fans at the FA Cup semi final between Liverpool and Nottingham Forest at Hillsborough.

I had tickets for the game, through Sheffield Wednesday as the host club, for a couple of friends from Liverpool, Terry Miles and Gerard Johnson, and myself.

I met them at a pub near the ground. The pub was absolutely heaving with Liverpool fans, and on our way to the ground, there seemed to be some aggravation outside, an air of disorganisation. There were people everywhere, not really in any orderly structure, desperately trying to get into the ground, with or without tickets.

Our seats were opposite the main stand, and we took them at about 2.45. We could see the Leppings Lane end was filling up quite quickly – remember at the time that it was partly terracing, partly seats.

Just as the match kicked off, I can remember seeing a lad somehow climbing over the fence, and his arm appeared to be snapped above the elbow. It suddenly started to dawn on everybody how bad the situation was behind that goal.

And to make matters worse, it was impossible, because of the shape of the fences, for people on the side of the pitch to climb over and help people escape the massive crush.

Terry was panicking, because his son was in that end, and obviously he didn't know whether he was in the thick of it all or not.

The referee stopped the game, took the players off the field, and after about ten or fifteen minutes, I decided to go to the dressing rooms to see what was going on. I went out the back of the stand, and had to climb over a dozen bodies to get to the gym. It suddenly started to dawn on me that here was a terrible, terrible tragedy taking shape.

I walked across the pitch to the changing rooms, and everybody in there was completely stunned, because word had filtered through that people had been killed.

I went round the back of the stand, and there were about fifteen people, all covered by blankets on the ground. At first, I thought they were injured and were awaiting further treatment, until the truth suddenly hit me.

I went back to Terry in the other stand, and we tried to find his son. By now, he was obviously extremely worried that his son had been killed.

I took him out of the stand, making sure that he avoided the dead bodies out the back, and we tried to find his son. We failed, but maybe that wasn't too surprising considering all the confusion and trauma. People were wandering around everywhere, shouting and screaming.

Gerard and I persuaded Terry that it was best he went back to Liverpool, where, thankfully, his son arrived a few hours later safe and sound. You can imagine the relief when he walked through the door.

Beverley was working that day as a beautician in Cole Brothers in Sheffield city centre, so I drove in the car to the other side of Sheffield and picked her up.

Our journey home took us past Hillsborough, and it was then the scale of the tragedy really hit me, with ambulances and police vehicles everywhere. The following day, I had to report to the ground for training, and it was horrifying to see all the mangled barriers where the Liverpool fans had been crushed. There was a smell of death in the air, one I never want to experience again.

Thank God football grounds have been made safer, and hopefully a tragedy like that will never happen again.

A couple of days later, Alan Smith asked that as an ex-Liverpool player, if I could go to the local hospitals and offer some comfort to the injured.

It was the least I could do, although it was a big shock to see the state of the injured in those hospitals. It was a big relief to know that most of the injured people I saw that day survived, and my thoughts, so many years on, go to those who lost a loved one.

Meanwhile, my life started to take a turn for the better off the field.

I was still living in a Sheffield hotel, with the club paying the £1,000 per week hotel bill, so the club agreed that I could move into Kelham O'Hanlon's house for £350 per week. The club was delighted at the reduction in cost, and Kelham was delighted that he was getting help with his mortgage. Kelham, a goalkeeper, was an old mate of mine from my Boro days.

Mind, there never seemed to be any heating on in the house; it always seemed to be cold!

Kelham was married to Michelle, whom I'd also known from my Boro days.

On many occasions I called into Cole Brothers – a big department store in Sheffield – to see Michelle, and on one of these visits I made eye contact with a rather attractive girl working on Helena Rubenstein cosmetics. Luckily, the girl concerned was very close friends with Michelle, and I made it very clear to Michelle that she had to make Beverley aware of my interest, but she had to do it in a subtle way. Once Beverley was aware of my interest, she pestered Michelle to introduce her to me, and after a few weeks, I finally gave in to her demands. That was in November 1988, and we were married four years later, on August 16th 1992. (This is my version of events, I'm pretty certain you'll get a different version from Beverley!)

We didn't splash out on a big ceremony, we just decided to walk into the registry office one day and get married, mainly because I was pretty busy at the time working as an agent, but more of that phase in my life later.

Beverley's mother and stepfather agreed to be witnesses, and we celebrated with fish and chips and a bottle of Dom Perignon champagne in our house in Todwick. It was one decision I've never ever regretted, and we've now got two great girls, Brogan and Alessia. Two of the greatest moments in my life was seeing them born.

So if it hadn't been for Frank Burrows and the delayed train, I would never have met my wife. I'll be eternally grateful to Frank.

I still had a year left on my Wednesday contract at the end of the season – Ron had steered the club away from relegation – when we went for a week in Marbella.

On the beach one day – we spent a lot of time on the beach and in the clubs as you do on these end of season trips – Big Ron said: "Hodgy, we're really pushing for it next season, can you do it for another year?"

To which I replied; "Ron, I won't be able to. I can't play forty games because of all my injuries."

After some thought, Ron suggested that if I wanted to pack in at Sheffield Wednesday, then he could put me in touch with an agent who was sending players to Japan.

The wages on offer were amazing, and Ron helped by sorting out the rest of my signing on fee from Wednesday. I couldn't thank him enough.

A club called Sanfrece Hiroshima, which was owned by the giant car company Mazda, were interested in me.

They made a very good first impression. I'd been on holiday with Beverley in

97

Cyprus, returned to Manchester Airport, and there they had arranged a Porsche 944 hire car for me to collect so then I could drive south and meet their representatives at Heathrow.

I struck a one year deal with them over a couple of days, although I signed the deal blind, which was a risk considering my earlier venture to Spain. I didn't know what sort of facilities the club had, or how good the standard was in Japan, but it was a very appealing challenge for me. I felt as if I was some sort of pioneer, and it was a great opportunity to see another part of the world.

Beverley was very supportive. We'd only been together for six months, and it was a huge request for her to go to the other side of the world. But she was all for it, and to be honest, she has been extremely supportive ever since.

Japan wasn't new to me, because I'd played there with Boro in the Tokyo Cup, and there were going to be a couple of other Brits out there with me, Alan Irvine and Tony Henry.

I flew out to Japan and after staying in a very impressive hotel for two or three days, a couple of people from the club showed me to my apartment.

It was very cramped, halfway up an apartment block, and with hardly any amenities, no television, no fridge, nothing.

But I didn't complain, unlike some of the other lads. It was clearly a block of flats used by all the Mazda car factory workers. And I think the Japanese respected the fact that I kept quiet and got on with things. Just after Beverley arrived a few days later, there was a knock on the door, and two club officials, Mr Ito and Mr Iminishi, presented me with a load of equipment. "You never ask for nothing, you never complain," they said.

It was great. There was a state of the art television, CD player, video system, microwave and cooling fans, just what we wanted to furnish the flat.

I unpacked everything, turned the music up full volume, and invited the rest of the lads round. Their mouths dropped wide open, and I joked; "What you agree is what you get!"

Bill Foulkes, who won the European Cup with Manchester United in 1968, was the manager, and I got off to a bad start in my first training session.

I'd only been in Japan for two days, when Bill insisted that I did plenty of running, which was difficult after a long haul flight. I pulled my calf, and I had to miss training for a couple of weeks.

Bill, with his hard centre half upbringing, liked to play an aggressive style of football, which didn't suit the Japanese players in the team, or my back come to that! And lifting weights in the gym didn't help the injury either. Maybe it was the unlucky number six that I'd been given. Six to the Japanese is the same as thirteen to us Brits.

The club sent me to six or seven different specialists, looking for a cure. I could hardly sleep, and could hardly lie straight.

It was when I made a phone call back to England to an old friend, Harry Hawes, that I was able to discover exactly who and where the best chiropractor was in Japan.

It was amazing that he was only forty miles away from Hiroshima. How Harry knew somebody on the other side of the world, I don't know.

I was sick of all the injuries and was contemplating retirement, but I decided to give it one last go. Desperate times call for desperate measures, I figured.

I drove to the address Harry had given me, and this huge Japanese guy opened the door. He had an equally huge amount of equipment, much more than I expected. When he started working on me, I thought that he was going to snap me in two!

Then he put me on an arthritic bed, strapped me into it, hit a pad above me and my body was wrenched all over the place. Bit like the old Batman programmes.

Sounds daft, but after two weeks more treatment, it worked. After hobbling into that bloke's house, I eventually came out straight as a dye. He had equipment I've never seen since. Wish he lived near Darlington!

Socially, we had some good times in Japan. There were some really good banquets, and we played one social game in particular, using a spinning table with a chicken's head on it. Whoever it ended up in front of, that person had to eat it. I was lucky, it never happened to me, but I wish I'd thought of that one when I was Liverpool entertainment manager!

Results on the field didn't go well for Bill, who used to come round and see me often in the flat. We had long chats, and then when Tony or Alan visited, I discovered that Bill's team talks were based on what I was saying when I was out of the side!

However, yet another injury came along, this time a knee injury that made me miss the last six weeks of the season. I went for an operation, and it was the first time that I'd ever watched an entire operation on my own knee being relayed on to a huge screen.

There were only two points in the operation which the surgeon refused to let me watch on the grounds that the surgery itself could have stayed in my mind for the rest of my life. The first was the actual cutting of the knee, and the second was the screw being drilled into the joint.

I had to spend several weeks in hospital, and Beverley had to smuggle food in for me, because the meals were awful. There were no English-speaking doctors, the knee didn't seem to be improving, and when Phil Collins came to Hiroshima for a concert, I had to sign a document saying that I was going to see him at my own risk.

The season had finished when I came out of hospital, and since my contract had ended, I made plans to go to Lilleshall for rehabilitation, which I paid for myself.

However, a few days before I was due to return, Mr Iminishi, a really friendly chap, approached me and asked if I fancied the manager's job. "We listen to you," he said.

I turned him down flat, because it was Bill who had taken me to Japan, and I didn't want to betray him.

On my last night in Japan, I had one last get together with the other Brits, and after a few drinks, we all wrote down on a piece of paper how much our wages were.

The other lads were mortified to learn that I was earning twice as much as them, and Tony Henry kicked up a big stink, because he'd played in every game that season, and I'd missed over half of them!

I got a great send off, there was a good farewell party, and lots of people turned up at the railway station to see us off. We even got a cheap upgrade to first class on the flight home, which the other British lads didn't get!

I returned to England on April 4th 1990, which gave me tax problems! Because I returned before the end of that tax year, April 5th, there was a problem with my tax return that fortunately Beverley managed to sort out.

I spent thirteen weeks at Lilleshall, which somebody told me was something of a record, paying for it all myself to get my knee injury sorted. I was there Monday to Friday, returning to Sheffield for the weekend every Friday evening.

You wouldn't believe it, but I still managed to get injured while I was there. We had a light training session one day, and Steve MacKenzie – remember him as the country's most expensive teenager when Malcolm Allison bought him for Manchester City? – injured me in a routine block tackle.

The injury was the last thing I needed, because FC Metz had shown interest in me, and asked me over to France to play in a friendly against Saarbrucken. I had a great game, but I struggled with my injury. They asked me to play in another friendly, but I refused, saying; "I don't play for anybody on trial after playing for Liverpool." I didn't dare risk an injury that could jeopardise any signing. Hard-faced I know, but I had no choice.

I signed a two year deal for them, just managed to pass a medical – I would have had no chance nowadays – and I managed to survive the first week's training.

However, the knee then went completely, and I spent two weeks in hospital in Strasbourg, and took another three months to recover.

I returned to training at Christmas 1990, and picked up yet another injury. This time I scored a goal in training, and one of the other players, Albert Cartier, just for fun, jumped on my back in mock celebration. The moment he did it, my back collapsed, and I was ruled out for the rest of the season.

It was one injury after another, and to be honest, it was getting me down. I was seeing the world and meeting some great people, but I wanted to play football and couldn't. If it wasn't my knee, it was my back, or my hamstring or my calf.

To make matters worse, some of my money went missing. I wanted to kick up a stink about it with the club president, Monsieur Molinari, but it wouldn't have helped the other foreign players out there, because they were on the same payment arrangements as I was. I spent an entire season on just my basic salary. The club didn't provide a car until five games had kicked in, so I brought a left hand drive mini and drove that around instead.

In the summer of 1991, I worked really hard to return to full fitness again, and in a friendly against Juan-les-Pins, I came on as a substitute, and had a very good game which prompted reporters to question why I wasn't in the starting line up for the opening game of the season.

But the president wouldn't budge, even though the coach, Joel Muller, wanted me to play, and Joel actually admitted to me that the president had instructed him not to play me.

So for a full season, I just trained either on my own, or with the squad, while I was in deadlock with the president.

Neither of us budged. He wanted me to leave, and I refused. Why should I? I was fit enough to play for his team.

Joel was great towards me, and he allowed me to go on loan to Swansea, then managed by my old friend Frank Burrows, for a month. I made my debut for them as a sub against Bradford City, and started the game at Preston the following week. I made one more appearance for them, as a sub at Peterborough, which turned out to be my last ever competitive game in English football.

Frank suggested that we talk about a contract at Swansea when my French contract finished, but then I snapped my hamstring in training one day. Frank was distraught – it was the second time he'd missed out on me!

I now had to return to France, knowing the end of my playing career was nigh. I'd been injured in more countries than a war veteran. Beverley and I packed all our belongings, furniture and a hundred bottles of wine (for personal consumption). I then flew to Stansted, obtained a transit van from Budget car rental, drove all the way back to France, loaded everything up – making sure that the wine was at the front – had a couple of hours sleep and travelled back to England. It was au revoir to France.

The injuries had finished my playing career, but what was I going to do next?

The mobile phone pioneer; "Why doesn't it ring?"

By that summer of 1991 I was shot. Both my Achilles were bad, and my knee was not much better. Come to think of it my back had gone too.

An agent offered me the chance to go to Germany and join Hanover. He had set it all up. They wanted me to go over, train with them, and take it from there.

But it wasn't for me. I was not in the right frame of mind, nor was I fit enough because of the injuries. My career was over. There was no way I could play competitive football.

I wanted to call it a day, and my body did too. I guess that between them, my mind and my body made the decision, and it was a definitive one, or so I thought at the time.

But still the offers came. Frank McLintock, and an agent called Graham Smith, offered me £150,000 tax free to go to Qatar in the Gulf. I had earned a fortune in Japan, but this was even more money.

By then, through my contacts throughout the world, I was already dabbling as an agent, helping players and clubs with moves.

But a figure like £150,000 made me forget about my injuries. I said that as long as they got me a return ticket, insurance and a watertight contract, I would seriously consider it.

The documentation didn't come through when it should have done, so I didn't turn up at Newcastle for the flight. When Frank phoned me I said I was in Sheffield and going nowhere.

Rochdale manager Dave Sutton asked me to train with them, and as it was fairly local, I did, just to keep fit. But his assistant Mick Docherty asked me to sign for them, and once again it was decision time. The game just wouldn't leave me alone. But I knew deep down that it was over, and I came clean, telling him that my Achilles had gone.

That was the last time I had to say 'no,' and I didn't bat an eyelid. I went home and the next day I said to Beverley. "I'm not going training today. My playing days are over." I was 31 years old.

Instead we went shopping – but if she thought that I was now a househusband she couldn't have been more wrong. We didn't go round the boutiques this time. I went out and bought a fax machine and mobile phone.

But nobody rang me for a month, which was hardly surprising, as not many people had a mobile then, and no-one had my number, so what did I expect?

Mine was a great brick of a thing. I stuck with the company and became such a good client, that they moved me into the Sony Diamond club, and gave me some incredible benefits when the new phones came out.

I sat in Beverley's flat in Sheffield with my mobile phone and the fax machine on the floor. I had a few contacts, the likes of Kenny Dalglish, and big Ron Atkinson, while I also knew Howard Kendall and Joe Royle. And the Professional Footballers' Association had my number. Gradually a bit of business came my way. I had helped to send a few young players over to Scandinavia, through an agent called Patrick Mork, who only a few months earlier had tried to get me to Scandinavia to play again.

He asked me if I was interested in playing still, but I told him that unfortunately my playing days were over and I'd retired. He couldn't believe it, but our relationship developed from there. We are still in touch, and he later helped me with Jason De Vos.

He was the agent who sent videos of players over from Canada. One of them was of Jason. I liked what I saw, and I initially took him to Bradford City, but he suffered an ankle injury and didn't play. It was a couple of years later that I brought him to Darlington.

Later Patrick and I fell out briefly over Nolberto Solano, who was one of the players with me when I took over at Darlington and had to wind up the agency work.

Once the agency work picked up it almost became too much for me. I was working for eighteen hours a day and came close to a breakdown. To give an indication of how much work I was getting through, my phone bills were £1500 – a quarter!

I was doing a lot of the work for nothing, to help out players I knew. Word got round and more and more came my way. At the time it was not the done thing to exclusively sign them up, but if I had done I would have cleaned up.

I remember trying to get a move for Mark Hughes (the Tranmere centre half, not the Manchester United striker). I was going on holiday the next day, but was still up at 4am sending faxes to York boss Alan Little who was considering taking Mark. Even though I was due to leave for holiday at 7am, I was determined to get the deal right.

I was impetuous, perhaps trying too hard, wasting a lot of time returning calls, instead of waiting for people to phone me back. I was doing it out of politeness, and to show that I was genuine, but in hindsight I was pushing myself too hard and running round in circles.

However it stood me in good stead for later in life, and when the business took off a lot of people wanted to work with me. I became only around the fifth or sixth agent to become licensed by FIFA. But despite the licensing system, it was becoming a bit of a free for all – though nowhere near as bad as it is today. There were around twenty agents in the country then, at the last count there were around 270, and by the time you read this, probably a lot more than that.

I began to get myself organised, and setting up a proper office at home helped. We lived in a village called Todwick, near Sheffield, in a house called Rectory View. The house overlooked the church, though sheer hard work, rather than divine intervention, was the root of my success.

I worked non-stop and built up a massive network across Europe and South America, with clients from Portugal to Croatia to Argentina. I was the only England based agent to have Europe so well covered, and could speak Spanish and French. Dozens of players, from several nationalities, went through me. I took a lot to English and Scottish clubs.

Often two agents were involved – one abroad and me in England. Sometimes they would move the goalposts at the last minute to stitch me up. Often it left me fuming, but it was all part of the learning curve.

On one occasion I was offered David Ginola. Kevin Keegan wanted him at Newcastle, but Roy Evans was just as keen to take him to Liverpool. My former Liverpool teammate, Terry McDermott, was Newcastle assistant manager and he asked me to make sure they got him. "Don't let us miss out on this one," he said.

I didn't get closely involved. I let the French agent Marc Roger finalise it, and Newcastle got their man.

Terry was delighted, and phoned to ask me what I wanted for my part in the deal. I said that a lovely bottle of claret would do nicely. To this day, I'm still waiting for it.

Kevin was always a fair and honourable bloke. On one occasion I took a stunning 19-year-old striker Vladan Lukic for a trial at Newcastle. He was a brilliant player from Red Star Belgrade, who had already pushed aside the likes of Darko Panchev. The fee was to be £1.25 million.

The player's agent, a German, came over with the player, and they stayed in a Durham hotel, near the Newcastle training ground at Maiden Castle.

The lad did exceptionally well in training, but when he was due to play for the reserves at Sheffield Wednesday, he developed a mysterious hamstring injury. But Kevin still wanted him.

The agent told me that there was a £250,000 fee in the deal for me. But I had my doubts; there was clearly something wrong. He also asked me if I would speak to Kevin to see if he wanted anything from the deal. I went to see Kevin, and I told him that I felt awkward about the question I was going to ask him.

But Kevin was fuming and said that he didn't need the money, nor would he want the money. I was relieved when he showed his disgust, because it was clear the Croatian club wasn't going to see much of the transfer fee.

Even though it was a lot of money, I was well within my rights to be paid that amount of money by the Croatian club. But £250,000?

Kevin and I pulled out because we were both very uncomfortable, and the deal broke down. When we sat down and thought about it, £1.25 million was going out of

Newcastle, but the money was not going to go to Red Star, which we felt was wrong.

But to be fair to the agent, he had the right to negotiate. Equally, however, Kevin and I were within our rights to say 'No'.

I rang Beverley, and it's fair to say that my decision didn't go down too well. Twelve years ago that was a phenomenal amount of money. But it was clear in my head at the start of my new business venture that I didn't want to be a 'dodgy' agent in any way. Of course I had to be clear in my mind what I meant by dodgy. Others may have done deals that they considered fair, and I felt were dodgy. No matter what code of conduct you work by, personal discretion will always have a role to play.

However, my stance was to take a standard ten per cent, and sleep easily in my bed, knowing that there was nothing to come back and haunt me.

The deal I have just described was not the biggest that I didn't do.

In the time between my first two stints as Darlington manager (1995/6) I took £826,372 in commission. My phone bill was £25,000, travel costs £31,000, third parties were paid, and I was owed £31,378 – a bad debt that was never paid. Add that lot to the forty per cent income tax I paid, plus corporation tax, and the amount left over was not so impressive.

But it was a good living and I loved it. The wheeling and dealing captured my imagination. However, being Darlington manager captivated my mind even more. It must do or I wouldn't keep returning to it!

I did an awful lot of deals, so many I have lost count. I travelled more than many agents did, because I always tried to see players first hand, rather than just on video, before I recommended them. When I had to rely solely on video, I would watch them again and again before committing myself.

I built up a good reputation, and prided myself on honesty. If somebody told me a lie, I wouldn't deal with him again. I'm like that to this day.

I had a particularly good rapport with the Portuguese. I watched the likes of Luis Figo, Rui Costa and Jao Pinto in the World Youth Championships, and saw star quality in all of them.

They were all with Angelo Martins, a fine agent and a good friend of mine. Because of the players he would pass on to me, I knew even before the start of the season that I would earn at least £50,000.

Pinto was the one player I badly wanted to bring to England, and I almost brought him to Liverpool. Roy Evans was the Liverpool manager when I first saw Pinto play. I sent Roy a video, and he liked what he saw, so he sent chief scout Ron Yeats over to watch Pinto in action.

That was in a match for Sporting Lisbon against Benfica, but unfortunately Pinto suffered knee ligament damage in the game.

A year later we went through it all again, and on the Saturday he damaged his knee again. So that deal finally fell through, as did a potential Liverpool move for Rui Costa, whom Roy also liked the look of.

The same season I spoke to Sir Alex Ferguson – or plain Alex as he was then. He liked the look of Fernando Couto, a Portuguese central defender who was playing in Italy. Perhaps I could have done a lucrative deal, but again my honesty came to the fore. I told Fergie that I didn't think the lad could head a ball well enough to play the English way. He was a dominating defender, quick and hard in the mould that United desired, but his one flaw was his heading.

I felt obliged to offer my opinion. Fergie accepted it, and pulled out. Fergie is a hard man, who has done brilliantly for Manchester United, but while he can rule with a rod of iron, and be single minded, he's shrewd enough to listen to the alternative view, as he did in this case. He wants only the best, and if a niggling doubt is put in his mind, he'll respect it.

When Howard Wilkinson was Leeds manager I recommended Pinto and Bruno Caies, a strong midfielder, to him. I sat up to 5am in Pinto's apartment in Lisbon, telling him how much he could earn if he went to Leeds. I was on holiday in Faro at the time, but flew up to Lisbon to try and sort out a deal.

I rang Howard to tell him the deal was on and both players would come. He was delighted. But an hour later he rang back and said it was on hold. I'm told that Leeds chairman Bill Fotherby had come in with a video of Caies saying that he was horrendous.

But that was an excuse. The Leeds board didn't want the deals to go through because they had other plans. A day or so later Howard was sacked.

I worked so very hard to get Pinto to England, and had my attempts to get him to Liverpool succeeded there was a six figure sum in it for me – from the Portuguese end, not from Liverpool.

I knew the Portuguese scene inside out, and my determination to get a Pinto to England finally paid off. But when it happened it was Jao's brother Sergio. I took him to Bradford when Chris Kamara was manager. Sergio was a big hit, but didn't settle in Yorkshire without his wife and baby.

A lot of foreign players don't sustain the high level of performance required in English football, and as an agent that was something I had to be aware of. I tried to look at the character of players as well as their ability.

I took Nicholas Riza from Australia to Liverpool, and he later played under Terry Venables at Crystal Palace. That came about by chance. I looked at a video of a striker, and it seemed Riza made all his goals, so he was the one I went for.

The lad was available on a free, and Liverpool were prepared to pay me £30,000. Not bad money for a flight and a couple of videos. But the Aussies wanted a big cut so in the end it wasn't all that lucrative for me. The goalposts changed when the Aussies decided they needed a transfer fee, which I then deducted from my commission. But the flights and the video were still worth £15,000.

Around that time I took on Tony Henry to work with me. I was so busy that I needed another person like myself. Tony fitted the bill perfectly because he was an ex-player with good judgment, and like me he was not afraid of hard work. He had played for Man City, Oldham and Bolton Wanderers, and had been in Japan with me.

I could not have picked a better partner. He was totally reliable, and put the hours in. He looked after the company, and later took it over when the lure of management struck me.

Sadly we fell out briefly, over money, the root of all evil, but have since happily made up.

As an agent when a deal fell through I didn't dwell on it, but got on with the next one. And there was always another one. I was offered several players a day from all over Europe, especially from the slightly less significant football nations, such as Poland and Yugoslavia.

I remember bringing one lad from a Polish side to Leeds on trial. He had just broken into the international side, and everything about him was spot on. When I went to the airport to pick him up, he was immaculately dressed. I felt I was on a winner.

You can tell by the effort people put into their appearance whether they have what it takes to impress. Some were incredibly raggy-arsed, and the first thing they asked at the airport was if they could borrow a tenner from me.

But this lad, Kazimierz Wegrzyn, was different. He trained with Leeds and Howard said that he had a brilliant attitude, which didn't surprise me at all.

He played for the reserves against Leicester and was magnificent. Other clubs were sniffing, so Howard told me that he wanted the deal tied up the very next day.

But the next day in training the lad badly fractured his jaw. It happened that his Polish club wanted him back to play in a very important league game, and although the Leeds club doctor said that there was no way that he was fit enough to play, he would do so whatever the pain. In fact, he was so desperate to play for Leeds – even though Leeds scout Paul Hart was planning to watch him play in Poland – that he wanted to sign a document stating that if the injury he sustained in training caused him any further damage, he would waive any blame on Leeds. He was the sort of character you wanted to work with.

Leeds nevertheless insisted that he went back to Poland for treatment and by the time Kaz returned to Leeds for a further trial period, they had moved onward and upward and had a title winning side. Although he again impressed, they decided that they were now becoming such a good team, that he would not have a starring role.

And as in those days you could not get a work permit unless you played in 75 per cent of your club's games, Leeds decided not to take him.

There was a time I even had African players, mainly Cameroon, but I rarely travelled beyond Europe. It didn't seem worth it then, though Mexicans, Chileans and Peruvians that I could have had on my books later played in Europe.

The player I was most pleased to bring to England was Jose Domingues, the Portuguese lad I took to Birmingham when Barry Fry was manager.

Angelo asked me to go to Portugal and look at a player from a Division Three side in Portugal. I thought he was taking the mickey, and declined, though I asked for a video.

The young player belonged to Benfica. They had around a hundred young players who they loaned out. They became known as the forgotten kids.

The video arrived and there I was watching this kid who was about five feet tall. The film was taken in a schoolyard, and to this day I vividly recall sitting there with a glass of red wine. The kid was phenomenal, and I decided that the best way to judge players was not to bother to go and see them, but instead have three glasses of wine and pop a video in!

I phoned Barry straight away and said that he must look at this video I was going to send him. He asked me to send it to the assistant manager Lil Fucillo. I did, and I remember Lil asking me why I had sent a video of a kid in a schoolyard.

I said I would pay for Domingues to fly over, if Lil met him. He agreed, but there was some sort of a mix up, and the next thing I knew Angelo was on the phone, saying that the kid was all alone at the airport.

Immediately I drove from Sheffield to Birmingham, and there was this lonely-looking kid standing there, all 5ft 2in of him – and that was with the highest heels you have ever seen. He reminded me of Alan Ladd, a short-arsed movie star of the fifties and sixties.

I thought: "What have I done. They'll crucify me. I haven't even seen him play live."

That morning he went training with Birmingham. They trained on the side of the pitch, because there was a match on later, and it was only a half hour session, so he didn't have much time to impress.

The following day I went to watch them train on a school pitch. There were around a hundred players, and my lad was warming up. Barry told me to tell him that he was to play for the last ten minutes.

He ripped the others to pieces and before the game was finished Barry had the contract in front of him.

But Karen Brady, who was chief executive, told Barry he had already signed enough players. He wasn't too happy and muttered something along the lines of: "What makes her think she can judge players?" Harsh, I thought, because I always got on well with Karen, and respected her business acumen.

I said; "OK, I'll take him to Blackburn Rovers, because Kenny Dalglish would like a look at him."

He trained with Rovers and again did brilliantly. Kenny wanted him to play a game for the reserves, but Barry had not given up, and wanted the same.

I told Jose to go to Birmingham, because he would have more impact there. He played and was great – so good that Karen changed her mind.

They paid £125,000 for him, and he was a big hit, loved by the fans. He played a lot of games for Birmingham, but after he made his Portugal under 21 debut, there was a problem for them.

Suddenly Jose was a star, and wanted his contract trebled. He was a teenager when I spotted him, and didn't demand big money when he signed for Birmingham. I advised Barry to sell him, because Benfica wanted him back, while Sporting Lisbon were ready to pay £1.25 million, so Birmingham were in effect making a £1 million profit.

Two representatives of Lisbon flew over to St Andrews to discuss the deal. Karen and I concocted a dodgy fax to make sure the deal went through. She wore a Chanel suit, with a short skirt, and swung round on a swivel chair during the meeting.

These two suave Portuguese guys were more interested in her than the deal. Then this fax arrived, arranged by us from another office in the building, claiming that an English club was prepared to pay £1.25million for Jose. That did the trick, and ensured the deal went through.

I'd arranged everything. All Barry had to do was sign. We all did well out of it, and my cut was enough to make all my efforts worthwhile. There was a clause about twenty per cent of our fee being paid up front, but Angelo and I waived it to make sure that the deal went through.

Lisbon did all right out of it, as they later sold him to Spurs for over £2million, but that was nothing to do with me, because by then I was at Darlington.

My first salary at Darlington was £25,000 a year, quite a contrast to the previous figure of £800,000 plus as an agent. Beverley went mad – but at the same time backed me.

I missed out on Emerson, after initially being the one who recommended him to Boro boss Bryan Robson. It was later that they followed up and signed him, and whoever was his agent at the time will, I assume, have got a fortune.

I took a lot of players to Scotland, and respected many of the people there. Rui Esteves was one of mine, and I took him for Dundee United to have a look at. I got on well with United chairman Jim McLean. He was as hard as nails, but straight as a die. I gained his respect because I advised him to pull out of one or two deals that I felt were not right.

But United manager Paul Sturrock (Lugs) dithered and nearly missed out on Esteves. He played one game while on trial and Lugs asked him to play another. The lad said he didn't want to, so I drove him all the way down to Birmingham, and told Barry to sign him.

He did, and he immediately won them the second leg of the Autoglass semi-final by earning a penalty.

Birmingham went on to beat Carlisle in the final, so they got an instant return on the money they spent on Esteves.

You can imagine how thick my contact book was, but in those days I could memorize phone numbers, and that's something I can't do now.

The deals came thick and fast, and among others, I took Robbie Slater to Blackburn, and Sebastian Rosenthal to Glasgow Rangers.

I also helped English players switch clubs at home. I helped my old mate Proc get a deal at Tranmere, as I knew their manager John King, having offered him a Bulgarian international midfielder.

By that stage in his career Proc had a bad knee, but I said I would try and get him a two year deal. We went to see John, and I said; "The deal will have to be as follows; £75,000 wages and £75,000 signing on fee," which I meant over two years.

John wrote the figures down, spent some time thinking it over, and came back with the reply, "I can't match £75,000 and £75,000, but what I can give you is £50,000 basic and £50,000 signing on fee, which makes it £200,000 over the two years."

At this point, I quickly kicked Proc under the table and told John that we would have to leave the room for half an hour to think it over. We just hung around outside, pretending that we were discussing the reduction in money, but really Proc couldn't believe it.

When the half hour was up, we went back in and said: "All right, but if we are going to do the deal, let's do it right now, or we will look elsewhere."

John signed Proc there and then, and I remember when we came out of the club, Proc running towards his wife Julie, and jumping up and down with joy. His knee injury had cleared up just like that.

He had got a superb deal when he had been on the verge of hanging up his boots.

Proc paid me £1,500, although it took a while for me to get it. His knee went before the two years were up.

That was the only time I pulled a bit of a flanker by misleading anyone. But I did it for Proc because he was like a brother to me.

I sometimes could have made a lot of money, but told clubs about players' injuries. That was at a time when medicals were poor, so I could easily have got away with pulling the wool.

I didn't like a lot of the people in the business, so I conducted myself properly because I didn't ever want any comeback. I refused to lower my standards to those of some other agents.

The Professional Footballers' Association respected me, and I remember on one occasion Mick Maguire of the PFA asked me to help a Finnish player who was having a problem with Doncaster Rovers. I was only too happy to help, because it showed how well trusted I was.

A lot of people who wanted to become an agent came to me for help and advice, and a lot of companies wanted to link up with me.

Paul Stretford, an agent who was big in America, wanted to team up with me because I was big in Europe. I didn't want to, but maybe should have done, because he later floated his business for £10million.

I was Steve Vickers' agent when he moved from Tranmere to Middlesbrough, and he too got a great deal. And former Boro goalkeeper Kelham O'Hanlon had me to thank for a few moves.

I had not long been an agent when Beverley and I married on a wonderful day, August 16th 1992.

I wanted to wake up next to Beverley the following morning, with nothing having changed. I worked that day and it was October before we went on honeymoon, because the season had just started when we got married, and I was particularly busy.

And I got busier and busier, until my life changed direction in May 1995.

Paul Futcher had been dismissed as Darlington manager, and a lot of people were linked with the job. It was Barrie Geldart, a long-standing friend of mine, and highly knowledgeable scout, who suggested to me that I might consider applying for the job.

I was interested; although Beverley asked why we should want to give up everything we had, to go into football management. It was a fair question, but by then I had been in touch with the club's directors.

I said to chairman Steve Weeks, that I was interested, but didn't want an interview. If they wanted me, fine, but I didn't want to travel up to Darlington only to be told after a long chat, that I was not getting the job.

Before I got an answer from him, Proc and I went to a Farewell to Ayresome Park event, held at Marton Country Club.

I was sure that I wanted to take Proc with me to Darlington, and we were laughing about the prospect, suggesting that we could be the Clough and Taylor of Darlington. Jim Platt wangled his way into the conversation, and two ended up as three.

The next day Steve Weeks rang, and asked me to come up and have a chat with him. I stressed that it must not be a formal interview, and he said, understandably, that he could hardly offer the job to someone he had not even met.

I travelled up, and went into the Blackwell Grange Hotel where four men – Steve, Bernard Lowery, Steve Morgon and Gordon Hodgson – met me.

They asked me all sorts of questions, but as the team had struggled badly I felt confident enough to promise that I would improve it by at least 25 per cent.

I said that I had been a player for a long time, understood exactly the character of players, and believed I could bring about a 25 per cent improvement in every player.

I said I would get them to play a passing game, cut out the long ball, and bring money in by selling the better players.

I remember Steve Morgon saying that improving the team mattered less than bringing enough money in to save the club. I had to live up to that promise for them to take me. At that time the most money Darlington had received for a player was around £150,000, for Jimmy Willis, who went to Leicester.

I repeated that if they had two legs I could sell them. That was good enough for Steve Morgon. He had just one more question to ask: "When can you start?"

John Hope and Eddie Kyle – who had managed for three games in a caretaker capacity after Paul Futcher had gone – had left the club, so there was no coaching staff.

I said I would bring Proc in with me, and Jim as youth team coach.

I rang Proc, who was still with Tranmere, and told him the job was mine. I agreed that the three of us would travel up to Feethams to meet the directors.

I met Proc and we drove up together. But at the Reg Vardy roundabout I had to pull over because we were laughing so much about various things that I couldn't see where I was driving because of the tears of laughter.

There's something about the two of us. We have such a great rapport that we can become helpless with laughter at the slightest of things.

The thought of the two of us managing a football club had us on the floor with aching ribs. At last as we edged toward some sort of control, I spluttered: "What would John Neal make of the two of us running a team?" That did it. We were off again for another few minutes, before we were able to drive the remaining couple of miles.

Jim had some managerial experience in Ireland, so would be a big help, although I knew how I wanted to go about the job.

The three of us then discussed money and I said we all should be on the same wage, even though it was a lot of money for Darlington.

But Jim pointed out that we could not be joint bosses as somebody had to make the decisions, and it ought to be me, as I was the most outspoken.

That wasn't strictly true, because Proc was certainly capable of standing his ground, but we agreed that Proc would assist me.

A day later Steve Weeks said he needed to see me in private and tell me something about the club. I tried to contact Proc, but couldn't get hold of him, so spoke to the chairman on my own.

He told me that Reg Brealey owned the club – but I already knew that because both Reg and I lived in Sheffield. But our private conversation didn't go down well with Proc, who felt he should have been in on it.

Next time I tried to ring him, I couldn't get him. I rang time and again over a three-hour period. Julie said he was in the bath, and eventually I said that he must have drowned by now if he was still in there.

When the two of us finally spoke, some nasty things were said, and we fell out big time. I decided not to take the job and rang Jim to tell him. But he wanted me to take it, pointing out that it meant a lot to me, and I might not get another opportunity.

Nevertheless I rang Steve Weeks and said I was not going to take it. Steve Morgon urged me to think about it for a day or two because I was by far the best man for the job.

Maybe at that point I felt that I could go back to being an agent – I hadn't taken any steps to wind up the business until I'd formally taken the job – while Jim wanted to give management in England a try after his success in Ireland, plus he had the opportunity to return to an area which he knew well from his successful playing days at Middlesbrough.

I suggested to Steve that he should give Jim the job, with our old Boro team mate Spike Armstrong possibly as his assistant, but Steve said: "Jim hasn't got a record of buying and selling players, and that's something we need."

Then Jim battered me again, and eventually Beverley told me to take it because she knew deep down I wanted to, and she would back me to the hilt. She reminded me that I had often talked to people about how I would train and coach players, and now I had my opportunity to do it.

So I rang Steve Morgon and said that I would come after all, but the money that was for the three of us must be split between Jim and me.

It was agreed, so I pulled the plug on the agency, and stepped into football management.

Beverley thought about the money we were giving up, but while she could cope with that, she cried because she knew I would be away a lot. But she did back me, and I appreciate that more than I have ever told her.

That morning, I left home and drove up to Darlington as manager of the club.

In some ways, it was just like the journey from Middlesbrough to Liverpool over a decade before. I was just as happy in my life as I was when I was a player at Middlesbrough. In fact, I had a great life – how could managing Darlington make it any better?

Arriving at Darlo;
"We can't afford to
win promotion."

So in June 1995, I drove up the A1 from my home in Todwick, through the gates of Feethams, and took my seat in the office that I was to share with Jim. I savoured the moment – manager of a football club!

However, the expected flood of phone calls didn't materialise, in fact, I didn't get any calls at all on my first day! I even made sure that the phone was working properly, by asking one of the staff to ring it. I wasn't used to people not ringing me.

Even though Jim and I were announced to the fans as joint managers, that wasn't the case. It was always the understanding that I was manager, and Jim assistant, on the insistence of the board of directors. The idea was that one of us had to liaise with the board.

One of our first jobs was to call the players together. The season had finished a month earlier, and the players were on their summer holidays. Eddie Kyle, who had been caretaker manager (Darlo's third manager that season after Paul Futcher and Alan Murray), had departed, and the players didn't know what was happening, which wasn't surprising.

So Jim and I introduced ourselves, took them into the boardroom, and poured them some champagne. They probably wondered what was going on!

We talked about what we wanted from them, what training was going to be like, how we intended to play. And then we drank a toast to the future.

We faced an immediate problem – a transfer embargo was in place, which was carried over from the previous season. That meant officially we couldn't bring players in, but unofficially we could still look at them in training and in practice games. I wasn't too concerned at that moment, because we hadn't seen our own players in action, and we couldn't make any decisions until then, even though plenty of players had been in contact.

We also had to sign up four of our own players who were out of contract, and wanted to keep on – Gary Himsworth, Sean Gregan, Robbie Blake and Paul Olsson.

The next problem we had was where to have training. Steve Morgon told me that in previous years, the town didn't want to help us, because the club had failed to honour its agreements, so we needed somewhere to train. The players had trained in South Park in the not too distant past – I've since heard the story of Kevan Smith, Fred Barber and the frozen dog mess – and I ruled that out immediately. We had to have somewhere with good facilities and a good surface.

Arriving at Darlo; "We can't afford to win promotion."

Corny O'Donnell, who was in the commercial department at Sunderland when I was there, suggested I try Jim Wood at Catterick army garrison. Jim, a fitness instructor who had represented Great Britain in the biathlon, really grilled me about my background, what our aims were, and we struck a deal. Sometimes, however, Catterick wasn't available, so we also agreed a deal with the Young Offenders' Institute at Deerbolt near Barnard Castle. Both facilities were excellent.

We also took the opportunity of a pre-season tour to Southern Ireland. I had a friend in Portugal who agreed to pay us £2500 in return for me putting a couple of Portuguese players in our squad with a view to placing them and selling them.

With the promise of money, a contact I had in Southern Ireland, John O'Driscoll, sorted out some accommodation and Jim arranged some matches against clubs he had contacts with over there.

By then, Gary Bannister, who had been freed by Lincoln, was on trial with us, while we arranged to meet a keeper, Ashley Stephenson, at the ferry port in Fishguard.

When we arrived at the port, Jim took it upon himself to go and find Ashley – typical keepers' union. Jim had left the coach for only a minute when a young Asian looking boy approached the bus.

I thought; "What is he going to try and sell us?" The driver opened the door only for the lad to utter the words; "Hodgy, I'm Ashley" in a very polite accent. I wasn't expecting an Asian looking keeper. I introduced myself and sat him down, waiting for Jim to return.

When Jim returned to the bus some time later he looked surprised when he was introduced to Ashley. Jim had obviously been looking for a figure that cut the image of a typical English goalkeeper.

There was a moment's silence, broken by Jim saying: "How was I to know that I was looking for a Pakistani."

It may not have been the most sensitive comment of his life, but there was no racial innuendo implied or taken. The whole bus burst out laughing – Ashley included. He had been accepted into the squad immediately.

We started to impose our authority on the players. We stopped them drinking on the ferry, which didn't go down too well on a long trip like that! We then drove in the bus to Waterford, and arrived at the hotel which had been booked for us at one o'clock in the morning.

However, the place was a shambles. They weren't ready for us, there were no refreshments, and there were drunks in the hotel foyer. There was no way we were going to stay in a place like that.

I immediately told the players to pick up their bags, and return to the bus. We drove to Waterford Town Centre where we found a clean hostel for the night.

At 6.30 the following morning, I got our bus driver out of bed – naturally he wasn't too pleased – and we drove to Dunmore East, a picturesque place just outside Waterford, where there were lots of hotels. None of them could accommodate a party of 24, but we were recommended some cottages near the bay. They had very good facilities, and had room for four players at a time. We found a nearby hotel to supply us with meals, and a pitch to train on. Our pre-season tour was taking shape.

We played our first game against Waterford and won quite comfortably. On the way back from the match, I told the lads that they could go out for a drink, as long as they were back in the cottages by 11pm.

Just to let them know I was keeping an eye on them, I sat outside my cottage at 10.50, watching them coming back up the hill. I thought it was important that they knew I wasn't going to allow them any leeway. They all arrived back on time.

The next morning, we made the lads feel better by allowing them to use a nearby swimming pool to relax. My idea was to treat them properly, on the basis of what was good enough for me during my career, was good enough for them.

We also beat Kilkenny and Cobh Ramblers on that trip, although Jim and I had to play up front at Cobh Ramblers because one or two of the lads had knocks. Jim scored a couple of goals, if I remember rightly. I was even asked by the press if I was going to make a playing comeback, but that was out of the question with the injuries.

On the last night of the trip, I told the lads that they could stop out until two o'clock in the morning.

As the deadline approached I sat on the window ledge like an owl, watching the lads come back. Then a car came up the hill and its headlights went out. Some people got out the car, so I asked Banno to pop over and tell the players concerned to send the girls home, and to take the drink with them.

The next morning, I had a word with the players on the bus. "You weren't clever and quick thinking enough," I said. "You should have sneaked over the fence at the back!" That was an expert talking!

The trip was a great success. We came home, and played some friendlies against Boro, Motherwell and St Johnstone, and didn't win any of them. But Pedro Paulo had such a good game against Boro full back Curtis Fleming that I was prompted to try and sell the little winger to Boro!

Everything about Pedro was good. He could pass the ball well, take on and beat a man, put in a good cross, but eventually the club just couldn't afford to keep him. I was really sad when I heard that he was killed in a car crash in Portugal a couple of years ago.

Pedro came with another lad called Rui Neves, who took on a babysitter's role. I don't think he got any goals for us, and he couldn't handle the Third Division on a regular basis.

They were the first two foreigners I brought to the club – there were plenty more to follow. I intended to use my contacts, whether they were in Britain or abroad, to the full.

When we played St Johnstone in a pre-season friendly at Feethams, we turned the heating up full blast in their dressing room, and put towels over the door to keep the heat in and attempt to dehydrate their players. Their manager, Paul Sturrock, an old friend of mine, wasn't too happy, but I told him that I had to find something to give our lads a little lift against them!

As the start of the season approached, the transfer embargo was still in force, so I had to sell before I could bring anybody in.

The most saleable asset at the time was centre half Adam Reed, a local lad who had come through the ranks, and was highly rated by Barrie Geldart, who had looked after the youth set up at Feethams.

Everybody told me that Adam had done well the previous season, and Sunderland had taken him on trial for a week to have a look at him.

When Barrie, who had left Darlington to become Blackburn's chief scout, made an enquiry, I told him that Sunderland had offered £150,000 for him and had taken him on trial again, when really they'd offered £75,000 and he was still at Feethams.

I told Barrie that they had to beat that, and Ray Harford, who had just taken over from Kenny Dalglish, offered £180,000, which I wanted up front, or if they couldn't do that, then it would have to be £200,000.

They agreed to pay £180,000, and the deal was done within days. I phoned Steve Morgon, who was on holiday, and he told me that I'd done something that he thought would never happen.

The embargo was lifted by the league, which was good news for the six former coaching staff who were owed money at the time – Tony McAndrew, Frank Gray, Ray Hankin, Alan Murray, Eddie Kyle and Paul Futcher!

And it also opened the door for me to sign Gary Bannister –the most important signing of the lot – Gary Himsworth, Phil Brumwell and Mark Barnard, who lived in the same village as me, and could keep me company in the car!

Phil was my first signing. He told me that he wanted £200 per week, so I checked with Sunderland, who told me he was on £50 per week, so I gave him £100. Good try, Phil!

My first league game as a manager was at Exeter City in August 1995. Because of the distance involved, we travelled down to our hotel in the south west the day before. After we met Bob Fuller from our club sponsors Orange, the penny dropped for me that this game was for real.

I'd often wondered what the feeling was like, sitting at the front of the bus, taking my team to a game. I said to Jim; "I'm pleased you're next to me," and he replied, "Don't worry, we'll be fine." Jim had done it before during his previous management days in Ireland, and knew what to expect.

I remember warming up the players on the field, while our fans were coming into the ground behind the goal and hoping that things would go well for everybody.

Hopefully, I said the right things to the players, because they started off well, doing everything we'd practised in training, and we won with a shot by midfielder Paul Olsson, set up for him by Banno.

At the final whistle, Jim turned to me and said: "That's your first win as a manager; let's hope it's the first of many."

Jim and I had a reasonably good partnership, although our approaches were different.

Training was done the way I wanted, and I think Jim accepted that. Jim's philosophy was maybe based on his years with Big Jack at Middlesbrough, but we didn't have the players for that style of play. He was very good at lightening up and explaining situations when I was trying to get my ideas over.

The winning feeling didn't last long, because then we failed to win for a few games. After the high of winning at Exeter, we were soon on a low, because we lost 1-0 to a late penalty at home to Rochdale. As a player, I'd never experienced such a range of emotions in a few days, and it was clear at that point as a manager I would have to start all over again emotionally.

I wasn't scared to ring the changes. I left defender Matty Appleby out in a league cup game at Crewe, because I thought he had a chip on his shoulder, and he needed to learn a few things from the stand. I figured that he would ask himself if he thought he was good enough to be in the team, why he was sitting in the stand. He was soon back in the team, because we lost 4-0. Rui Neves missed a couple of chances.

There was a considerable amount of media attention after the Scarborough home game. We lost 2-1, and we should have won – I think Gary Bennett scored for them.

We had outpassed them, but couldn't finish them off, so after the game, I announced on Radio Cleveland that I was putting the whole team on the transfer list!

I figured that nobody would come in for any of them, so I could say they had two choices, either find themselves out of football, or believe in themselves more.

It certainly caused a few rumblings. National newspapers, television and radio all latched on to the story.

Radio Five came along one day when the players were training at Deerbolt with Jim, and I joked; "The players are over at the prison training – I hope they're kept in!"

I took some stick from the fans, both verbal and in writing. I phoned a few up, quite good-naturedly. One bloke in particular, from Barnard Castle, was most disturbed about what I'd done, and I spent half an hour speaking to him. At the end of the conversation, he accepted my point that I was trying to make the players believe in themselves, and my reasoning behind it, and sometime later he wrote me a very nice letter.

I deliberately stayed away from the players all week. Jim spent a lot of his time with them, and he came back to me and said: "You've upset their families and the players are very low."

The following game was at Barnet. The players and Jim went on the bus on the Friday morning; I drove to Lincoln and met Reg Brealey face-to-face for the first time. Reg was the club's majority shareholder at the time, and had become involved in the club two or three years earlier. I had a good chat with him, and explained why

I'd put all the players on the transfer list.

On my way to the hotel in the evening, I stopped at an off licence and bought some wine, champagne and lager, then invited all the players to my room when I arrived at the hotel.

I apologised to them if I'd offended their families, but pointed out: "If you've lost your faith in me as a manager, then I'll drive home.

"If you don't believe what I'm going to tell you, then I'll leave. You're playing with the belief that you can't win games because you're at Darlington. You are thinking small time."

They were probably the most important words of my managerial career up till then. I took Jim out of the room with me, to let the players talk about it amongst themselves.

I named the team, leaving out Steve Gaughan and Gary Himsworth, and I took time out to explain to them why they had been dropped from the team. When I was a player and left out of the team, nobody explained to me why it had happened, something that annoyed me.

We drew the game 1-1, with Banno scoring, but I shall always remember that game for the sudden impact of Jose-Marie Quitongo, who came on as a second half sub, and nearly broke the bar with a blistering shot going down the slope which was a feature of the Barnet pitch. Unfortunately, we couldn't afford to keep him because he was on big money.

The following week in training, I could sense that there was more urgency about the players than there was before the Scarborough game.

The next game was Lincoln away, and we had a selection problem at centre back. We'd been playing 4-4-2, but Sean Gregan had missed the Barnet game because of injury, and it would have been an injustice if I'd left either Andy Crosby or Matty Appleby out because of how well they'd played at Barnet. So I decided to play all three of them as centre halves, with Simon Shaw and Mark Barnard as wing backs.

The formation clicked, and we battered Lincoln, opening them up for fun.

There was one problem, though, with Banno. He hadn't been firing on all cylinders, and some fans had started to turn on him. Jim said that we should leave him out, and Banno even agreed with the suggestion.

But I was adamant that he should stop in the team. "He's better than anybody we've got in the club. The other players must learn to think like him. We're not dropping him."

The Lincoln game was a big turning point, and we won our next five games to really set the place buzzing, and the fans changed their minds about Banno. He became a real crowd favourite.

But there were developments off the field that I didn't really like. Because I was still going up and down to Todwick, I didn't know what was going on at the ground for at least four hours in the working day.

Jim used to ring me every morning and tell me what was happening, particularly regarding the actions of Steve Morgon and Tony Kenworthy. Politically, that was very difficult, because it isn't healthy for people to have frosty relationships.

We relieved Tony Kenworthy of his youth team duties, on the basis that we didn't think it was working, but then Steve Morgon appointed him to the commercial staff instead.

We thought about bringing in Alan Kennedy and then Gary Megson for the youth team job, but the money, as you would expect for a youth team job, understandably wasn't enough for them. As it turned out, Alan is now doing well as a media pundit, while Gary has taken West Brom twice to the Premiership! My old mate from Boro, Billy Askew, agreed to take the youth team.

But it was clear that I had to sort out problems, while I was going up and down the motorway, on my mobile phone, and I was arriving home or at work in a bad frame of mind while a less than healthy atmosphere was developing off the field.

One of the highlights for the fans of my first spell at Darlington was the 4-2 FA Cup win at Hartlepool, but there were all sorts of developments off the field that day which ignited certain events later.

Notts County were interested in keeper Mike Pollitt, but I told them that we weren't interested until we had a replacement sorted out, particularly with the FA Cup in mind. However, I did say to them that if we lost at Hartlepool, I would consider doing business at £100,000 if they were going to sell Darren Ward, their number one choice at the time.

What I didn't appreciate was that Reg had a very close relationship with Notts County, and without me knowing, a deal was struck for £30,000.

When I found out – just a day before the Hartlepool game – I was furious. The deal was all but done, and Polly was to sign for County on the Monday morning.

Polly, who I suspect didn't know about the deal, had a great last game in a Darlo shirt, as we won 4-2 and were rewarded with a second round tie at Rochdale. On the day we were brilliant, and Kenny Lowe, the Hartlepool midfielder, applauded us off the field, which I thought was a very nice gesture.

For his part, Polly did well at County and then Rotherham, playing for them in the First Division.

Jim and I nearly resigned at the end of the game on principle. We thought that it was entirely wrong for the club to sell a player without our knowledge and permission. What was the point of being in charge of the team when our players could be transferred without us knowing?

Jim said that he would walk as well, and that we shouldn't let others dictate to us.

We decided to stay on because we were on a high after the Hartlepool game, plus we felt that we would be letting the fans down. It was a great feeling to play so well at Hartlepool, and receive the adulation of the Darlington fans. It was the best Darlo win there for many years, so I was told (there would be an even better one later!).

We needed a goalkeeper, so we signed the much-travelled and slightly eccentric

John Burridge as cover until we could sort something out. Jim was wary of Budgie, and so I made it clear to Budgie that his role was to play in goal and to help the youngsters around him, and then nothing else. No coaching or anything.

But by now there were several disagreements behind the scenes, and there was a really bad atmosphere between playing staff and non-playing staff.

And then we received a visit from Bernard Lowery, who became chairman that season.

The club was flying at the time. A five match winning run in October, plus two further draws, had catapulted us into promotion contention, something which the fans certainly hadn't tasted since the old Fourth Division days. Life was really good for Darlo fans.

Bernard said: "We can't afford to win promotion. You need to pull the reins on."

I was gobsmacked. What was the point in managing a football club if its directors wanted you to lose? How could I look the fans in the face and tell them that we weren't going to try hard in games?

So, completely disillusioned and in order to get away from it all, I decided to take Beverley and the girls away on holiday to Cyprus, to make a decision on whether to stay at the club or go.

I arrived back in time for the away game at Chester but I still hadn't made my mind up. I arrived at the ground only to see Jim and Sean Gregan arguing like mad about tactics, with strong words being said. Banno told me that there had been a lot of upset in the club whilst I was away, and he thought that Jim was getting used to the idea of being manager in his own right.

We lost badly at Chester, with striker Cyrille Regis causing loads of problems in their 4-1 win, ironically the only away defeat suffered by the team all season until the Wembley play off game.

The following week was the second round FA Cup tie at Rochdale, and I decided that I was going to quit, but I knew that if we beat Rochdale, then I would be in a position of strength to suggest to Steve Morgon that he should leave instead. Steve was involved in a few rows behind the scenes, and wasn't too popular with the fans. Jim led me to believe that he was going to do the same as me.

We led 2-0 at one point against Rochdale, and at half time, I asked Jack Watson, our chief scout, to come to the dressing room. I handed him a letter that contained my resignation, and asked him to pass it on to the chairman, with the request not to open it until the end of the game.

The saying goes that curiosity killed the cat, and I know that letter was opened before the final whistle.

Jim knew what was in the letter, and for the second half, he stood well away from me on the touchline, issuing instructions to the players.

I honestly thought, after all our discussions of the principles involved in the Mike Pollitt transfer and Bernard's visit, that Jim was going to walk away with me.

We drew 2-2, and at the end of the game, I walked into the dressing room, thanked the players, and Jim said he would give me a ring when he got home.

Steve Morgon rang, and asked me what was going on. I told him that I wasn't happy with recent events, which I guess he knew already. He asked me not to do anything else until he'd seen me in person.

I got a call from the press soon after the game when I was in the car on my way home, but those were the only two calls I received on the Saturday night.

I started to realise on Sunday morning that Jim, who was then back home in Ireland, hadn't quit as well, and the press confirmed it. Steve Morgon asked me to come to the ground on the Wednesday, with the press reports suggesting that Jim had taken over as manager, which wasn't what we had talked about. He was supposed to be walking away with me, not staying.

The draw was made for the third round of the FA Cup on Sunday afternoon and it provoked even more thought from me.

The draw for the next round? Liverpool v Darlington or Rochdale. My old club, a chance to go back to Anfield as a manager. Show Liverpool what I had learned from my two years there as a player and put into practice as a manager. A chance for Liverpool fans to see that a team in the lower divisions could play like them, well, a little bit anyway.

Beverley knew how much that draw meant to me, but on principle, I wouldn't budge. I couldn't go back to a club that was selling players behind my back and saying don't win promotion. "Go back," she shouted at me. But I wouldn't budge; I had made my mind up to leave.

On the Wednesday, I drove to the ground. Jim had returned from Ireland and when I arrived, he said; "Come into my office," which went down like a lead balloon with me. "My" office? It was our office until the previous Saturday.

I told him that I wasn't happy with the fact that he hadn't called me to talk about the situation, and that he hadn't supported me as we had agreed before the Rochdale match.

I also pointed out that the reason why I left was because other people were trying to dictate what was happening without my knowledge, especially with the sale of Mike Pollitt. Steve Morgon joined the argument, saying that the club needed the money, and I had a go back.

I also told Jim that I had kept him in a job when certain other people wanted him out, but I stood by him – and now I thought I was due the same from Jim. I left Jim in no doubt that he had done wrong, I didn't even shake his hand as I left.

On reflection, Jim probably did what he thought was best for himself. Maybe he needed the job for his own reasons, but I still maintain that if we had stuck together after the game at Rochdale, we could have made things happen for the better behind the scenes.

I stormed out the club, and went to meet the players at the Blackwell Grange Hotel on the outskirts of Darlington.

"I'm not coming back," I told them. "But do me a favour, win promotion because certain people don't want you to. It suits them to stay in this league. You owe it to yourselves to keep performing and winning matches." And then I pointed to Banno and said: "You make sure of it."

And that was it. I drove back to Todwick, and restarted work as an agent, although the lads continued to phone me. I never regretted leaving on principle, but I regretted having to do it. If only the sale of Polly hadn't happened, but overall, the club was more important than me or other people.

With Roy Evans, the Liverpool manager at the time, watching from the stand, we lost the replay 1-0, and it was Rochdale who had the privilege of playing at Anfield in the third round. It hurt me that we never got that far, and I know it hurt the fans too. Instead of going to Liverpool in the third round of the FA Cup, it was a home game against Northampton instead.

Jim was made manager in his own right after I left, Banno was appointed player-coach, and Tony Kenworthy came back as reserve team coach.

I returned as a guest of a sponsor for one game, and caused a stir. It was the 1-0 home win over Hartlepool, Steve Gaughan getting the winner with a tremendous shot from outside the box. Tony completely blanked me as he passed me in the corridor.

Naturally, I watched the results with interest, and at times wished I were there with the team and the fans. By this time, I'd been offered the Scarborough job, passed the interview and chairman John Russell had even called a press conference, but I turned it down.

I was a little concerned about the build up to the last game of the season at Scunthorpe. The players spent part of the week at the magnificent health club at Redworth Hall. It was supposed to help them relax and forget about the game, but I wasn't too sure about the effect the number of swimming sessions had on their legs. In my opinion, swimming is ok to freshen legs after a game, but not for training.

I heard the game on the radio, and at 3-3 we nearly won it, but Robbie Blake just missed from ten yards. Rumour had it that Steve Morgon celebrated the fact that we were in the play offs in the changing room, while the players were downhearted about missing automatic promotion. The play offs were just a consolation prize.

The players kept me in touch with what was going on. Matty Appleby, Andy Crosby, Banno, and Mark Barnard phoned me up regularly to tell me what was happening.

Full credit though to everybody concerned, the team reached Wembley for the play off final against Plymouth after beating Hereford over two legs. I must admit it hurt me not be there with them, and share a great day with the players and the supporters. My time would come, but under different circumstances, four years later.

Sadly, the day didn't belong to Darlington, because Plymouth's Ronnie Mauge scored the only goal of the game in the second half.

I would be lying if I said that I didn't miss the day-to-day involvement with the players and the matches, because after all, that is football life as a manager. Despite all that had happened, I still wanted the team to win every week.

I was willing them to win matches and win promotion, just to get back at certain people at the club, who I knew would be suffering if the team was flying high in the table.

There were one or two job offers. Falkirk suggested that I should apply for their managerial vacancy, while Ian Atkins asked me if I fancied going to Northampton as his number two. But I didn't know much about Scottish football – although I had supplied some players to Scottish clubs – while I didn't want to be an assistant, because it just wouldn't suit me.

So, I renewed my agent's licence, and turned my back on management – until Steve Morgon rang one day.

10

Outside looking in; "We'd like you to come back as manager."

BY the time the following season, 1996-97, started, my agency work was keeping me busy, but I found time to follow the team's progress with considerable interest.

I hoped they would do well, and I felt that Jim had inherited a side drilled in playing the right way and doing the job properly. He had added his own thoughts and signings, and I wished him well.

But there were things that niggled me, one of them being that after I had left, Jim appeared to have convinced everyone that while I was at the club, I was in sole charge of buying and selling players, and that made it look as if I had no impact on the coaching or the way we played, though I did.

After I left Jim signed, among others, Michael Oliver, Darren Roberts, and Brian Atkinson, who all went on to do well at the club. But Stevie Gaughan had left – a deal done by me – Matty Appleby had gone to Barnsley, Gary Bannister had quit as a player, Paul Olsson had quit through injury, and Gary Himsworth had joined York.

They were largely replaced with inexperienced players, on salaries around the £300 a week bracket. When you take into consideration the money that had been made from the game at Wembley, it seemed to me to be bad business not to invest more in the team.

The team had done well in a pre-season trip to Ireland. But they lost the first game of the season at Hull, which, when put into context was a lousy start because we had lost only once away from home in the whole of the previous season.

That was at Chester, before I left, and to Jim's credit they didn't lose another away game.

But once the new season started I was curious to see whether they would play the same way, taking the ball from the keeper, passing it and keeping it.

While I was angry with some of the things that had been said about me, I didn't want them to fail. After all, I knew a lot of the players, so of course I wanted them to succeed.

If Jim wanted to adopt the typical Division Three long ball game, that was his prerogative. But he didn't. He tried to get them to carry on playing from the back, and to be comfortable on the ball.

It was interesting to see that he encouraged that, because, remember, he was a goalkeeper, and not many keepers like to see the ball passed around in front of them on the edge of their own eighteen yard box.

But to be honest the public had now become accustomed to this style of play, and if Jim had changed to a long ball game, questions would have been asked.

As the season progressed the results picked up, and full credit to everybody involved for that fantastic 2-2 draw at Leeds United in the Worthington Cup. Was I a little envious at not being in charge that night? Damn right I was.

It was George Graham's first game in charge at Leeds, and I felt that the Leeds lads would be out to impress. I didn't think Darlington had a chance. When the result came through I was more shocked than delighted. I couldn't believe it.

And as I was in Sheffield at the time, I read in the papers about the match from the Leeds angle, which felt strange. But by then I had been away from the club for almost a year, so some of the closeness had gone, though I was in touch with several of the players.

Shortly afterwards Sean Gregan went to train with Crystal Palace with a view to moving there. I advised him not to go. I knew of a link up between Reg Brealey, who still owned Darlington, and Palace chairman Ron Noades. I feared that Sean's potential move there was a publicity stunt.

However, I'm not sure that he wanted to move that far south anyway.

Around that time several of the Darlington players were phoning me regularly to discuss things that were going on at the club, including the appointment of former Sheffield United manager Danny Bergara as coach.

But to be honest I wasn't interested any more in tittle-tattle. If the players were not happy, the only way to get out of the club was to play well and hope an opportunity came to move on to bigger and better things.

At that stage I had no indication whatsoever that I would soon be returning to the club. It was simply not on the agenda. I had happily picked up where I left off with the agency, and felt that my time as a manager was finished – brief though it was.

I didn't go for any other job, didn't have affection for any other part of the country, and didn't want to have to create that feeling elsewhere. Besides, I think Beverley would have taken a bit of persuading to let me go back into management. She was happy, and I had no desire to uproot her.

But then things kicked off with Sean Gregan again. He was a very good player and was starting to be in real demand.

It appeared that he was going to join Wigan, but this was a deal that concerned me. I wrote down the people involved and drew a circle round it. There was a link. Wigan owner Dave Whelan, who also owned JJB Sports, Darlington owner Reg Brealey, and the proposed Soccerdome project. I thought there was something that didn't add up, especially as the fee for Sean, was, according to speculation, nominal.

I recall that Jim said he knew nothing about the deal. Maybe he did, but didn't want the fans to think he was sanctioning the sale of one of the club's star players, especially to a team which at that time was in the same division.

I was working with Sean at the time, and became involved. I went to see the Wigan people, especially manager John Deehan. We knew each other, so the meeting was very relaxed.

Then I went to Dave Whelan's factory, and expected him to sweeten me up, with some clothing, but he didn't. I stuck to my guns with what I wanted for Sean, and the deal fell through.

I found out that the price was only around £100,000, which I didn't feel was anything like enough for a player of Sean's calibre at that stage of his career with so much time ahead of him. After all, I had sold Adam Reed to Blackburn for £180,000 just over a year earlier.

Sean was the most saleable asset at Darlington and I would have thought that £400,000 to £500,000 was a more realistic figure.

I rang Jim up – the first time we'd spoken since I'd left – and told him what the situation was, which was only right, as he was manager. I can't remember the conversation, so it must have been reasonably amicable.

That said, I bet my name was worse than mud in the club.

But that didn't stop Steve Morgon contacting me. He was ringing me regarding Sean, but I felt from his tone that he was considering me for a return as manager. But I nipped it in the bud, telling him not to even consider me while he still had a manager.

When the team lost at home to Barnet, the fans turned on Steve, possibly blaming him for the Gregan situation. The fanzine had been unkind to him at the time, and it's a fact of football that the public can be very demanding, and harsh. Some fans had learned that Reg Brealey was the man behind the club, and weren't too happy. Their feelings were taken out on Steve.

I said to him that if the team lost five or six successive games, then he was justified in questioning whether Jim was taking things forward.

It was not a happy team at the time, and in a 5-2 defeat at Cambridge, skipper Andy Crosby and Gary Twynham ended up fighting. Gary was sent off, and waited for Andy in the tunnel, then smacked him as he came into the changing room.

I got a call on the Sunday after a 2-0 defeat at Lincoln. Steve told me that Jim was going to lose his job, but at that point I wasn't sure whether he would, although I'm led to believe he knew that his time was up. But it was up to chairman Bernard Lowery to tell Jim, and I don't think he really wanted Jim to go, especially when the chairman had said: "If Jim goes, I go." (Now where have I heard chairmen say things like that before).

I told Steve that if I returned I had to say why I was doing so, and he had to honour the decision. It was a few days before I said 'yes', and I insisted that for me to return, Steve had to leave the club.

I felt that would be for the good of the club, given all that had happened and the problem he had with the fans.

He said he had had enough anyway, and was ready to quit, though he insisted that it would look wrong if he walked out the door the day I walked in.

I agreed with him. He said he would have a handover period of around a fortnight, while Ken Lavery took over his role.

And that's what happened. My role was clearly defined, and it was all done as amicably as possible.

We agreed that all buying and selling, contracts and football matters were to be handled by me, though the club was to set the budget. On footballing matters, it was agreed that I would do all the talking to the public and media.

At that time I didn't hear anything from Reg, even though he was the major shareholder.

Despite his unpopularity with some of the fans at the end of his time, Steve was not a bad man. In fact, regardless of what the public thought, he was a good man. He had a genuine desire to take the club forward.

The first impression I had got of him, was not what he was about. I grew to like him, and I felt partly responsible for him leaving, which hurt me, especially as he had a wife and children.

Of all the people I have worked with at the club, he was one of the best in terms of what he tried to do for the club. If he could give any extra money to the players, he did. He maybe didn't have a lot of football knowledge, but he worked at it very hard.

I have never tended to socialise with people at the club. I judge them on what they can do for the club, and he was good for it at the time he was there.

I got to know him very well around that time, as did club secretary Carol Barnett, and football secretary Lisa Charlton, and they liked him too.

I asked Carol just before I rejoined the club, what the financial state was. I needed that information because I wanted to make sure that I was not being conned, like I felt I was the first time I joined the club when I was immediately under pressure to sell a player, Adam Reed to Blackburn.

In typical fashion Carol said she could not disclose such information until I was an employee of the club. She knew I had been offered the job, and was going to accept. But she was absolutely right to refuse me. Even when I was at the club it was difficult getting anything out of her. At least I knew, that with Carol around, the financial affairs of the club would be kept safe.

There was something that I was frustrated about at the time, but it was nothing to do with Darlington.

My return had come just at the point when I had three deals, worth over £8 million (in total, not to me!) going through from my agency. Rosenthal was going to Rangers, Pederson to Blackburn, and Kvarme to Liverpool.

I had to write to the FA asking whether I could complete the deals, while still taking on the Darlington job. The deals were worth a lot of money to me, so it was important to conclude them.

I was told that I could complete them, as long as I didn't sign a contract at

Darlington, or get paid until the deals had gone through. Steve had to write to the FA confirming that I was working for nothing, even expenses. He was probably hoping that the deals would take many months to go through. In fact they took around a couple of months.

I did everything by the book. I surrendered my agent's licence, which was passed onto Tony Henry. I even had to resign as a director of my own company, though Beverley continued in the same role.

She also said that if I was going back to Darlington, we would have to move there, as she didn't want me driving up and down the motorway – especially on no salary, albeit temporarily.

She said if I was in the Darlington area I would be totally committed to the job.

In my first training session back with the club I spent just half an hour with the lads. I knew who I needed to help them along – Gary Bannister.

He had left the club, and moved to Cornwall. After a lot of persuasion he agreed to return as coach, and eventually bought a house in Croft. He got it cheap, because at that time there were a lot of floods, and nobody would touch the houses there, as they were so close to the river.

Banno felt that he was getting it really cheaply, and his family wanted it. But it took him six months in finding a company that would give him a mortgage, and by that time the authorities had built an embankment to keep the floods out and make the properties more secure.

As Beverley had suggested, I went house hunting too, and we bought the one we still live in. It's in a village outside Darlington.

But it was quite a job finding one Beverley liked. I worked on it after training each day, but the more brochures I took her, the more she disliked the houses that I had thought were possibilities.

I was by now convinced that she didn't want to move. But as soon as she saw the details of this house, she agreed to it immediately.

Maybe it was a woman's intuition, but whatever it was, she knew straight away that this was the house for her.

The trouble was I couldn't find it. All I had done was pick up a brochure and had never seen the house. Jack Watson, a great servant to the club down the years, went out of his way to find it for me.

I drove out with Banno to have a look. It was no more than fifteen minutes from Darlington, but driving along the winding roads, it seemed to take forever.

Eventually we saw Jack standing on a raised piece of grass at the end of a lane. He was jumping up and down and waving his arms. He looked like the village delinquent.

But he had found the village, which we would never have managed in a million years, even though he didn't know which house it was. As we drove into the village – which is really a hamlet – I noticed that there was no shop, or pub or Post Office, but plenty of cow muck and horse manure.

There was only around half a dozen houses there, and a few Raby Estate cottages, but I still didn't know which one it was that I was supposed to be looking at.

There was no estate agent's sign and the picture in the brochure I had was taken from the bottom of the back garden, so from the front I could not recognise the house.

In a way that was a good thing, because if this was the house Beverley liked, then nobody else was going to be able to find it. Therefore we would get it at a good price, as we would be the only people bidding.

Eventually we sussed it out. Not only was I not sure about the house, but the village didn't suit me. I had visions of the children dragging cow muck into the house on their shoes.

I came back three or four times, looking for the owner. There were net curtains up and I couldn't see in. I tried to make an appointment, but the estate agent said that the woman who owned the house was out of the country.

It belonged to an Indian couple, who had built it to sell on, but to avoid capital gains tax.

When we finally agreed a viewing date we were extremely surprised to find that virtually all the furniture was brand new and still wrapped up.

The place was unlived in. It appeared that it was no more than a weekend home. There was a double bed in one bedroom, and a kitchen that had all the normal appliances for a weekend stop over.

After viewing the property on one more occasion, Beverley was convinced that this was where she wanted to move. I couldn't believe it. The house was going to cost me a fortune, but I was convinced that I would spend even more on the children's shoes.

We had gone from a small development in South Yorkshire with manicured lawns and immaculate road, to a garden like a bombsite and enough horse manure out the front to keep the leeks growing in all the gardens in the north east.

What was she thinking of?

After a brief private discussion outside, Beverley made it clear to me that I had to get this house at all costs.

I asked Beverley to stand in amazement, giving the impression that I was disagreeing with her about buying the house. Put simply, we had a mock argument. I knew that the owner was looking on from inside, and I was hoping to give her the impression that I wasn't interested.

I gave a quick knock on the door, thanked her for letting us view the house, and off we drove. As it was March and she was due to move in April, we had obviously made her worried.

The asking price was well over £200,000, and when I got back home I phoned the owner and made it clear that personally I didn't want the house, but my wife did, and I made a point of saying that I was only prepared to go to a certain price.

I also made a strict point of saying that I needed an answer in thirty minutes. After I put the phone down, Beverley said I was horrible to put the young lady in such a position, and there was no way that they would accept our offer (which was considerably less than she wanted).

But within ten minutes the lady had phoned back and said 'yes,' on the condition that we could exchange in three weeks, basically setting a date of April 1st.

Being the superstitious person I am, that was a no go. I would settle for the 2nd, 3rd or 4th, but April 1st – no chance!

I assured her that it would be concluded on the timescale set, with no problems. We agreed to come up one more time before shaking hands on the deal.

It was on this last visit that I found out that her husband was in the clothing business. In fact he manufactured Warner Brothers jeans for children.

I wouldn't be me if I hadn't negotiated for a few pairs of jeans to be thrown into the bargain.

We have been here over seven years now, so once again I was wrong and Beverley was right. It's a beautiful house and we are still very happy here. It was nice to be settled again in a family home, though seven years for us in one place is a miracle.

I have dragged Beverley from country to country, and never believed that I would stay in a place for such a long time. But she has a great ability to adjust.

But having finally got the house, our problems were not over. Our elder daughter Brogan, who was four at the time I think, failed to settle at nursery. I had always taken her to nursery at Todwick, and she always skipped off happily.

But the nursery in Darlington didn't suit her. She was all right for the first couple of days, but was in floods of tears on the third day and said that she was not staying. The teacher advised us to stick with it, but the next day I saw one child hit another, yet nothing was done about it.

It seemed to be that environment that had upset her. The nursery teacher had insisted that I drop Brogan off and leave immediately, not allowing her the time or opportunity to upset me. I made the feeble excuse that I had to go quickly to phone mummy. There was no way that Brogan was letting go. I will never forget the simple words that she said to me: "I will come with you daddy to ring mummy."

I knew at that point that I could not leave my daughter for one more day at that nursery.

Even a long time later when we drove past, Brogan would frown and say: "It's not nice there."

We took her to Ferndene, off Cleveland Terrace, and she loved it there.

That was one problem solved, but I had another one with a bunch of older kids – the football team! We were scrapping to stay out of the bottom three or four and it was anything but plain sailing.

My first game back in charge was at non-league Runcorn in the FA Cup first round. Our physiotherapist, Mark Riley, picked the team. He had been with Lincoln as a player, and was knowledgeable. Obviously he knew the capabilities of some of our lads better than I did.

Straight away we played the wing back system, my favoured option. I was nervous. There was a slope on the pitch and it was pretty muddy. I wondered whether the lads were fit enough, and Treacle (Paul Newell) the keeper didn't fill me with confidence.

But I knew the nucleus of the team from my previous stint a year before. I had faith in Andy Crosby, Gregan, Simon Shaw, Robbie Blake, Mark Barnard and one or two others.

I was in the hotel the night before the game, when Tony Henry, my business partner, phoned me and said that one of the deals was going wrong.

I could have told him that it was his problem now, but I made a couple of calls to smooth one or two things over, and he managed to pull the deal off.

And we won 4-1 the next day – the team's first in seven games – so suddenly things didn't look so bad. It was a massive relief. Ironically my first game in charge third time around was also in the FA Cup, against Hornchurch.

I got only a lukewarm reception from the Darlington public, which wasn't really surprising. I had walked out a year before, and Jim had taken them to Wembley, and to that great draw at Leeds.

They were two of the proudest moments in the club's history. They were Jim Platt's moments, not mine, and I fully accepted that.

We lost 1-0 at home to Exeter in the next game, and the fans had a go at Steve Morgon, who at that stage had not announced that he was leaving. I was trying to do an interview for Radio Cleveland with Ray Simpson while that was going on.

Then we lost 3-2 at Scunthorpe and I was furious at the manner in which it happened. I got very angry with the players, telling them that it was performances like that, which had cost Jim his job. The players responded and we beat Northampton 3-1, Daz Roberts grabbing a couple of goals.

A crunch game was looming, a night match at Brighton, who were, like us struggling at the foot of the table. But they had worse problems. There was a major fans' revolt at the time, because of the way they felt Brighton was being run.

It had generated national publicity and feelings were running very high – so high that our fans had been told to stay away. Fortunately we won 3-2, however the result cost Brighton boss Jimmy Case his job.

Again the result was a big relief for us, because the omens had not looked good. We had stayed in the Grand, where I believe the mods and rockers film Quadrophenia – another battle of Brighton – had been filmed.

The hotel was freezing, and the old windows needed replacing. I put my experience to good use, by taking a leaf out of former Liverpool boss Bob Paisley's book, and let the lads have the better rooms.

We had to wait all day for the game, and I never like hanging around in those circumstances. I have a belief that the less time players have to think about the situation, especially at Third Division level, there's a greater chance that they will perform better in the game.

And this was a big game for Brighton. A win for them could turn their fortunes, and having a game in hand on us and being only a few points behind, it was critical that we got at least a draw.

Trying to find a good surface to train on – except the beach – in Brighton was never going to be easy. The best that we could come up with was a nice grassed area, but with a rather large slope.

The training went exceptionally well, and that told me things would go to plan on the night.

But all of our plans could have gone up in smoke within moments of the game kicking off. The police had informed us that there was a possibility the fans would invade the pitch at some point.

There was nothing for us to be alarmed about, because any protest would be aimed at their own directors, who were deemed responsible for selling off the ground. To say the club's future was at stake is an understatement. The protest duly arrived as predicted. Even Brighton manager Jimmy Case kept his head down in the dugout – and he was an old school hard man.

All the hostility worked against Brighton, we played well, and won. Glenn Naylor bagged two goals, and Robbie Blake the other. That gave us important breathing space over the teams below us.

But after the game we were hanging around again, for the coach was delayed an hour while police cleared fans from the pitch.

I honestly didn't know whether we would escape relegation. I could see ups and downs ahead. But Banno was calm and relaxed. "Don't worry, we'll get out of trouble," he said.

I knew there was a lot of work to do, but Banno showed confidence in the lads, while I felt that I had to keep them on their toes all the time. So we were an ideal partnership.

But things were not good financially at the club. We needed an income boost, and the best answer I could see was to try and sell Sean. My old friend Adrian Heath, who was manager at Burnley, and I, managed to conjure up a good deal.

Gary Peters, who had not long taken over from John Beck as manager of Preston, had rung me about the availability of Sean. Another mate of mine, Kelham O'Hanlon, let it slip to Gary Peters that I was about to sell Sean to Burnley. I didn't want to give Gary the impression that it was a one horse race for Sean's signature.

Fortunately Gary was a big fan of Sean's. Now that he was aware that I was prepared to sell Sean, I knew it would only be a matter of time before the phone would ring.

Fortunately for me when he called I was shopping with Beverley in Meadowhall centre in Sheffield.

As you could probably guess I was in a ladies' clothes shop, and the call was the perfect chance to cut my shopping short. I explained to Beverley that this call was more important for the club financially than buying clothes was.

Gary initially offered £200,000, but I dropped into the equation that a club not too far away had already made a better offer. I made it clear to him that the first club that offered me £300,000, would complete the deal – subject to Sean agreeing to the transfer.

He wanted us to meet to discuss terms, but I said Sean was only coming over to Preston if he was signing for them.

Obviously Gary had to discuss it with his directors first. It was in the interim that a reporter in the north west had dropped it nicely into Gary's ear that Burnley was the mystery club. Within an hour we had an offer of £300,000 from Preston.

But Preston got a great deal, and were to make more out of Sean than Darlington did, because he later moved on to West Brom for over £1 million – a deal that I set the ball rolling on. However from our point of view it was not a bad bit of business either because we got more money than we would have done from Wigan.

However there was a sell on clause, though by the time Sean moved to West Brom, George Reynolds was in charge at Darlington so it was under him that the club reaped the benefit (more money for George on the back of my deals).

Of course I didn't take too much of a risk in selling Sean when we were still in danger of relegation. I already had a replacement lined up – Jason DeVos.

I had earlier taken him to Bradford for a trial, which fell through because he picked up an injury, so knew all about his ability. I sold Sean to make money for the club, knowing that I could sign Jason. As soon as Sean went, Jason came in for 14 days' trial, but he didn't need to because I knew that he could head a ball as well as Sean, he could pass, and had a presence about him.

He was raw, and lacked Sean's aggression, but for 10,000 dollars (around £7500), it was a great bit of business for Darlington. I paid it, the money coming out of my cut from Sean's deal, though in the end I never got it back.

Beverley had wanted me to buy a conservatory out of the money we were due, but I spent it on Jason instead. I used to wind him up by telling him the conservatory would be a better investment than him.

Jason made his debut the game after Sean left. We were at home to Northampton, and when a Northampton striker broke clear, Jason halted him with a tremendous tackle. In that one moment, he won the Darlington fans over, and they knew as well as I did that we had signed a quality replacement for Sean.

After the game Jason did radio and press interviews. The media wanted to talk to him, as it was unusual for Canadian players to join lower division clubs over here. He is intelligent and articulate, and was immediately accepted as a potential memorable Darlington player. His preparation for games was meticulous, and he was clearly here to make a name for himself.

He was keen to make as many appearances for the Canadian national team as possible, and the only downside with him, was that he put country before club. But I couldn't hold that against him.

However I wasn't happy when he opted to return for treatment after injuring his foot in a game at Barnet. He got it pinned, and returned a few games later. I brought in Richard Hope from Blackburn, a local lad recommended by Barrie Geldart. He did well and we finished 18th, well clear of relegation, though had Jason been an ever present we would probably have finished higher.

Considering that we picked up £450,000 when he signed for Dundee United, it was perhaps my best ever deal for Darlington.

At one point Crystal Palace boss Terry Venables was looking at Jason, and a potential deal was discussed, but never finalised. Ironically the discussions took place in my conservatory, which by then had been built.

Just before deadline day that season I sold Robbie Blake. Bradford manager Chris Kamara wanted a striker and rang me. I remember it clearly because I was sitting in the garden at Todwick on what was a lovely day (we didn't move north until a few weeks later).

Chris knew nothing of Robbie, but a mutual friend, sports writer Alan Nixon did, so I asked Chris to ring Alan and he would back me up. But Chris said that it was Bradford chairman Geoffrey Richmond I had to convince, so I did, telling the chairman of Blakey's close control and goal touch. I said that he would go on to be a £1m player – just what Geoffrey wanted to hear.

The problem I had with Blakey was that the better he got, the less of a team player he became. He would dribble the ball rather than release it. So even though he was a constant handful for defenders, we were losing our fluency.

Blakey went down to Bradford with his agent Bob Moss, and another of our players, Michael Oliver, a good mate of Blakey's.

Olly went just for the ride, but ended up concluding the deal. Blakey kicked Bob Moss out and said that he would do the deal with Olly. I told Bob everything that Blakey needed, such as insurance, car etc. I asked him what money he was asking in terms of wages for Blakey. He wouldn't tell me, but I insisted, saying that if he didn't I would pull the plug on the deal. So he revealed the amount – which was far too low. But it proved unnecessary because in went Olly, making out he was the agent or brother, or whatever. As far as I'm aware Blakey got a very good deal.

The deal was £300,000 to Darlington, and the fax went through on transfer deadline day. Ken Lavery asked if it was for real. He couldn't believe we had sold two players, and raked in £600,000 that was a fortune to the club.

And it was a big rush getting the striker we needed to replace Blakey. Carl Shutt, of Bradford City, was the man. We got him because Reg Brealey had promised him a signing on fee, and there were other lads travelling up each day from Yorkshire who he could come with.

I met him at the Post House Hotel in Rotherham, the day before transfer deadline day – so the clock was ticking. Once we had agreed, he had to go to Bradford the next day to finalise it.

We only just got the deal through. I confirmed his £7,500 signing on fee in writing, and Carol, the Darlington financial secretary, just squeezed the fax through in time. Shutty then rushed to Bradford. But the Queen was visiting Bradford that day, and the city had come to a standstill for security reasons. I was going to sue her if the deal had been blocked!

In the end the club didn't pay the signing on fee, so I did.

Shutty had a fantastic career, playing in cup finals at home and abroad, and played for Leeds in the European Cup.

Yet despite that wealth of experience, he was ever such a quiet, and gullible lad, and the other players sometimes took the mickey out of him, even though some of them were lucky to be in the Third Division and he had scaled the heights.

He took over the role that Gary Bannister had vacated, as he had similar attributes. He formed a good relationship with Daz Roberts, and was brilliant on the training ground, very fit for a lad of his age.

But believe it or not, he was very nervous before games even though he had played in front of much bigger crowds. I learned that it was best not to tell him until the day of the game that he was in the team.

In fact it was John McClelland who told me that. John was 40 when Jim Platt had asked him to help out in the centre of the defence, and unfortunately he broke his leg in his Darlington debut at Hartlepool.

It was the only game he ever played for the club, but I kept him on as reserve team coach, and he knew Shutty's character. Even though he was quiet, Shutty was a very clever lad, who went on to manage non-league clubs. He got his first taste of being in charge at Darlington, for after John left, he ran the reserves.

He could communicate better as a coach than he did as a player. He was great at putting ideas up on the board and then explaining them.

When his playing days ended, I wanted him to stay at the club and run the youth set up, but his wife didn't want to move up from South Yorkshire so he had to decline.

We had some memorable games that season, some for the wrong reasons, including a 6-0 hiding at Fulham. That day I was really angry, because we had two or three triallists in the side, and they were not helped and supported by the other lads as much as they should have been.

The pitch was frozen that day, but I insisted that we should play, which Fulham boss Micky Adams appreciated.

My reasoning was that I didn't want to winge that it wasn't playable, because that would have made it look like I was making excuses, for we had some key players missing. Also, our club was hard up, and I had to consider the cost of having to travel back to London for a re-arranged game.

As I recall, Glenn Naylor missed a chance early on, but it probably wouldn't have made any difference had he scored, because we collapsed and were ripped apart.

Before the following game, at home to Cambridge, I stressed to the lads that there must be no repeat. I ordered them to make their mark from the kick off and not let their commitment drop for the entire game.

Daz Roberts took it even more literally than I had meant. Cambridge kicked off and Daz threw himself at the man in possession, making probably the only crunching tackle of his career in which he won the ball cleanly.

He was never a great tackler, tending to arrive a touch late, but on that occasion against Cambridge he was spot on, and that set the tempo for the whole game. We won 2-0.

Avoiding relegation was the target that season and we did it, Daz weighing in with 16 league goals.

We had some bad days though, none worse than a 4-1 defeat at Scarborough when we had three players – Andy Crosby, Mark Barnard and Phil Brumwell – sent off.

Referee Eddie Wolstenholme gave us nothing, even though the Scarborough players were more aggressive than we were.

Mark Barnard was scythed down, and when he got up, he gave the Scarborough lad the slightest of clips. The ref saw only that and sent Barney off. And I remember Gary Bennett, who of course later played for us, piling into Brian Atkinson, without so much as a booking.

If we had lost one more player, the game would have been called off. I could have told one of the lads to go down 'injured,' but that would have been the coward's way out.

Mick Wadsworth, the Scarborough manager, said in an interview that the ref got all the decisions right, and I had a right go at Mick. I felt he could have been more honest and defended us. I later got to know him better, and liked him.

We beat Brighton on a very windy day at Feethams. I remembered that Kenny Dalglish always said the best policy was to let the opposition play with the wind first. See how they fared – then do it better.

We got the results we needed to retain our League status, including a 3-0 win at Colchester on Easter Monday, Glenn Naylor scoring a hat-trick.

That victory made it three wins and three draws in March, good enough for me to win my first Manager of the Month award. At that time the award was a beautiful bronze owl, and I later won a silver salver for my second award. I've kept both of them.

We were safe from relegation by the time Hartlepool visited Feethams three games from the end of the season.

They desperately needed to win to stay clear of relegation, and grabbed a 2-1 victory courtesy of Joe Allon's goal, when the ball fell to him when he was on his backside. He prodded in one of the most important goals of Pool's history. I was fuming, because I had just put Gary Twynham on as a substitute, and he ran with the ball instead of passing it, lost it, and Pool won a corner from which they scored.

The word went round that I had struck a deal with Hartlepool manager Mick Tait. There is no truth whatsoever in that. I may have said that I wanted Hartlepool to stay up, but there was no way I arranged it.

The only reason I wanted them to stay up was so that we could take six points off them the following season. It turned out that both games with them the next season were draws, but we did do the double the year after that.

Besides it was better to have Pool in the league rather than have to make a trip to Exeter or somewhere like that.

Any of the lads will confirm that I was gutted to lose to Pool. I had a right go at Gary Twynham in the dressing room, and he had a go back. He had once thumped Andy Crosby, but if I had backed down I would have lost the respect of the players. In the end the lads stepped in to make the peace. But that's how angry I was at losing.

But I handed him a start in the next game, at Mansfield, because he wanted to move back to the Chester area, and a team from over there was looking at him. Besides I wanted to show I bore no grudges.

We played at home to Cardiff in the last game of the season, a game they needed to win either to get into the play-offs, or to get the home leg second. I can't recall which.

Their manager Terry Yorath reminded me before the game, that it meant nothing to us, but did to them.

I went to Bernard Lowery, our chairman, and told him I would like £1000 in the players' kitty if we won. I said I wanted us to finish the season on a high by beating a team up near the top.

That emphasises that I would never send a team out to try and do anything other than win. We did win, 2-1 with goals from Shutty and Daz.

The season had been a learning curve. I had come in with only six months of experience as a manager, and with a team that was struggling.

Gary Bannister was a huge help that season, and his words of wisdom, and the experience as a whole stood me in good stead – for some of the trials and tribulations to come.

The Peden era; "Can I borrow £50,000?"

I had plenty of time for Reg Brealey. At the time of his handover of the club to Mike Peden in the summer of 1997, there were rumours that he was bankrupt, and he needed the money from the sale of his shares because of business problems he had in India.

But I think that was just typical Darlo gossip, I believe that he had decided it was time to move on. After all, he had been involved with the club since 1992.

Not very many people who were part of the club had a good word to say for Reg, but to be honest, I admired him. I'd always adopted a policy of see as you find. Whenever there was a moment I thought he had to call me, he was always extremely positive, especially throughout the early days when there was a string of draws on the pitch.

He was well-connected in the media world and the reporters whom he'd known from his days at Sheffield United said very positive things about the standards that Darlington Football Club was setting.

On the business front, whenever I had to sell a player, Reg would always make a call to show his appreciation of the funds I had raised. At that time, without doubt, I was keeping the club alive.

He never had any problems with me if I requested his permission to bring in a new player because he knew I had the intelligence to understand the balancing of the books.

I was quite happy not to buy players. What was the point of paying out big money for a player, when that money could be used to bring in free transfer players on good salaries? Reg used to let me get on with it, and kept his nose out.

My idea of a perfect chairman would probably be a mixture of three people I worked with at Darlo. Mike Peden's plans and ideas, George Reynolds' money when he took over, and Reg for the way he conducted himself and provided support.

I didn't do much team strengthening during the summer of 1997 when Mike first came along, because we had finished the previous season so well, and I didn't think we needed to add many new faces. Plus, there wasn't all that much money for new signings, only about £500 per week in terms of wages.

I only brought in two players – keeper David Preece, who had been released by Sunderland, and midfielder Lee Turnbull.

Lee's signing had nothing to do whatsoever with the fact that he rated me as the best Boro player ever and I was his schoolboy hero – honestly!

Lee hardly ever played for us, but he was tremendous in the changing room, very good at motivating and lifting the lads. One of his best ever games for us was at Brighton, when Preecey was sent off for a professional foul, and after Carl Shutt went in goal, Lee went into the centre of defence and led us to a 0-0 draw.

We didn't do much in the league that season. We had some good results, but we had some bad ones as well.

There are three games that I will always remember from that season.

In the first round of the FA Cup, we were drawn at home against Solihull, a midlands club playing in the Southern League.

Because they were only a part time club, everyone assumed that a win would be a formality for us, especially after Glenn Naylor scored in the first minute at Feethams.

But it became farcical after that. Our players became far too complacent, thinking that they would score seven or eight, but that never happened.

Instead, Solihull scored in the second half, and nearly snatched a winner.

But there were events after the game that shaped my thinking about referees in Darlington games for several years after that, and possibly shaped the thinking of referees towards us.

Because the old East Stand had been demolished and we were using portacabins on the west side of the ground, the club used the upstairs bar in the Quaker Sports Centre for after-match refreshments.

Two of our directors were in there, and saw the Solihull chairman give some money to the match referee, Mr Robinson from Hull.

Our people took the action to be some sort of bribe, when instead all the Solihull chairman was doing was handing him some money to buy a round of drinks. There was nothing sinister going on.

The usual procedure in replays is for the same referee to be appointed, but instead Mr Robinson was taken off the match while the FA launched an enquiry, which a few weeks later completely exonerated the referee. No doubt he, and his family, were extremely relieved.

To me, he hadn't even done anything remotely suspicious during the game that had cast doubt upon him. Our bad result wasn't down to any of his decisions; it was just our bad play and poor attitude.

Because we had made the complaint, we had to pay all the costs of the enquiry.

Whether I'm being sensitive or not, I don't know, but for a long time afterwards I had the impression that we never got the marginal decisions from referees.

Because of the enquiry they were obliged to set up, the FA appointed Uriah Rennie as the replacement referee for the replay. Rennie by this time was working his way up the refereeing ladder, and was on the verge of the Premiership.

After the first game at Feethams, Mike Peden offered to provide free transport to Solihull for all Darlo fans, but he never got round to paying the bill. When he departed, the debt was left to the football club.

It was a strange setting for the game, because a couple of years earlier, Moor Green, who owned the ground, turned the pitch ninety degrees so then the main stand was behind one goal.

As every Darlington fan knows, Rennie added five minutes stoppage time in the first half, and an amazing twelve in the second half. Mario Dorner scored in almost the last minute of the ninety, but then they equalised in the 11th minute of stoppage time. Fortunately, we won the penalty shootout.

I acknowledge that there was some stoppage time to be played. There had been a few substitutions, while Lee was dismissed for elbowing their keeper in an aerial challenge.

I asked the referee why he'd added so much time on. "I couldn't remember whether the match kicked off at 7.30 or 7.45," he replied. Draw your own conclusions.

The match was decided on penalties. Some of our fans weren't happy about the team's performance, and one of them, Dave Hardisty, had the daggers out for me and made sure I knew about his feelings in no uncertain way, but was then slapped, I am led to believe, by one of our female fans!

We also learned more about Mike on that trip. By now, the players were finding him a laughing matter, and any respect they had for him quickly diminished while we were away for the Solihull match.

The team travelled down the day before the game, and we stayed in a Stratford hotel. Mike said he would treat everybody to a meal in a top Italian restaurant in the town, and we ended up in a Beefeater! The food was poor, and I ended up having to pay for the desserts and drinks because Mike said he was only paying for the main course.

Then there was a problem with the hotel. I went for a walk around Stratford early the following morning, only for Banno to ring on my mobile, asking me to dash back to the hotel because the bill hadn't been paid, and everybody had been asked to leave their rooms.

Mike owned a company called Chaddington's, and I found their office in Stratford town centre, but Mike wasn't there, but he appeared at the hotel before I returned.

Mike tried to persuade the hotel manager that because he was the chairman of a big company that was running a football club, he would pay later. But the manager refused to budge, and wanted us all out of the way.

So to prevent any further argument and disruption on the day of a big cup tie, I stepped in between them and paid the bill with my credit card. You can understand why I was becoming more and more dubious.

Our game in the next round was at Hednesford, one of the progressive teams in the Conference.

They were a new club that had worked its way up a couple of leagues, and played in a brand new stadium that had still to be finished on one side. Mind you, there weren't many places for the press that day, some of them, including Andrew Wilkinson from the Gazette, had to sit on a chair a couple of yards away from the touchline.

The manager, John Baldwin, had spent quite a bit of money on bringing in some ex Football League players, and because we didn't have a good away record at the time – we hadn't won away in the league up to that point – then they quite fancied their chances.

Baldwin had a few things to say in the media beforehand, but that only served to gee up our players. Needless to say, there were words exchanged between us on the touchline.

The match was decided by a penalty, for a foul on Brian Atkinson, but there then followed a bizarre incident.

Daz Roberts beat the keeper from the spot, and when the ball hit the back of the net, it bounced back out towards him.

Daz, in his delight, then accidentally kicked the keeper's hand instead of the oncoming ball, resulting in referee Phil Richards sending Daz from the field of play. No doubt his decision was made by the fact that the keeper was rolling around on the ground and he got the impression that Daz had deliberately kicked him.

We went ballistic, but the referee wouldn't change his mind. Fortunately, we held on to win, partly thanks to young Paul Robinson who worked very hard closing players down as a lone striker, and helped to earn a third round game with Wolves at our place. And to give the referee credit, he was genuine enough to change his mind when he saw the video. Good job we won, wasn't it?

Some people saw the league game against Doncaster as a crunch game for me.

Doncaster were having a wretched season, and were well adrift at the bottom of the table.

When we played there in March, we were still without an away win in the league all season, plus the away game before we had lost heavily 5-0 at Mansfield.

There was talk of me getting the sack if we lost, and that Brian Little, who had just resigned from Aston Villa, was being lined up to take my place.

I travelled in my car to the game with Keith Agar, our commercial manager. Mike phoned Keith, without realising that I was in the car next to him, and indicated that he would consider sacking me if we lost, and suggested replacements, Brian amongst them.

However, Mike was in no position to sack me, because even though he had taken on the club from Reg the previous summer, he still hadn't paid for his shares. In effect, he didn't even own the club, Reg still did.

There was a turning point in the game. Doncaster hit the post early on, but we recovered and won the game with goals by Mario Dorner and Paul Robinson. Mike called a board meeting afterwards, but nothing came of it.

There were always problems with money in one way or another.

One day, Mike came into my office in the old portacabins and asked if he could talk to me privately, as Barrie Geldart and Banno were both in the room.

That was pretty pointless, as the walls were wafer thin, and even whispers could be heard through the walls.

Mike wondered if it was possible for him to borrow £50,000 from me because there was a "short term cash flow problem," a phrase heard many a time around the offices of Darlington Football Club.

By this time, I had a reasonable insight into Mike and how his businesses were running, so in order to protect myself I suggested that any money was to be loaned through my solicitor, Bill O'Hanlon from Crutes, directly to his solicitors in Stratford. By doing this, I virtually guaranteed that should there be any concern on Mike's situation, his solicitors wouldn't enter into any sort of agreement. He didn't seem to be keen on conducting business that way.

Of course in my own head, I was asking myself that if Mike was a millionaire as he claimed to be, then why did he want to borrow £50,000?

Mike offered to pay me back with interest but I suggested once again doing it through the solicitors.

Within thirty minutes of Mike leaving the office, our chairman, Bernard Lowery, came to see me. It was amazing. Bernard asked the same question as Mike regarding the £50,000. So I said: "Do you know, Mike has just been in and asked the self-same question." Bernard looked very embarrassed, apologised and quickly left. He didn't need £50,000 for himself; he was quite simply trying to raise funds for the club. In all due respect, Bernard shouldn't have been put in that situation.

Not everybody got on well with Mike. I had my disagreements with him, but I was disappointed that we lost Barrie as youth development officer.

Barrie's knowledge of youth and junior football was excellent, and he was very good at spotting talent. For Darlington, he discovered Robbie Blake and Sean Gregan, and I persuaded him to return to the club from Blackburn to improve the youth system.

By this time, Barrie had drawn his own conclusions as to where the club was heading.

He had left the security of Blackburn Rovers, and had found himself in a club that was already in a financial mess. He wasn't a fan of Mike's either, and unfortunately for Darlington Football Club he handed in his notice and returned to Blackburn.

There were also times when certain directors wanted me to leave players out. There were instances when directors made loud comments about certain players from the directors' box, something that I would never accept. That's like a red rag to a bull to me, because directors should show their full support for the players and the team in public.

On one particular occasion, Bernard popped into the office after lunch at Sardi's restaurant and decided to take it upon himself to ask me to leave full back Simon

Shaw out of the team.

My response was instant. I shouted through to Banno in the next office to bring me one of the official team sheets, and I deliberately wrote Simon's name down in the team. There was no way anyone was going to dictate to me on who was, and who wasn't, going to be in the team.

I also had words with Mike about sponsorship of players and raising funds.

Mike had the idea of asking companies to sponsor individual players, but I was strongly against the idea, because it could have meant that a sponsor, by threatening to withdraw his backing, could make sure that the player he was sponsoring was in the team, regardless of his contribution to the team and how well, or badly, he had been playing. Imagine dropping a player one week, and then his sponsor threatens to pull out the next. Mike saw the sense in that, fortunately.

At the end of season 1997-98, I had to look for a new assistant.

Banno, who had returned to the club with me in November 1996, wanted to leave. He admitted that he struggled as a number two, and couldn't get the right and proper response from the players when I wasn't around to take charge of coaching sessions. Banno was a quiet lad, and not really a leader on the training ground.

So with his agreement, I sacked him as my assistant so then he would receive three months' pay as per his contract.

As his replacement, I contacted Ian Butterworth, a defender, who had been forced to quit the game at my old club Norwich because of injury.

I'd known Butts for a while, and in fact he had played for us in a friendly at Spennymoor earlier in the season when he was trying to overcome a knee injury. On the way to the ground, we spoke about a few things to do with coaching, and we seemed to be on the same wavelength.

Butts slotted in just right, because then we could do our coaching evenly for the defence, midfield and attack on the training ground. We had played Cobh Ramblers in Ireland in a pre-season friendly, and they were looking for a manager. I suggested that they appointed Butts, knowing that I would be able to monitor his progress. Their goals against reduced dramatically.

This was also an era in which I brought a few foreign players to the club. We had all nationalities coming for trials and reserve games, and certainly the fans seemed to enjoy coming to see these unknown quantities.

My logic for bringing foreign players to the club was simple – they were cheaper on the continent at the time, and so they were worth having a look, especially if they paid their own airfares.

A pair of Austrians were recommended to me, Mario Dorner and Franz Resch. A friend of mine called Edi Bruner was their agent, and he told me that Alex McLeish, who was then manager at Motherwell, had released them because they couldn't pay any signing on fees.

I asked Eddie if I could look at them in one game only, having already made calls to Paul Sturrock and Jim McLean in Scotland to give me an insight into what sort of players they were.

It was very important that I had the opportunity to see them play in one practice match at Durham, and they showed enough to suggest that they were better quality than we had already. In fact, the pair of them combined for our first goal, when Mario scored from a pass by Franz.

I made my mind up I wanted the pair of them. But the deal almost collapsed because Edi demanded a rather large signing-on fee, something that we couldn't afford.

Franz and Mario both made it very clear that they wanted to join the club. To be honest, they couldn't have gone anywhere else because the transfer window was about to close. Rightly or wrongly, in the interests of Darlington Football Club, I asked the pair of them if they could find an agent who could make the deal go through. They used the services of an Austrian lawyer, and I paid him a finder's fee, out of my own pocket, of £7,500 that he passed on to the players. The club never repaid me.

They both settled in very well. Franz was an Austrian international, but he picked up an ankle injury that he couldn't quite shrug off, and he went back to Austria. Mario – or Super Mario as the fans dubbed him – decided to stay, and he did well, scoring fifteen goals in two seasons.

Loukas Papaconstantinou was a goalkeeper from Canada, who had Greek parents, and was a friend of Jason DeVos.

In the summer of 1998, we brought him over from Canada and he trained with us at Catterick. He was brave, a good shot stopper, but he admitted that his kicking wasn't very good. "Don't worry, we'll work on it," I told him.

And boy, did we have to. He just couldn't kick the ball out of his hands straight, nor could he kick the ball properly off the ground either. He either miskicked it, or the ball only went thirty or forty yards upfield. He played only one game for us, and we told him not to kick it if he could help it, and instead, just pass the ball square to one of the wing backs. At least when he played for us, he kept a clean sheet. Loukas-aid helps Darlo, I suppose you could say!

He was accident prone, as well, and suffered probably the most unusual injury I have ever come across. I wasn't best pleased about it at the time, but I can laugh about it now.

During one training session, there was a huge water hose running the full length of the pitch. It was virtually impossible not to see it, so we all thought.

Everybody managed to see it and jump it, but Loukas came right down on top of it, and was left rolling around on the ground, clutching his ankle, which in no time swelled three times its normal size. It was quite serious, and at one point we thought he'd broken his ankle, but he was out for the rest of the season.

Willie Guimarra was another Canadian lad, who came over at the same time as Loukas, but I never really had enough confidence in him. But he did have a very good game against Swansea, when he tortured their right back, and set up victory.

Willie and Loukas weren't with us long, leaving Jason DeVos as the only Canadian at the club.

At the start of season 1997-98, with the club under pressure to improve the ground in line with the Taylor report deadline, Mike announced that he was going to rebuild the old wooden east stand.

This meant that the club offices and dressing rooms had to move across the field next to the west stand, and Bernard kindly provided some bright orange portacabins which the fans dubbed the "Olympic Village".

In order to symbolise the end of the old stand and the construction of the new, Mike announced that the old stand would be blown up as part of a magnificent firework display.

What a fiasco, probably the most embarrassing episode in any of my Darlington careers.

There was a big build up to the moment itself, and Mike arranged for "Blond on Blond" – otherwise known as Jodie McCourt and Peter Grant – who were probably the best of the entire night's entertainment.

With the fans expecting the stand to be blown to smithereens somehow, a crane removed just a small section of the roof with a few fireworks. Everybody in the ground rolled around with laughter, but to be honest it was a huge embarrassment. It didn't reflect well on the club at all.

As the construction of the new stand progressed, it became more and more obvious that money was tight. There was talk of people not getting paid, both contractors and staff, so something had to be done.

One of the biggest deals I've ever been involved in as Darlington manager was the sale of Jamie Coppinger and Paul Robinson to Newcastle.

Jamie, who was a striker, hadn't even played in our first team, but had shown loads of promise in our reserve team. He'd also played for England Under 16s, and on one occasion when he came back, the England coach told me that he thought Jamie was a stone light in weight, which I laughed at. In response, I asked why they didn't add a stone of weight on his football shirt. It was simply a sarcastic remark to the authorities.

The lad had loads of ability, and to me it didn't matter whether he was a stone light or not. Jamie had a real football brain, and I tipped off Kenny Dalglish, who was then at Newcastle, about him.

Robbo had made a few appearances, and scored a cracking goal at home to Peterborough from about thirty yards out, in front of several scouts.

When we played at Leyton Orient, their manager Tommy Taylor actually offered me £100,000 for him after the game, but I told him that clubs from higher divisions were interested.

But not only were clubs sniffing around him, there were also several agents who had seen his Peterborough goal on television.

He was very exciting on his day, but sometimes he couldn't get the consistency, which would possibly come at Newcastle with better players.

We played Newcastle behind closed doors and both Robbo and Jamie did well. Kenny and I agreed a deal, but first I had to speak to the parents of both players. Surprisingly, nobody outside of the club knew about Newcastle's interest. Barrie went with me to meet them.

Jamie's parents were quite shocked that Newcastle were prepared to sign their son at such an early stage of his career. However, they were excellent, taking on board everything that was said to them, and I asked them for an answer within a day as to whether Jamie could sign for Newcastle. After thinking about everything the move entailed, they said yes.

That meeting was completely different to the one we had with Robbo's parents. I found Robbo's father ignorant and arrogant, his first words were "It's nothing more than my son deserves" which was quite a shock to Barrie and me. How could he come to that conclusion? Robbo had only played a handful of games in the first team, and even at this point wasn't ready to demand a regular place in the Darlington line up.

Robbo quite simply had a talent, which given an opportunity to train and work with better players, might help him progress up the ladder.

Sometimes we found it very difficult to get Robbo to accept the instructions we gave him before reserve games, and it came to my attention that he always seemed to be looking across and talking to somebody in the stand – it turned out his dad was also giving him instructions! Shall we say that I had a few words with him. No wonder his dad thought he was ready to move on to a big club, he had such a high opinion of young Robbo, and clearly thought that the Newcastle interest was nothing more than he deserved.

I managed to strike a deal with Newcastle secretary Russell Cushing for £600,000 for the pair, and passed on the news to Ken Lavery, our general manager.

Ken thought it best to have £500,000 up front for the pair, but with the club facing financial problems and the summer coming up in which there would be very little income, I contacted Russell and asked him to spread the payments, half on the day of the transfer, and the rest in July, and he agreed.

Both of them played in the Newcastle first team, and for a spell when Ruud Gullit was manager, Robbo replaced Alan Shearer in the starting line up, although there was an element of politics in that.

It was in the spring of 1998 when I made what I consider my best ever signing, Craig Liddle.

I regularly watched reserve team matches, and I liked Lids, when he played for the Boro. His first team opportunities under Bryan Robson were very limited – I think he'd played only a couple of games and been on the bench a few times – and I took him on loan until the end of that season.

He was strong, could pass the ball and read the game well, and could play at right back or in the centre of defence. He became an instant crowd favourite, and I

147

wanted him to stay at the club on a permanent basis.

Anybody who has been to Cardiff knows that it is a 300 mile trip, at least five to six hours on a bus. With it being the last game of the season, I allowed the lads to have a few drinks on the bus coming home.

The atmosphere on the bus became naturally more and more relaxed as the journey went on. When we came off the motorway on to the A66, I asked Lids, who by now had consumed a few drinks, to come and have a word with me at the front of the bus about the following season.

I told him that I would offer him the same deal that he was on at Boro. Words didn't come out of his mouth, just babble and hand signals. This was probably down to the fact that he'd consumed around ten pints of lager on the way home.

I didn't just need to convince Craig, I also had to convince his wife. It took me a few trips up to his home in Chester-le-Street to convince the pair of them that it would be the best decision he ever made to join Darlington. Eventually he agreed, and the signing of Lids was a big, big plus for Darlington Football Club. I made it clear to him that other good players would be following, and I was after one in particular who could ignite the team and the fans – Marco Gabbiadini.

Gabbers was, and still is, a hero to Sunderland fans, firing them to promotion before he moved to Crystal Palace and then Derby County. But his career then seemed to go downhill, and things weren't working out for him after he returned to his first club, York City.

I went to a York reserve game one night with Barrie to have a look at him, but I knew that other clubs were interested in him, so I made it known that I was looking at Wayne Hall, a left back.

I hadn't see Gabbers play for a long time, but I had a picture in my head of what he should be. Gary Bennett was in touch with Gabbers, and he told me that he wanted to leave York, possibly for Scunthorpe, who were managed by Brian Laws.

Gabbers was exactly the type of player we wanted, somebody who would create goals out of nothing, and would be selfish around the box when the chances came along. I watched him in another reserve game at Bradford City, and he did things that I knew would do us a power of good.

On this night when we were watching him play for York, Lawsy, who left Darlington as a player to become manager of Scunthorpe, came up to me and asked whom I was watching.

I told him that I was keeping an eye on Wayne Hall, but I would probably only have about £400 per week to spend on wages. Lawsy told me that he was after Gabbers, and he had enough in his budget to offer him a one-year contract. (Thanks Lawsy, that's all I needed to know!)

I told Lawsy that Gabbers was the "laziest fat b....." that I'd ever seen, and personally I wouldn't touch him.

My problem was that Scunny would blow me out of the water with the wages they could offer him, so I was on the phone to Gabbers the following day. He told me that Scunny had offered him a one-year deal, so I countered that by saying I would offer him a two-year deal.

Benno also phoned Gabbers to have a chat, and eventually Gabbers agreed to come up to Darlington on the train. So he arrived at Bank Top station, we made sure that we picked him up, and he made the short trip to Feethams.

He told me that he had received a good offer from Scunthorpe, but I responded by telling him; "They're concerned about your weight, they're having second thoughts."

I gave him the best package we could afford, a two-year deal with bonuses, and he signed.

But there were more than just Lids and Gabbers. I set my sights on bringing more good quality players to the club, with Mike's backing.

Just before the end of the 1997-98 season, we also signed defender Steve Tutill.

Tuts was available on a free from York after giving them some great service over the years, and we signed him on loan with a view to a permanent transfer. But before we did so, I went with Barrie to have a look at him in a York game. He had been out for most of the season with a knee injury, and we wanted to make sure that he was all right.

I'm pretty sure that York manager Alan Little had tipped Tuts off that one good performance would earn him a move to join the rest of the former York players including Gary Himsworth and Glenn Naylor at Darlington.

His performance that night was just what we had expected and there were no doubts in my mind that the loan deal was with a view to a permanent transfer.

Tuts was a big presence at the back, the sort of player we needed to help keep the defence tight.

He played well for us for a few games, and he signed a two-year contract with us just before we played Leyton Orient. It was just before transfer deadline day, though something in the back of my mind was niggling me.

There was no question of his attitude, his ability or his desire to win, but there was something that I couldn't put my finger on.

The next day he proved that I was right to have doubts, for he broke down early in the game at Orient, with the knee that had troubled him at York. He admitted that he'd been playing through the pain barrier for several weeks. I had to admire him for that, and it summed up Steve's character – although we had a worrying summer wondering whether he'd be fit for the new season.

But how could I criticise him when I had done the same when I was playing at Metz. I had put my manager Joel Muller in exactly the position that Tutts had put me in.

I also knew that Adam Reed was available because he had finished his contract at Blackburn. Adam came back to us on loan for three months at the end of the 1996-97 season, and he'd been playing for Blackburn reserves at right back, where he'd been doing quite well.

Paul Jewell, who was manager at Bradford City, rang me and asked for my opinion about Adam as a right back, knowing that he had played under me at Darlington.

Paul was obviously not aware that I was in talks with Adam about a move back to Feethams. And Adam was not aware that I was giving him the worst recommendation to Bradford City that I possibly could.

When Paul asked if I thought that Adam was capable of playing at right back, my response was: "You're joking aren't you?"

I also pointed out that he wore contact lenses, which kept dropping out when he was playing, and that his passing from right back was nowhere near the standard expected from a good Division One side.

When I put the phone down I turned to Barrie and said: "That's Adam in the bag now."

He wanted to move back to the north east anyway, and as Paul didn't make a follow up call, Adam had no option other than to sign for us, though I think he must have lost his contact lens the day he headed into his own net against Cambridge!

He maybe cost me a little bit more than I wanted in terms of wages, but he was Darlington through and through, and after three years away at Blackburn, he would be a much better player.

So I admit that I told a couple of white lies to Brian Laws and Paul Jewell, but they were both in the interests of Darlington Football Club!

Another player to come along in the summer was an old friend of mine, Gary Bennett.

Benno had just helped Scarborough into the play offs the previous season, and was keen to come, not only as a player, but also to help with the coaching.

I spoke to Benno at the end of that season, and in turn he told Scarborough that he wanted to get back to the north east. I agreed a deal with Scarborough, but then when I was on holiday Mike decided that he wanted to give the fans something to get excited about, and so took over the deal himself.

And instead of paying nothing for a 35 year old, he paid Scarborough £20,000. The chairman, John Russell, snatched his hands off.

I went berserk, telling Mike that nobody except me did a deal at Darlington.

But the upshot was that the squad was definitely much stronger than the previous season. Gabbiadini, Liddle, Reed, Tutill and Bennett had all been signed, and with the new stand completed, we were set for a real assault on the Third Division. There was a real sense of anticipation in the air.

We were buzzing in pre-season, and at short notice we arranged a game at Scottish club St Johnstone. Because it was arranged so hastily I had to ask the players to travel in their own cars. There was not a single complaint. In fact no sooner had I got the words out than the players said they couldn't wait to get up there and play.

Considering that they had to drive for around four hours, their attitude was magnificent, and they put in a magnificent performance, especially Jason DeVos.

Ian Butterworth and I were convinced that at last the football club was moving in the right direction. But such optimistic thoughts were somewhat hasty.

The night before the opening day of the season, at home to Barnet, I resigned on a matter of principle. It sounds trivial, but it was about the background music for the team when they ran on to the pitch.

Benno said that the players wanted their own theme tune as they ran on to the pitch, and I gave it my blessing – I can't really remember what the name of the tune was. Benno then went to see Helen Coverdale, the commercial manager, but she refused. Benno came back to me, and I went to see Helen, who told me that Mike had already chosen the music, Eye of the Tiger, and he wasn't going to change his mind.

I rang Mike on his mobile, and asked him why the players couldn't have the theme music they'd asked for.

"I own this football club, and they will run out to whatever tune I want. If they don't like it, then I'll sack them," he said. He told me to tell them that they would all be getting letters on Monday morning telling them that they no longer had a position at the club.

I told him that I assumed the letters would be sent first class, then added that I could save him some money because he didn't need to send me a letter because I was resigning.

I returned to my office where I had to ask unsuspecting journalist Ray Simpson to leave.

Benno went white, Jim Montgomery went grey, and Butts was lost for words.

It sounds impetuous, but I was determined to stand my ground on principle. If I didn't stick to my principles on this issue, then I figured that Mike would try and steamroller me on more things to do with team affairs, and I wasn't having that.

Word crept out that there was a problem, and Ian Parker, one of the directors, went to great lengths to persuade Mike to speak to me on the issue.

He eventually did later in the evening. He explained that he'd always wanted to own a football club, and the team to run out to "Eye of the Tiger."

I told him that if the players said no, it wouldn't happen, and besides that, he still hadn't bought the club from Reg Brealey, who was still technically the owner.

Eventually, we reached some sort of agreement. Eye of the Tiger was played just once, and it was consigned to the dustbin. The players' choice was the next record on the public address system.

But come the game it was the same old Darlo. The new East Stand was opened, adding extra spice to the occasion. There was a big crowd, but once again we let everyone down, including ourselves.

We lost 2-0 to Barnet, their keeper had a blinder, and their second goal was top class, a volley at the far post from a deep cross. I had a go at the players, because 4,200 fans had turned up, and I felt that they'd been let down. Another 4,200 crowd turned up for our next home game against Halifax, so the fans obviously forgave us.

Unfortunately, there were one or two other things wrong with the new ground. For example, there were no dugouts in front of the new stand, so we had to sit in front of the old West Stand and the away fans.

Our changing room was slightly dangerous, mainly because of a massive low beam across the middle of it. One day, Andrew Scullion, one of our sponsors, split his head when he bumped into the pillar.

The water ran out of the showers into the changing room – that was nothing compared to the next water problem that was in store – plus there was only one toilet in the middle of the changing room. Not exactly the best. We asked for a bath to be installed, so three showers were removed.

My office was the best of the bunch, but was originally designed as a creche. Mike must have assumed that there would be demand from only four or five toddlers. There was hardly room to swing a cat.

Mike even bought a bus, which had previously been used by Everton, for around £75,000 plus VAT. Add the hire purchase and the club was looking at £130,000 or so. And the bus looked so old that it had probably been around in the time of Dixie Dean. All car buyers know that you should have a good inspection before you buy anything. I don't think anybody checked the bus over; it was a in a right mess.

Mike decided that the bus needed to be re-sprayed black, presumably to give it a better look.

We assumed that the letters DFC would be sprayed on the sides. Wrong. It was to be a moving advertisement for Chaddington's, Mike's company.

Mike had it spray painted in Chaddington colours, with hardly a mention of Darlington Football Club, which didn't go down too well with the supporters, not to mention me.

It was a lot of money to pay for a bus, and our transport bill for a season was nowhere near that much. And we still had to pay for fuel and the driver.

It was the biggest heap of rubbish I'd ever travelled on. We went to Sheffield United for a midweek League Cup game, but it wouldn't go above 60 mph. It made a grinding noise when it was moving, and the tyres were badly worn. Nothing seemed to work on it. The television and video broke down, and then one day, the microwave blew up!

At least we were getting paid on time anyway.

We thought we were in for a good season when we played Sheffield United over two legs in the Worthington Cup. We lost 3-1 at Bramall Lane, Daz Roberts scoring in the last minute, and in the second leg we led 2-0 with ten men, after Glenn Naylor was sent off early in the first half. Jason DeVos scored a great goal with a towering header that night, after Stevie Gaughan's deflected shot had put us ahead on the night.

But Sheffield took control in extra time, Dean Saunders scored a great goal to give them the advantage, but Steve Bruce, who was manager at the time, said "Take the p... out of them!" which wasn't very respectful I thought, and told him so. I like to think it was out of character for him to say something like that, because he's doing well in management.

We found our form in the league. When Gabbers and Jason scored to give us a 2-1 win at Plymouth in the middle of September, we were top of the league and looking strong.

And after we beat Shrewsbury the following week, came the first turning point of the season – Brentford away.

It was payday when we travelled down on the Friday.

We got down to the outskirts of London, and I could hear some mumblings from the back of the bus. Jason, who was the unofficial spokesman for the players, said in his Canadian drawl: "Gaffer, we've got a problem, our money's not in the bank."

We pulled over at the next service station. Several players checked with their banks, and sure enough, nothing had been transferred into their accounts.

I rang Carol in the club office, who confirmed it, and she also revealed that she had been instructed by Mike not to tell me before we set off for London.

I then rang Mike, who told me that there had been some sort of financial hiccup, and the bank wouldn't let us exceed our overdraft. He said that the wages would be paid as soon as possible.

I was fuming, because the situation put me in a bad light with the players I'd brought to the club during the summer. I'd sold the club to them on the basis that we were going places, and now less than two months into the season, they weren't being paid. What sort of message was that sending to them, and the supporters? Plus, I was sitting on a bus that cost £75,000, listening to Mike telling me this.

There was a frosty atmosphere that day when Mike turned up at Griffin Park, and we lost the game 3-0. I don't think it was because of the non-payment of wages, but purely because Brentford were a better team than we were. They were too strong, though we were not right mentally.

It was at this point when people started to look a little deeper into Mike's background. Searching questions were asked by the fans, people started to surf the internet looking for clues, there were arguments with the cricket club over rent and there appeared to be no substance to the companies he said he owned. It was starting to build up. The players sensed it, and I tried to keep them informed, though it was vital that they still focussed on the job.

The money problems were growing. There was a problem with obtaining kit, because apparently a bill from the new kit suppliers, Biemme, hadn't been paid.

So in order to solve the club's financial problems, I decided to sell Jason, our Canadian international. Mike tried to overrule me, saying that we needed him for a promotion push. My reaction to that was if we didn't sell Jason, morale in the club would plummet because people weren't getting paid, and that would paint a black picture.

And there were considerably more people on the payroll than the previous season. Mike had recruited loads of people to work in the restaurant and the bars, and there were more non-playing staff than playing staff. There were assistants for this, that and the other. It was more like a Premier League club.

There were plenty of clubs interested in Jason. Liverpool were certainly interested, as was Terry Venables, who was then manager of Crystal Palace, and Paul Sturrock of Dundee United.

Liverpool sent their chief scout, Ron Yeats, to come along and have a look at him in action, and Lugs at Dundee United sent John Blackley, who used to play for Hibs and Newcastle. Terry offered £400,000, but Jason felt that he couldn't live in London, although I pointed out that we might be keen on doing business at £600,000.

Lugs was very keen, but not keen enough at one stage to offer what we wanted. So I told him that Liverpool were going to buy Jason, and he was going to play against Peterborough so that Liverpool could check him one last time.

Lugs then offered £400,000 up front, and after Jason played for most of the game against Peterborough, with Ron Yeats in the crowd, he moved to Dundee United two days later.

Jason still wasn't the finished article, but he'd come on in leaps and bounds since he'd joined us, and would benefit from further coaching.

He did well at Dundee United in the Scottish Premier League, and after three years there, moved to Wigan Athletic, and helped them to the Second Division championship in 2002-03.

Results started to go against us after the Brentford defeat, and we slipped down the table.

We lost 2-1 at home to Brighton after Lee Ellison was red-carded for elbowing one of their players, and I had strong words with Brighton manager Brian Horton about some incidents in the game.

I was in the dressing room after the game when a message came from Mike that he wanted to speak to me and Butts in one of the executive boxes.

Ken Lavery and Ian Parker were also in there with Mike, and before anybody else said anything, I told the pair of them to keep their noses out! They were in no position to talk about football.

Though to be fair to them they are both good men, and just because I was angry on that occasion does not mean that I don't respect them. Ian was, and still is, a big supporter of the club, and works for Reg Vardy, who supplied all the club vehicles (apart from the notorious bus!).

Ken was general manager of the club, and while not a football man, worked hard for the club. And with respect to both, they were only dragged into the meeting to give Mike moral support.

Mike's first words were; "The club is going down the pan."

To which I replied: "If I hadn't sold Jason De Vos and brought in £400,000, then we wouldn't have been able to pay the wages."

Mike retorted: "I'm not happy with the football."

And I replied: "I'm not happy that you're the chairman and being unable to pay the wages" and walked out with Butts. Mike still hadn't paid Reg for the shares, over a year since he'd walked into the club. I knew, because I'd checked with Reg only a few days previously. So as far as I'm concerned that was a battle I had won.

It was one problem after another because we then had severely embarrassing problems with the pitch.

Tommo, the groundsman, did his best, but he was working against the odds. The drainage had been renewed during the summer of 1998, but probably because of 200,000 tonnes of concrete for the new stand, water was unable to drain into the River Skerne. The water table had altered completely. The pitch was in a right state, there was hardly any grass on it, and groundsmen from Middlesbrough and Sunderland had both been along, and came to the same conclusion, that the pitch was thatched and there was no root growth.

It was in a mess. Tommo tried to re-seed it, but in our first home game of the season, it was clear that the ball wasn't going to roll properly, because there were so many bobbles. Every time it rained, water would stand at various places on the pitch, and would take ages to evaporate.

To make the situation even more embarrassing, Mike decided to buy thousands of worms, which he thought would help to aerate the soil and allow the water to drain away. These worms were supposed to be of the same pedigree that had helped to solve Manchester United's pitch problems at Old Trafford, although all worms look the same to me.

They couldn't get through concrete, though, and all of them drowned. The media coverage was totally embarrassing, and made us a laughing stock. Mike should have been charged with cruelty to animals.

Mike even talked about bringing in Uri Geller to use his powers, but I blocked that, because it was becoming a farce. It seemed as if the water couldn't escape, and we were hardly into November.

However, we were then drawn at home to Second Division Burnley in the first round of the FA Cup.

It was clear that we couldn't play the tie at Feethams, so after talking to Middlesbrough, we agreed to switch the game to the Riverside Stadium. The FA and Burnley were fine about it, but I don't think we made much money out of it because of the cost of staging it, plus gate receipts had to be split according to the rules of the competition.

It was a dream for me, being an old Boro player, albeit I'd never played for Boro at the Riverside. We had the home dressing room, which gave me a buzz standing in the same place as manager Bryan Robson would – and not banging our heads on any low beams.

Kenny Dalglish trained with us at Durham University a few days before the match. His visit was at my request, because I wanted him to look at our setpieces –

after all, he knew enough about them! There was one setpiece in particular, involving our left back Mark Barnard, which Kenny said wouldn't work because of the angle involved.

We went into the game knowing that if we won, we would be live on Sky tv at home to Manchester City in the Second Round.

Knowing that £75,000 would be in the bag if we saw off Burnley, Mike decided that the pitch would be resurfaced.

We seemed to be down and out in the game, with Burnley leading 2-0 midway through the second half. Even though Burnley had scorer Andy Payton – also a Boro old boy – sent off, there seemed no way back for us.

But we came charging back, and I believe that the press lads had to rewrite their reports three times in the last twenty minutes!

Goals from Brian Atkinson and "Super" Mario pulled us level at 2-2, and I remember Burnley manager Stan Ternent, standing next to me and panicking, wondering what to do next. He was looking for help from his staff in the dugout, but got none. He seemed to be on his own.

I felt for him. He was a friend of mine and I respected him, and when he pleaded for help, and received none, it was a sad sight.

In the last minute, Mark Barnard scored from the same free kick we'd worked on in training, and which Kenny said wouldn't work. Brian Atkinson rolled the free kick down the side of the wall, Mark let it roll past him, stepped over it, and then fired across goal into the bottom corner.

It was a great fightback, without doubt one of the greatest in the club's history, to earn us a home tie with Manchester City. We even did a lap of honour to salute the fans on what was a really special night.

A day or so later, it was confirmed that the Manchester City game would be live on Sky, and would be pulled forward to the Friday night for coverage.

Then there was another embarrassing moment. As a publicity stunt leading up to the game, Mike announced that we would be making a new signing.

Unfortunately, some of the fans believed that we would be parading a new player, even though I dropped hints that we weren't really. All sorts of names were mentioned, such as John Barnes and there was even talk of a record fee being paid!

The new "signing" was Billy Bubbles, a foam mascot dressed in a Darlington strip. With a machine blowing bubbles everywhere, Billy Bubbles was paraded on to the pitch as the new signing – to a loud chorus of boos. Another public relations disaster, and the bloke who provided the bubbles never got paid either, to my knowledge.

Nevertheless, the fans turned out in force for the game. Because the club was being paid well by Sky, we were able to finish returfing the pitch, and it looked quite good for the occasion.

Joe Royle was Manchester City manager at the time, and was receiving some criticism from their fans because the team hadn't started all that well in the old

Second Division after being relegated the year before.

Plus they were playing in the early stages of the FA Cup for probably the first time in their history, so if we beat them, then Joe could have been out of a job.

As I mentioned earlier, our dugouts, for want of a better word, were on the far side of the field in front of the Manchester City fans. Joe decided to stay in the main stand, opting to listen to the stick from Darlington fans instead!

We played well that night. We took the lead from a setpiece, when Gabbers made a dummy run to the back post, and then ran back to the front post where he flicked on a corner for Benno to head home. It was great for Benno, because it was his birthday, and he celebrated in style later with champagne.

We held the lead until midway through the second half, when their substitute, Paul Dickov, scored with a great volley from the edge of the box.

There was controversy right at the end. There was a break down the right, and the ball was crossed into the middle, where Glenn Naylor appeared to be a certain scorer, but was pushed in the back by Jeff Whitley. The referee, Barry Knight, didn't give the penalty, so Steve Gaughan ran after him in frustration, swung him round to protest, and got sent off.

We gave as good as we got in the Maine Road replay eleven days later. Glenn missed a good chance early on when Gabbers' shot hit the bar, and he put the rebound wide.

But I thought the referee held a grudge against us. There was one incident in which City had a corner and we broke away in a three onto one situation, and the referee called play back so Jamie Pollock could receive treatment for cramp. I went ballistic, because it was a disgusting decision to make, and in my opinion the referee should have continued with play. If Jamie had suffered a head injury, then fair comment.

Gabbers was also sent off. Danny Tiatto came on as sub for them, and he headbutted Gabbers, who went down, quickly followed by Tiatto. But the referee sent them both to the dressing room.

I followed them a couple of minutes later, for using foul and abusive language. I was fined £2,500 by the FA, and I suppose they left their sense of humour at home at the hearing when I grabbed the linesman around his stomach and wondered whether he was fit enough to officiate in games! I paid the fine, and was banned from the touchline for a few games.

Losing Gabbers was a major blow to us, because he was our attacking force, and could turn the game in an instant. As it was, a former Hartlepool player, Michael Brown, dribbled through in extra time and scored the winner for City.

Our pitch was all right for a few weeks, but because the water didn't seem to be draining away, it stood on the pitch, despite Tommo's best efforts.

Games had to be postponed, particularly against two struggling clubs, Hull and Carlisle.

We kept battling away for the play offs, and we had a very good 3-2 win at

Hartlepool, but we dropped points when we managed to play the games against Hull and Carlisle, plus we lost other games. I felt that I must have come back from our win at Hartlepool with eleven ghosts, given our results since that battling performance.

After the Hull match, I was actually spat in the face by one of our own fans next to the tunnel, which was absolutely disgusting and unnecessary. But the pitch was in such a state for that game, that it was a real battle, won by Gary Brabin of Hull in midfield.

When we were due to play Carlisle originally, they had several players missing, and their manager, Nigel Pearson, and chairman Michael Knighton put pressure on the ref to call the game off, which he duly did.

We lost our momentum because of the pitch. Exeter came to our place at least twice, but the match officials postponed the game with their players standing next to the pitch. It was a significant night, though, when the game was finally played right at the end of the season because that was when new owner George Reynolds was introduced to the crowd and given an amazing reception.

I think Exeter were awkward with us in return. We were due to travel to their place on the same day England played Poland in a World Cup qualifier near the end of March, so we suggested switching the game to the Sunday, because we didn't fancy a long journey back to the north east in the middle of the night.

But Exeter insisted on playing the night before, and even though I had a forty five minute discussion with their chairman on the phone, the League ruled in their favour. We drew 0-0, but had Michael Oliver sent off.

I even had to bring in players who would suit the pitch. How Gabbers managed to score goals regularly on it, I don't know, but it was no good for ball players. I signed Martin Carruthers, because it was his style of game to chase after long balls, instead of trying to dribble through defences.

Mike suggested players to buy who were way, way out of our reach.

I think he read in one of the Sunday papers that striker John Spencer was available at Chelsea, and he suggested to me that we could go and buy him, because in his opinion, he was the type of signing we needed to grab the imagination of the fans.

I just laughed at him, and told him that we couldn't afford his wages of £5,000 per week.

Mike suggested that we should obtain a sponsor for his wages, but I wondered who was going to pay out £250,000 for a season?

Plus, having a big earner in the dressing room would only cause resentment and jealousy, as well as a queue of players at my office door wanting pay rises.

Mike finally lost interest in the deal, but to be honest, it never really got going as far I was concerned.

Mike also suggested that we restructure the bonus system as a promotion incentive for the players.

He came to me and suggested that if every director put in £10,000 for an insurance policy, then the players would get a £50,000 per man bonus for winning promotion.

But that didn't happen. The Football League allow clubs to take out an insurance policy to cover large bonus schemes. I asked Mike later if I could see the document, but he refused. As far as I'm aware, no insurance was taken out.

So it's just as well we didn't win promotion, or we would have been faced with a bill of almost £500,000. We slipped up at the final hurdle, and I'm sure that there must have been some relieved directors when it became mathematically impossible for us to go up.

With the financial problems still rumbling along in the early part of 1999, my relationship with Mike became more and more frosty, and after a row with him over something, Scarborough offered me their manager's job. John Russell was chairman at the time, and knew I was having problems with Mike. He offered me a salary of £100,000 per year, plus the use of a driver, plus a cut of the transfer fee if I managed to sell their best player, Steve Brodie.

When approached by the press, Mike said that he wouldn't stand in my way if somebody else wanted to employ me. There was uproar amongst the fans.

But I turned Scarborough's offer down, and instead pledged my future to Darlington. Mike and I called a press conference, at which it was said we were both working very hard in the club's cause, but our body language didn't convince many people. We virtually sat with our backs to each other.

Mike also wasted money on a Christmas party for the staff.

He hired the Blackwell Grange Hotel, and paid for everybody at the club to go with their partners. Sitting at home ten minutes before it was due to begin, I couldn't make my mind up whether to go or not, because I knew that the hotel wouldn't get paid, and we'd end up in trouble of some sort.

I only decided to attend minutes before it was due to start. Keith Agar, who was working in the commercial department, met Beverley and me at the door, wondering where I'd been and that Mike wanted to see me. I told him to go and sit down, that I was in the bar if Mike wanted to see me, and that I, and not the club, would pay for my own drinks all night. In my opinion, it was a sham, a publicity stunt – and I was proved right because Blackwell Grange were still owed money several months later.

One of the other directors put money on to each table for players to buy drinks, and Mike had the audacity to claim that he'd done it. The comedians whom the club had booked were poor, and the lads slaughtered them. It was a terrible night, remembered for all the wrong reasons.

So you can see how the financial wheels were about to come off. Mike had failed to pay the wages on time twice – he also hadn't paid us at Christmas – plus other people and firms were asking for their money. There was even a story that Hartlepool hadn't received the money that was rightly theirs, for the tickets we had

159

sold to our fans for the game at their place the previous September.

Everything seemed to be going wrong. Even when we had a club dinner, which was supposed to be an uplifting event, the comedian we had booked was very poor. The players, who by now had had a drink and were in high spirits, decided to slaughter the poor bloke. Normally a comedian can win these battles with a bit of banter that cuts down those who take him on – but not this one. He'd lost it, and fell flat.

A bit like the state that the club was in.

Kings of Europe: Alan Kennedy helps me crown Paul Walsh with the European Cup

Three times a Quaker

Wembley Wonders: Liverpool with the Charity Shield in 1982

Celebrating Liverpool's European Cup win in 1984. I was only the substitute – but made sure I was closest to the camera

In the red and white of boyhood heroes Sunderland

Three times a Quaker

Hornchurch horror: Looking on as we lose to the non-league side in my first game back in charge

Dynamic duo: But my double act with Jim Platt was not to last

Hartlepool are silenced. Benno celebrates with Gabbers after scoring at Victoria Park

Bottoms up: The fourth official makes an arse of himself as we clinch safety at Lincoln

Two of a kind – except for the hair. Proc's has gone already and he's not a manager yet

By George: Happy days, a never to be repeated era, as our new signings meet the colourful chairman. Lee Nogan, Martin Gray, Neil Heaney, Neil Radigan, Neil Aspin

Tommo's Turf: A pitch to be proud of

The other loves in my life, my wife Beverley, and daughters Brogan and Alessia.
Below: Brogan (left) and Alessia

Happy snap with Brogan and Alessia   Portugal – our favourite holiday haunt

Kids stuff: Me with three children! Guess which two are mine

No hiding place – even in New York. Just checking to make sure George isn't following me

The arrival of George Reynolds; "That's who should get the club."

Money at the club appeared to be running short, because club owner Mike Peden asked for access to the youth funds, which he claimed were there to be used for the benefit of the club if necessary.

I stressed to him that it was for the youth set up only, as it was given solely for that purpose. I warned him that if he took it, I would phone Micky Burns at the Professional Footballers Association, and tell him what was going on.

I didn't want Mike to take that funding to right his own mistakes. By the end of March there was no money available to pay the wages. Iain Leckie, who was youth development officer, and vice-chairman Gordon Hodgson, were the two signatories to the youth team money. I told them that if they touched it, I would walk out. I made a point of saying to them that if that money was released they would drop the club into big trouble. It would possibly lead to an in-depth Football League investigation.

Though to be fair to them, they may have had no intention of releasing it. But there was no doubt that Mike was desperate. He said that if I helped out he would get a re-financing package. But that would be to finance the re-financing package that we had already done!

As I saw it, a couple of months down the line we would be back in the same boat, except that this time the youth funds would have gone as well.

By this time George Reynolds had made his initial plans to become involved in the club. I knew that if Mike got his hands on more money, whether from the youth set up or from re-financing, he would have remained in charge until the wages were delayed again.

George wanted to buy the club, and being impatient, he didn't want to wait another couple of months.

I didn't want that either. I wanted Mike out, because I couldn't see the club going anywhere except down if he stayed.

I make tough times like this easier for myself by never letting it get personal. I try to make decisions that will benefit the club. Personalities don't come into it.

I don't socialise with people involved in the club, because if you become close friends it makes the job very difficult. And all that matters is the club. On a personal level, therefore, I had nothing against Mike, but felt that he had done his time at the club, and we were ready for a new era.

However, it was getting personal between him and the players, because they needed their wages. They were getting disgruntled, even though I had told them to be patient and they would get paid.

But by then Mike's nickname among the players was Saddam Hussein. As Mike bore a physical resemblance to the former Iraqi leader, with his moustache and brushed back dark hair, footballers being footballers, it was inevitable that they would make the link.

At the point when George arrived the players were behind with wages, even though I had raised well over £1 million in the transfer market. That proved we were in a mess financially.

Coach and senior player Gary Bennett knew George, as he was a Sunderland fan at the time that Benno was a player there.

As far as I'm aware, Benno advised George to speak to me to get the full picture of the state the club was in.

I understand that the directors had approached George just before Mike had taken over, and that George had sent them packing, because at that time he didn't want to know.

I was disappointed that they had done that behind my back. In the past when the club was in a mess or facing 'short term cash problems', as Bernard Lowery put it, they would tend to come to me first. Maybe at that time George wanted to buy Sunderland, though whether that was within his league financially, I don't know.

But for whatever reason, by the time Mike left, George was very interested, and it was Benno who alerted me to that.

Ironically, the first time I ever spoke to George, I was driving along the Darlington bypass, and was exactly at the spot where the new stadium is now. I was with youth team coach Stuart Gibson, for we were returning from watching Halifax play. I remember that Matt Clarke, later to play for Darlington, was playing in attack for Halifax and looked very useful on the day.

I was straight with George. I told him that I would meet him, only if he was very serious about buying the club. If he wasn't I would not reveal any details of the club because it was not his business.

He said he was very keen, so I agreed to meet him. I dropped Stuart off, spoke briefly to Beverley, and then rang my father to ask him what he thought about George, because I was aware that my father knew a little about him. He told me that Bobby Snowden, a tough former Northern League footballer, and a friend of my father, had given him an insight into what George was like. When my father passed on the details to me, I knew I was in for an interesting meeting.

However, my father suggested that I form my own opinion of George, rather than take his word for it: "If you make your own judgement, you can't blame anyone else if you get it wrong," he said.

However, by the time I got to Shildon to meet George, I had some idea of a part of his background. But I didn't care as long as he did the right thing by the club.

Personalities didn't come into it.

There were six Mitsubishi Shoguns outside the offices that gave me the impression that here was a man who looked after his staff. That was just what we needed at Darlington Football Club.

As I went up the stairs one of the staff came out to meet me, and show me to George's office. As soon as I met him that was the moment he became George, rather than Reynolds. He then introduced me to his staff. They all had individual desks of the highest quality, and if his taste in furniture was anything to go by I could tell that we were in for a good meeting. He seemed controlled and organised in every aspect of his business.

They were my first impressions, and they were very good ones. Everything was kept in immaculate shape in a spotless room.

After a few minutes he suggested that we continue our conversation at his home in Witton-le-Wear, so I followed his car. It wasn't all that far away, but seemed miles. We drove through the gates and up the drive, and I noticed a beautiful Bentley parked in an open garage.

Once inside I could see that his house, like his office, was in splendid order, with the trappings that you would expect of a man of wealth.

I took my shoes off at the door, for I had lived in Japan for a spell, and it was quite natural for me to do that when I walked into someone's house – especially one with expensive carpets that probably cost £100 a square metre. He told me to put them back on, adding that there was no need for that.

I was then introduced to Sue, his wife, and Alexis, his daughter. I didn't warm to Sue, or her to me. I don't know why, but in all the time I have known her we have never really clicked.

George asked whether I would like tea or coffee, but somehow I couldn't see either of them making it. Then a butler appeared!

This was my first meeting with the chairman, so I had no idea what he was like as a man.

We talked for around nine hours – me for ten minutes of it. The rest of the time I listened. At the time every story he told was new to me. He showed me every room in the house, every door being complete with nine carat gold hinges and handles.

He even had a lift in the house, though I've no idea whether he ever used it. He had a piano that played on its own, though he sat there making out it was him playing. He amused me. He was a refreshing and amazing character.

He then showed me round the grounds and it was 3am before I got home. Beverley was none too happy, especially when I woke her, then went back downstairs to put the kettle on. I didn't feel tired, and wanted to tell her everything we discussed throughout the entire evening in the whole conversation with George. If Tino Asprilla and other star names he wanted had met him at the same time as I did, they would have signed for him.

I told Beverley that we shook hands, and I would make sure that he would get the club. He had asked if I was prepared to work for him, and I had no hesitation in saying that I was. He wanted to know if I was loyal, adding that all his Shildon staff were loyal. He added that even if I was the worst manager in the world, he would look after me. However, that sort of promise didn't wash with me, because managers are judged on results and nothing else.

Even at that point he was talking about building a new stadium, though he made it clear that we would not be paying transfer fees for players. I was no different from a supporter of the club. I wanted to hear what everybody else wanted to hear. Darlington FC now had a future, and that was all that mattered.

Ironically, just before George arrived on the scene, I had made a programme for Boro TV with pundit Ali Brownlee and former Boro star Bernie Slaven. Ali said I had no chance of making a success of the club unless I found somebody with millions of pounds. Then out of the blue came George.

George and I worked together to enable him to take over from Mike Peden. I held the ace card because I knew Mike wanted the youth money – and he owed me £118,000 plus compound interest – to try and keep the club afloat. I would not let the youth money be touched, and with George coming in, I didn't need to.

However, with the players' pay being slow to come through, there was even talk of a strike by them, though I would never have let that happen. I would have dragged them out onto the pitch myself, because a strike would have gone beyond the boundaries of what was right and what was wrong. It would have let the public down, and I couldn't let that happen.

I got the players together and told them: "We're safe." I told the players everything. I was on such a high. I told the players that if we could struggle by for a week or so, then the end result would be what we wanted, a new owner, with the security for the players of knowing that they would get their wages for many years to come. I would ask George to meet the players. I knew that the players trusted me.

Before he became involved I'd only really ever heard of George once before. I was on my way back from pre-season training with our physiotherapist Mark Riley in the car. We used to train at racing trainer Denys Smith's gallops near Bishop Auckland, a deal arranged by Jack Watson, a tremendously helpful and knowledgeable chap who had been associated with the club for years.

As we drove past George's Shildon factory, Mark had said: "That's who we should get at the club: George Reynolds. I've heard he's a character with a slightly dodgy past, but worth millions."

Little did we know that a year or so down the line it would become reality.

Once he had made his mind up to buy the club, George was very businesslike about the whole thing, and very decisive. I remember the first big meeting in the Amec offices. Bernard Lowery, the club chairman, was there, along with Gordon Hodgson, the vice chairman, Ken Lavery and George's men Luke Raine, Mike Metcalfe, and Mark Hayton.

We discussed the ownership of the club's shares, how much debt was outstanding, and all manner of financial matters. George declared that he would write out a cheque for £1 million to pay the wages, and get the club out of debt. It couldn't all be paid, because there was still some haggling to do with Gallifords, the company that had built the new east stand at Feethams.

There were different views among those in the room of how we should proceed, and I sided with George. He said he wanted to buy all the shares, so that he couldn't be stitched up. He wanted control. Mike Metcalfe asked George if he was sure he was doing the right thing.

By now there was no stopping the man. "Yes, get the cheque book," he said.

There was also money owed to me, from the sale of players and purchase of equipment for training. It added up to £118,000, and on the agreement of Mike Peden, compound interest was being added at a rate of four per cent above the base rate. That agreement had been in place for two years, long before George had any involvement, and I had to get experts to calculate what I was owed. There were two separate invoices, and I was told that one amounted to £6 million, and the other £2.8 million. It was all legal and above board.

The rate at which the debt was growing was mind-boggling. I remember that I had inserted a clause into the contract of Jason DeVos, prior to his move to Dundee United. He was entitled to a percentage of the transfer fee, and I knew, hand on heart, that if I had not inserted the clause, he would probably never have seen a penny of his money.

The club was one day late in paying his first instalment, and was quickly reminded of the clause. A quick phone call to his lawyer and the club bank manager let Mike know that interest was accruing at £1000 a day.

So I was pretty convinced that the exact same clause in my agreement would stand up in a court of law. So in theory I owned the club, and could have gone to Mike, held out my hand, and said: "You owe me more than £8 million." Though in reality it was money I knew I was very unlikely to ever see. What mattered to me most was the club, and it appeared to be in safe hands.

But when I came clean with George about what I was owed, he said that prevented him from buying the club, because at any time I could hit him with the bill.

I said that if I trusted him to buy the club, he must trust me to tear the documents up. He agreed, and I tore them up. But I kept copies, which are legally binding. I've since been offered money for the documents, for legally I could sell them on. But I declined.

Occasionally I would remind Beverley that we had no worries for we were multi-millionaires – on paper. Sometimes when I had a glass or two too much wine, I would stick the documents on my forehead, and walk around the house saying: "We are worth millions. I've got a head for money!"

Perhaps George used my position to pressurise Mike, pointing out that if he tried to block George from buying the club, I would hit Mike for £8 million. Bernard tried to tell me it wouldn't stand up in court, but I was assured it would.

And the directors probably believed it, because they had been quick enough to settle with Jason.

The debt I was owed was money I had never asked for. When I joined the club I didn't want any commission for selling players. But Steve Morgon had insisted on a clause giving me ten per cent. Later it was changed to five per cent for youth development, and five percent for the players' pool. That agreement was reached so that if we ran short of money, we didn't have to go cap in hand to George for more. However, by then I was already owed the sum that was to escalate so rapidly.

When George bought the club, I received a lovely letter from Mike. He thanked me for the last two years, wished me all the best, and passed on his best wishes to Beverley and the girls.

As far as I'm aware George was more generous to Mike than he had to be. George held all the aces, and could have driven a much harder bargain than he did. A lot of companies were owed money, and George settled a lot of debt. I can't say whether bailiffs were actually on the verge of coming in to take goods, though that was a story doing the rounds. But neither Mike nor the chairman had hinted to me that we were in such debt that the bailiffs were poised to swoop.

All I could see was a bright future for the club. I was told by some people that George's involvement would lead to problems and it would all end in tears. I didn't think so. In my intrigued opinion everything was going to be fine.

George captivated me. He could turn a simple story into a book; he could talk for England. He thrived on it. I could never remember him sleeping. He seemed to eat, drink and breathe hard work. I tried not to get carried away, but believed that he would build the new stadium, and that we would climb the divisions.

So much for the vision, now came the task of trying to turn it into reality.

We decided to keep the playing wage bill the same, and to do that release eight players and sign five, but on better money.

Assistant manager Ian Butterworth and coach Jimmy Montgomery were given pay rises by the new regime, though George was later to claim that it was my doing.

And George cut the non-playing wage bill by offloading several people, getting his way by making it clear he wanted them to leave.

He justified doing it by explaining, by way of one of his stories, how staff levels can increase without any more efficiency.

He told me of two men running a fire station, with one engine and one phone. Both would clean the engine after they came back from a fire. They took on two more men; one to answer the phone the other to clean the engine. Then another two arrived, to make tea etc. They ended up with three engines, but had three times as many people employed.

From a business angle he made a fair point. He liked to run a tight ship, with everybody being necessary.

But George sometimes seemed to overlook the fact that I was not only a football man, but had a keen eye for business as well. I knew as well as he did that if you only brought £1 in, you couldn't spend £2.

For years I had helped run the club on a shoestring. If there was something we couldn't afford, that I felt we needed, I bought it out of my own pocket.

George brought some of his own people in, and that's when Luke Raine, who later became PR director, arrived at the club. But already there were signs that things might not be plain sailing. For example Butts (Ian Butterworth) was given a deal that included clauses for the club to pay his stamp duty, relocation expenses etc. But George wasn't happy and pointed out that none of the workers in his factory were given such deals, so why should Butts. George didn't accept the unwritten rules of football, and in a way he was right. Why should football be any different? But it wasn't my generation that applied these 'rules'. They were in place long before that, and were introduced to help smooth the business of moving clubs, something that players did more than most workers.

When players were given cars, most asked for the car to be written into their contracts. Fortunately I had already done a deal with Ian Parker from Reg Vardy, to the effect that only new players coming into the club would have the option of leasing a brand new vehicle from Vardys. But in order to protect the motor company's relationship with the club, Carol, the club secretary, would deduct the amount owed for the cars, from the player's wages.

But George later blamed me for draining the club's finances by giving all the players club cars. But other members of staff were given pay rises, and as far as I was aware, nobody in the club doubted that George was worth the £240 million that he claimed.

Just before George arrived, Bernard had offered me a salary of £80,000 a year, then urged me to wait for the takeover as George would probably offer me more. But I thought it was a fair amount, and didn't want to move the goalposts. I had brought money into the club by selling players, and justified a wage of around that amount.

George badgered me to get a Mercedes club car, but I don't know why and I didn't want one anyway. So I declined. One day when I parked my own car at Darlington station to take the train to Doncaster to seal the transfer of Manchester City midfielder Neil Heaney to Darlington, my car was scratched right down one side while I was away.

I went to see George because it was on the club's insurance. I told him it would cost £2,500, but he told me it was my fault as I shouldn't have parked there.

One of the clever things about George was that he didn't simply accept a situation. He had the vision to look at it from a different angle. That's one reason why he had been so successful. There seemed to be another dimension to him that few other people have.

As it turned out I had a run of bad luck with the car, getting two or three burst tyres. In the end I got rid of it, and replaced it with a Mercedes club car – a 250 turbo diesel sports.

Around this time I was invited by my friend, Darlington businessman Alan Noble, to a party at his home, and a rather splendid party it was too.

On a quick visit to the loo, I heard a couple of outspoken chaps, who had obviously had a drink too many, make a comment directed at me: "Here's one of Reynolds' boys". I made it quite clear that I was nobody's boy.

I was delighted that George had taken over the club, and was willing to work closely with him. But I was still an individual, and didn't take kindly to any suggestions otherwise.

13

Chasing promotion;
"Let's stuff these
big time Charlies."

The hunt was on during the summer for players of better quality than we already had.

I believed that I needed five players to build a squad capable of winning not only promotion, but also the Third Division title. I had them earmarked – Neil Heaney, Lee Nogan, Neil Aspin, Martin Gray and Geoff Clark, though there were one or two other possibilities.

I spent my entire holiday on the phone from Portugal, trying to make sure that the deals for the new players were completed. My bill was £1180. It was all itemised, and I took it to Shildon to try and reclaim it. The lads in the office there laughed, and told me that I had no chance.

I had been told to get well-known players that the fans would warm to, and that's what I had spent my holiday doing. I lost out, however, on Paul Simpson and Tommy Widdrington.

When I saw George, he said that I had been on holiday, and shouldn't have been working. He added that he didn't think Beverley would have been too happy. He was right, and I couldn't argue with him.

But already I was learning that I was dealing with someone a little bit different. He was always looking for a good deal.

Because of the George factor and his promises to take the club to the Premiership, we were strong favourites to win the division, and I had to get good players to give us a chance of living up to the expectations.

I spent a large part of that summer with Mark Hayton, the company accountant, discussing permutations for reducing the bonuses that Mike Peden had written into the contracts. They were legally binding, and Football League rules stated that bonuses could be changed only if all the players agreed, or the team was relegated.

And there were incentives as well as bonuses, for example Marco Gabbiadini was on so much a goal.

Under Mike's deal, the players were on £30,000 a man to win promotion, and £300 for every win. I pointed out to the accountant that the previous season we had finished six points short of the play-offs, the games we should have won, but didn't, being against Hull and Carlisle.

I told him that subject to the Feethams pitch being right – because we had endured a load of problems with it – we would finish in the top six, and maybe win automatic promotion.

We worked out what we could expect the average home gate to be, and how many games we might win, to work out what we could afford. But I knew that whatever formula we came up with, we would still face a hard job convincing the players to take it.

In the end we agreed on £1000 a man for each win – but only when we were in the top three. The win bonus was £500 when we were in the play-off positions, but nothing if we were below that. The players got nothing extra for drawing a home game, but £250 for an away draw while we were in the top seven.

George put the case that we might miss out by a point after paying out all that money. But Mark and I pointed out that it might work the other way, with us creeping into the playoffs on the last game after paying out no bonus money.

Then after the players agreed it all, George cut the admission fee for the fans. All our calculations were scuppered!

As for the new players, Neil Heaney was probably the biggest name signing of the summer. He had been at some big clubs. He'd started his career at Arsenal, played for Charlton in that famous play off final against Sunderland, before he'd moved on to Manchester City. Neil took a bit longer to sort out. It took me a while to persuade him to join us, but it was reasonable enough for him to take his time, for he was walking out on a good contract at Manchester City. Our two year deal was half what he could have got there. I believe he was on £150,000 a year at City and came to us for £70,000.

I'd tried to sign him the season earlier on a loan deal, and Barrie Geldart had gone with me to watch him in a reserve game, but instead Neil had gone to Charlton, and played for them at Wembley.

Barrie and Keith Agar both knew Neil very well from his younger days at the Boro. He was exactly the player we wanted, somebody who could link defence and attack. His skill, technique and ball control would make him completely different from anybody else in the Third Division.

The problem I faced was getting him to play every week, because in the previous five years, he hadn't even played fifty games, so making sure he was fit every game was going to be a big challenge. But if we got him right, physically and mentally, then I was sure we would get all the games we wanted from him.

He was an instant hit with the fans, scoring twice in a pre-season friendly at Durham, but then he picked up a knee injury, and started to complain about it.

At the same time, I was having a new conservatory fitted at our house, and the lad who was fitting it all together, said he had a bad knee, the same sort of injury that Neil had.

I invited him to come along to Feethams for treatment one morning, and I made sure that he was in the treatment room at the same time as Neil.

John Murray, our physio, strolled in, and I pointed at our guest's knee and said; "Isn't that injury just like Neil's?" John clicked straight away, and replied, "Yes, you're right; it's almost exactly the same."

I then pointed out; "But it doesn't prevent this lad from playing every Saturday, and he doesn't moan about it."

At that, Neil lifted himself off the bed, walked out of the treatment room, and went training! Neil wasn't trying to pull a fast one; he just needed convincing that he could play with niggling little injuries that other players would shrug off.

In the past, Neil had suffered from pulls and sprains, and I was convinced it was because he used to warm up with training shoes on, and then switch to boots.

For my birthday, Beverley bought me a new mountain bike. Unknown to her, I took it to the training ground to be used by Neil every morning when he would go on a four mile ride before training got under way. He would come back from his ride, jump off the bike and immediately put his boots on and join in the warm up.

Did the idea work? Well, I'd like to think so because we got forty three games out of him in all competitions that season, more first team games I believe than he'd played in the previous five seasons.

He was nicknamed "Large" by the lads, because he had been involved in a couple of big moves, or maybe it was the Boro swagger that Matty Appleby and Michael Oliver had shown in earlier years!

Opposing defences were scared stiff of him, but Neil needed to play to the crowd. So at home when we attacked towards the Tin Shed, he played on the right so then he was in front of the main stand and away from the mainly unoccupied west stand, and when we kicked towards the Polam Lane end, he played on the left. Revelling in a free role, he scored some great goals that season when he cut in and curled the ball over the keeper with one foot or the other.

He was a down to earth lad, no airs and graces, and fairly even tempered, until one day he had a bust up with Peter Duffield on the training ground.

I thought he was quiet while he sat in the changing room. Suddenly he got up, walked back on to the training ground, and head butted Duff!

So in order to sort out their differences, I locked the pair of them in a room so they could cool down and talk things through.

I don't know whether my idea worked completely though, because when they emerged, they were talking, but the air didn't seem to be completely clear. Little Duff could pick a fight in a telephone box some days.

Welsh international Lee Nogan had a pedigree from a much higher league. He had been offered a deal by First Division Grimsby Town, but wasn't sure whether to accept it or not. Nogs was a really clever player; he had very good control, and knew exactly where everybody was on the pitch. He was a great example to others.

The idea was to try and pair him up front with Marco Gabbiadini, but the partnership just didn't work. Nogs would try and create things, but Gabbers, being a typical goalscorer, was selfish around the box, which was understandable. To Nogs' credit, he persevered with the partnership and was convinced it would work, but unfortunately it didn't. It had to be Nogs or Gabbers in the team, and I had to stand by Gabbers, because of his goalscoring potential.

Nogs instead had to be content with reserve team football, and he was magnificent as the reserves won their league and the Durham Challenge Cup. I couldn't fault his attitude at all.

Martin Gray was a key signing. I suppose I wasn't too different from George, in that I took a hard line with Martin. He was on the golf course when I phoned him, and he asked for this and that. I said 'no' and the conversation ended. But he phoned back and agreed to come.

The club agreed to pay Martin's removal expenses, but I had to sanction it, because George said he wouldn't pay it because he could find a cheaper firm than the one Martin wanted to use. That was another indication of the way George thought and worked.

I badly wanted Martin because during the previous years when I'd been at the club, the team had lacked a midfield player who could break up the opposition's style of play.

I'd known Martin for a few years, and I'd tried to sign him when he'd left Sunderland for Oxford on loan. He was a local lad from Sedgefield and I knew he wanted to return to the north east. I was well aware that Denis Smith, the West Brom manager, was trying to take him to the West Midlands, so I knew the competition for Martin's signature was going to be difficult.

All the other players I signed took pay cuts from their previous employment, but Martin was a little bit different – I had to offer him more money to leave a bigger club and come to a smaller club.

He proved to be worth every single penny. He didn't give anything other than 100 per cent, whether it was a five-a-side game, sprint work, cross-country or a match day. You got complete determination and enthusiasm from him. He's still the same now on the coaching staff.

He was a crucial signing. Defensive players are always judged by the clean sheets they get, but before the opposition got to the back four, they had to bypass Martin's defensive wall.

He wasn't the quickest player, but he always managed to get there to make the right tackle.

I've never seen a player stand like him before a match in the tunnel and put himself eye-to-eye with the player he was going to be competing against. He had the amazing ability to stare without blinking for a minute or two. I knew for sure it would put some doubt in the other player's mind.

The signing of Neil Aspin took several weeks of my time. He was a vastly experienced player, and had just finished the previous season at Port Vale in the First Division before he was released. He knew one thing, and one thing only – how to defend.

It took me nearly a month to sign Neil. You would have thought that at the age of 34 he would have the ability to negotiate his own deal, but instead I ended up speaking to a close friend of his, who wasn't even an agent, and didn't have much idea on how to negotiate a footballer's contract. It was probably Asp's way of avoiding confrontation over money with his potential new employer.

I had already earmarked exactly how much I was prepared to pay every player. Knowing full well Asp was on better money at Port Vale, I knew he would have to take a cut in order to further his career by another two or three years.

I couldn't really speak to many people about him because he had been at Port Vale for ten years, but I trusted the word of John Rudge, the former Port Vale manager who moved on to Stoke City. I knew he'd give me the exact details of how Asp was as a player and as a character. He was the exact same mould as Marco Gabbiadini and Lee Nogan. We'd agreed £70,000 a year for Neil Aspin, but when George went to meet him, he tried – according to Asp – to knock it down to £50,000. But Asp stuck to his guns and got the full amount.

The biggest problem we found with Asp was getting him to accept the ball at the back, whether it was from one of his defensive partners or the keeper. When he did receive it, the ball was going in one direction only – as high and as far he could possibly kick it towards the opposition box.

On many occasions, I asked him to take a little more time and be prepared to play out from the back. His response was straightforward and simple; "I spent ten years booting it. You can't expect me to change overnight."

With a lot of hard work from assistant manager Ian Butterworth, who with all due respect wasn't much older than him, Asp eventually accepted the ball in tight situations and tried to play out from the back. On many occasions his new-found skill found him breaking out from the back and taking the ball beyond the midfield players. It was only when he reached the halfway line that he ran out of ideas!

We also signed keeper Andy Collett on a free transfer from Bristol Rovers. David Preece, who had been keeper for two seasons, had several clubs interested in him, and I needed a replacement.

Andy was a Boro lad, which suited me, because I wanted to sign people from the north of England. Plus, he was also prepared to come to the club for the same wage as Preecey.

I hadn't seen him play, but I checked him out, and was told that he had been the Player of the Year at Bristol Rovers and was very popular. He didn't have any other clubs lined up, so he accepted our offer.

His agent was the first agent to ask George for a fee. When he phoned up, I passed him to George.

"Hello, I'm Andy Collett's agent. I'd like you to pay me a fee of £10,000 for arranging his signing."

"How good a goalkeeper is he?"

"He's brilliant."

"Ok, then, I'll give you £100,000 if you sign an agreement. Every time he lets a goal in, and the team loses, you pay us £10,000."

"You're joking!"

"No, I'm not. My manager is giving your client a job. We're going to pay him wages for two years, and you're asking us to pay you the money for us giving him a job. Why don't you give us £10,000 for giving him a job?"

The conversation went backwards and forwards for a while, and the agent eventually gave up.

George was right in a way. He was giving somebody a job, and couldn't see why he should be paying somebody a fee. The agent waived his fee, and we signed Colly, just as Preecey departed for Aberdeen.

When all the players had been signed up, George went to Durham to meet them. He had his photo taken with the new boys, and it was a great picture, with everybody laughing. George had it blown up because he liked it so much. At that time all was sweetness and light, though there were undertones of what was to come.

When we transferred Preecey to Aberdeen the fee was £300,000, of which he was entitled to £30,000. George would not pay it. He said if I had not signed him for Darlington he would never have got such a lucrative move – another example of George's ability to take an unexpected angle.

But it was an agreed deal, and I had to fight Preecey's corner.

In the end the Aberdeen chairman paid him, and Preecey sent me a bottle of champagne and a lovely letter. As I had Colly lined up to replace him on a free transfer, things worked out for everybody.

So those were my signings during the summer after the chairman bought the club. We were very high profile, not surprising I suppose considering all the press coverage, not just locally, but nationally as well. He promised the fans a new stadium, and that the club would rise quickly through the divisions to the Premiership in five years. It promised to be the stuff that dreams were made of.

We were red-hot favourites to win promotion, and to our fans, it was a case of who was going to be second.

I thought it would take us six or seven games to get going, to really gel together, but we started the season well, in front of a huge following at Halifax on the opening day of the season, every single one of them cheering the chairman to the rafters, when he raised his scarf in front of them.

Nogs pressurised the Halifax keeper into hitting a clearance straight to Gabbers, who rolled the ball into the net for the only goal of the game, and we were off. But in a way, my problems started before the game. Usually a bonus scheme doesn't kick in until after the third or fourth game, but because the chairman had hyped the bonus up so much, the players asked in the changing room if they were going to be paid it that day if they won.

The chairman responded that he would pay it, so at the end of the game he was £13,000 out of pocket, the eleven players plus the two subs that went on the field.

George had wanted the bonus system to come into play after the third match, but I insisted that it should apply from the first game of the season. He agreed and there was a hell of a buzz among some of the players when we won at Halifax, because the bonus was far more than the wages that some of them were getting, as some of them were on only around £300 a week.

We won our first three league matches, also beating Shrewsbury and Macclesfield, so the chairman was the best part of £40,000 out of pocket by the end of August, when all the other clubs hadn't paid a penny.

It became obvious that some players had a little scam taking place. We were winning games on a weekly basis and without fail at least two of the players would go down with injuries, leaving me with no option but to make substitutions so late in the game. No wonder the chairman thought that there was a syndicate going.

Luke asked me to go to the Shildon office and see the chairman.

"Do you know the hamburger stall next to the Quaker Sports centre?" he asked. Yes, I replied, slightly mystified.

"Well, its profit is getting wiped out every time you put a sub on the field."

I pointed out that there wasn't much I could do about that, if a player claimed he was injured or I thought he looked tired, because I didn't want to risk an injury later.

The chairman insisted that I should think about the hamburger man.

I tried to put a stop to it by saying that anybody who went off injured would not start the following week. Then I tried to apply the bonus only if a player was on the field a certain length of time. If not, the bonus would be split among the five substitutes.

One thing was certain. The opposition was aware of how much money some of our lads were getting, and they used it to their advantage. A game against us was like a cup final to the opposition. Some managers were earning less than our bonus, and I'm sure they fired their lads up by ordering them to pull out all the stops to make sure we didn't get our money.

As much as George was being very generous at that time, it had a negative effect in a way, though you couldn't blame him for that.

The hype was phenomenal, especially with all the statements of going all the way up to the Premiership and a new ground. Feethams was bouncing; everybody was on a high, and getting on so well with each other. The club was how it should be. The chairman was recognised everywhere we went.

We travelled to an FA tribunal in London on the train to appeal against the decision not to grant a work permit to Geoff Clark from Canada.

Geoff, a midfielder, was the fifth player I had identified to come during the summer, but the government wouldn't grant a work permit for him on the basis that he hadn't made enough international appearances, but we tried to argue that a player of his ability in his position wasn't available in this country.

The chairman believed that he could swing any decision. He took a huge amount of folders, which included the plans for the new stadium, and threw them on the table in front of the tribunal. The tribunal members, who included journalist John Sadler, former Nottingham Forest manager Frank Clark and PFA official Brendan

Batson, couldn't believe what they were seeing.

The chairman then pointed out that Geoff spoke English, that his grandparents were English, and Canada had fought on our side during the war.

But even though the chairman thought he'd won the case, the tribunal found against us, and I had to forget about Geoff.

The chairman made sure he showed us his new apartment in London. The security guards in this magnificent old converted hospital knew who he was, and let him in. Of course, the chairman's apartment was bigger than everybody else's! It was very tastefully decorated, and I understand had been designed by Versace.

If he told us once, he told us a hundred times that Baby Spice of the Spice Girls also had an apartment in the same building.

The chairman took us to the fitness centre in the building, and there was a blond girl doing some exercises. George was adamant that she was Baby Spice and in his normal brash loud manner was going to make sure that the blond girl would hear his comments.

The young girl concerned eventually became a little annoyed and said "I'm not Baby Spice – who the hell are you?" She obviously didn't know George, but Baby Spice would have.

I started to get an indication of what was coming when Colly injured his shoulder at Rochdale in a 0-0 draw.

I had Mark Samways on the bench as a replacement, but after him, I only had youngster Keith Finch as back up, so I decided to go for Mark Prudhoe, who as you all know, was part of the Darlington team that won promotion twice under Brian Little. Prud would also be useful for some coaching.

I went to see the chairman, and told him that I wanted to sign Prud.

He said no, and pointed out that we had a youngster already, plus I'd already signed four players. My response to that was Finchy wasn't ready for the first team, and if we had to rely on him for two or three games and something went wrong, then the whole season might come off the rails. Also, it would also look bad from the fans' point of view if we couldn't bring in a player to replace an injured one.

The chairman then agreed – but only if I created a space for him. I tried to argue further with him, but he wasn't going to budge. No space, no player.

He reminded me that I was supposed to be the expert and if I wanted a player in, another one had to go out.

So I had to work out quickly whom I could sell or loan out, and I decided that it had to be Martin Carruthers, who was behind Nogs, Gabbers and Duff for a place in the forward line. We had signed him for his pace at a time when our pitch was bad, and the best tactic was to play the ball over the top for him to chase. He's since gone on to score a lot of goals and I'm delighted for him. I never really wanted him to go.

I loaned him to Southend with a view to a permanent transfer, which eventually brought us £50,000 a month later. "You're not bad at this business," said the chairman.

Chasing promotion; "Let's stuff these big time Charlies."

The Prud signing was an early sign of the chairman having his finger on the financial pulse. He knew what the players' wages and bonuses were to the penny.

I had no real arguments with that, after all, it was his money. But I couldn't see the late Jack Walker at Blackburn stopping Kenny Dalglish from signing a player on loan for a month – were these the early signs?

But then we had problems paying for little bits and pieces, because the chairman wouldn't pay bills. I split the ten per cent I was due from all sales – as per my contract – to be split between the youth policy and the first team pool. By doing this, I knew I would never have to go to George for any financial help in the event of an overnight stay, if new balls were required at Christmas or any other minor things.

People would hear George say that he was paying out big money – which was true – but in order to pay for one player's wage, we had offloaded two from the previous season. Eight players left Feethams who had been in the budget for season 1998-99 – Mark Barnard, Mario Dorner, Steve Gaughan, Lee Ellison, Darren Roberts, Johnny Leah, Carl Pepper and Martin Carruthers.

Plus, we'd sold Preecey to Aberdeen for £300,000 just before the season started, brought in Colly on a free, the second part of the transfer fee came in from Newcastle for Coppinger and Robinson, plus Southend's £50,000 for Martin. So the bonus money for the season was covered.

George also said that he wasn't bothered about running the club at a loss, because he would put the money in to cover it.

But my opinion of the chairman was starting to change. We'd had the problem of bringing in Prud, while the lads in the office at Shildon marked my card about the chairman's attitude towards different things. I was in his office one day when he was looking at his video monitors and saw one of his staff scratching a heart on one of his expensive machines. In response to this, the chairman, using a can of spray paint, sprayed a heart on the bonnet of the car belonging to the young guy who had scratched the machine.

The chap concerned was made aware of this, and in no time at all was banging on George's door.

"What the f... are you doing spraying a heart on my car?" he demanded.

George's response was extremely calm, not showing any sign of emotion, and he quite simply said: "If you're going to scratch a heart on my machine, I'll spray a heart on your car."

The lad wasn't on a winner. "You can't spray my f...ing car."

"You can't spray my f...ing machine."

"But that's my f...ing car."

"But that's my f...ing machine."

"I only scratched a little heart, but you sprayed a f...ing big heart."

"My machine cost me half a million pounds. Your car only cost you a couple of thousand. I'll do a deal with you – you respray my machine, I'll respray your bonnet, and we'll call it quits." There was no response to this, and the guy just left the office, beaten. George's philosophy was simple – an eye for an eye, a tooth for a tooth.

George had ten rules and theories, but at times I wondered whether he practised what he preached.

We started the season really well, and by the time we played Hartlepool at their place, we'd won five, drawn three and lost just one of our opening nine league games. The defeat was at Peterborough on Bank Holiday Monday, when our defence wasn't at its best.

I felt very confident that we would beat Hartlepool, and I told the chairman in Strikers Bar before we set off that we'd easily win, after all, they were struggling near the bottom of the league. There was even a whisper that my mate Chris Turner would lose his job as manager if they'd lost.

But how wrong I was. We were dreadful and lost 2-0.

My approach was complacent and therefore completely wrong, and in turn the approach of the players was wrong. We thought that all we had to do was turn up and beat them. Hartlepool outbattled us all the way though the game, and that really hurt everybody.

George told their chairman that we'd lost deliberately to keep Chris in a job, but we didn't throw the game, we just got it completely wrong. I didn't see Chris after the game for a chat, and maybe that was a relief.

But that was nothing compared to the stick I got from our fans on the Internet message board. It just goes to show that losing to Hartlepool hurts badly with our fans, but I like to think that we made up for that defeat later in the season.

Our next game was at Lincoln, where John Beck was manager. He knew all the tricks on how to unnerve the opposing team and to upset their preparations.

There were a couple of speakers in our dressing room, blasting out rap music, so I cut them down. The next thing, we heard music outside the door, coming from another strategically placed speaker, and so I cut the wire to that.

I had just started the team talk, when we heard music coming from the shower – there was even a speaker in there! We cut that down, but we could still hear the music coming through the walls from the Lincoln dressing room.

I told the lads instead to go and stuff them, but even though we created a hatful of chances – and Craig Russell missed most of them – we had to settle for a goalless draw.

Craig had very good work ethics. He had a good scoring record at Sunderland, but then he went to Manchester City and was played out of position as a left wing back.

It worked out just right for Craig to play on loan at Darlington, because he was still living in Sunderland. When his loan spell ended though, I felt that we couldn't keep him permanently, because by this time the team was playing very well.

Jesper Hjorth came along in November and was awesome for us in a trial game against Middlesbrough. He'd played for Denmark's Under 21 team, but had lost his way.

I decided that I wanted to sign him, and so George said that he'd deal with the negotiations and took Jesper and his wife to his house at Witton-le-Wear. I went home, half expecting a call.

George offered him a nine month contract to the end of July, but told him that he wouldn't get paid in May, June and July!

Sure enough, I received a phone call from Luke Raine, who asked me to pop up to George's house and sort things out, which I did in less than fifteen minutes. George promised that he would leave future negotiations to me.

Jesper won us a few games, and rescued us on one memorable occasion, a great strike against Shrewsbury that helped us back into the game. If Jesper had stayed fit, then he would have been a big asset on a heavy pitch, especially in the play off final at Wembley.

The away game at Swansea was eventful, and will always be remembered for the red card of Walter Boyd, the Swansea substitute.

It was a very hard game, as it always seems to be for us at Swansea. In the second half, Swansea had a free kick, and before play restarted, Boyd, who had only been on the pitch for a few seconds, got involved in a confrontation with Martin Gray, who went down holding his face, so Boyd was dismissed before play had even restarted. Sent off after zero seconds, and it was claimed to be the fastest ever sending off.

We drew 0-0, but after the game, I gave Gabbers the biggest bollocking he'd ever had for the way that he'd played. He'd given the ball away far too much, our attacks broke down regularly, and he didn't play the simple ball.

I thought his legs had gone, and I had it out with him nose-to-nose in the changing room.

We stayed overnight at a hotel in Bristol, and Gabbers blanked everybody, teammates and management, all night.

It was a psychological game with Marco – I was determined to keep the upper hand. He was certainly the strongest personality in the changing room, and was the unselected leader.

After the game, I agreed to do a radio interview with Ray Simpson on Radio Cleveland by climbing an old rusty ladder to reach a gantry about fifty feet above the ground – apparently I was only the second manager in history to dare climb the ladder! The first had climbed up in order to jump off again after his team had been beaten 3-0.

Our next away game was at Southend, where I had to call in the police.

Just before the game in the tunnel, a person who I thought was a spectator that had climbed the barrier confronted me and said; "Will you sit down, you c..." so I called the police over, and I was then informed that he was the fourth official.

I reported him to the FA, but the case dragged on. The League Managers' Association and the FA's Compliance Officer, Graham Bean, got involved as well.

A couple of months later, we were invited to Soho Square for a hearing, but in the end the LMA managed to convince me to brush it all under the carpet. It was a pity nobody wanted to brush any of my hearings under the carpet.

There was trouble after the same game. One of their lads was sent off for a foul on Gabbers, and he waited for Gabbers in the tunnel at the final whistle. There was a short scuffle that was soon sorted out.

Mind you, the home side were maybe a little annoyed before the game. When we laid the shirts out in the changing room a couple of hours beforehand, we deliberately left those of Gabbers and Neil Heaney on the bus, and when they looked around our changing room, Southend assumed that they weren't going to play. But they not only played, they each scored in our 2-1 win.

Victory was a good reward for what had been a tiring week. We'd won at Southend, drawn at Swansea, and the Saturday before, we'd made another long trip to Second Division Gillingham, where we'd lost 3-1 in the second round of the FA Cup. Our interest in the Cup was over, now was the time to really concentrate on league games.

This was the season in which, for political reasons regarding the venue of the 2006 World Cup, the FA insisted that Manchester United play in the World Club championship in South America, so there was a place for a Lucky Loser in the FA Cup. Whichever of the second round losers won a separate draw, would play at Aston Villa.

The draw was made the day after the midweek replays had been sorted out, and to be honest, I'd completely forgotten all about it, especially as we were in the middle of a training session when the draw was being made.

We were working on setpieces, when John Murray, our physio, came sprinting (for him) across the training ground shouting; "It's us! It's us! We're the Lucky Losers!"

Pandemonium broke out, the training session almost fell apart, and television and radio crews turned up wanting our opinions.

The FA brought the Cup to Darlington, and there was a big press conference at Feethams, in which the chairman said he'd sorted it all in a phone call to God.

I suppose it was inevitable it would be us; with the way the chairman's luck was going at the time, because everything seemed to be going our way. The only negative was that Gabbers would miss the match because of suspension, so he summarised for Radio Cleveland.

The Lucky Loser certainly gave us a boost on the pitch. We thumped Halifax in our next home game 4-0, with Gabbers scoring twice from the spot, and we were then unlucky to lose at Stoke in the Auto Windscreen Shield in golden goal extra time.

We went to Villa on the Friday. It rained heavily overnight, and I was hoping that the match would be off, so that Gabbers could play in the re-arranged game.

But there was no chance. Villa's pitch was covered with a rain protector that rolled away, dispersing the water as it went to the side of the pitch.

I thought we did well that day, and we certainly gave our travelling fans, around 2,000 of them, plenty to cheer about. Aston Villa keeper David James pulled off two or three good saves for them, but we lost 2-1. Benito Carbone scored a great goal from thirty yards, and they went 2-0 up through Dion Dublin.

But we pulled one back through Paul Heckingbottom after James had blocked Duff's penalty to set up a grandstand finish. Our fans were magnificent that day, and when Hecky scored, the place lifted.

Not all was well between John Gregory, the Villa manager, and I, though.

There was some history between us, going back a few years. When I was at the Boro, we played at Brighton and I put a ball out wide to Mark Proctor, and then made a run up the middle for the return ball. I tried to go around John, but he thumped me on the blind side. Alan Mullery, the Brighton manager, later came in to our dressing room afterwards and insisted I told him who'd done it, but I came from a background in which squealing isn't looked upon too kindly.

Funnily enough, when I met up at Liverpool with Mark Lawrenson, who was playing for Brighton that day, he hoped that I realised that it wasn't him who'd thumped me, but I told him not to worry, I knew who the culprit was.

The next time I came up against John was again for Boro, this time against QPR at Ayresome Park.

Early in the game, I went down on the edge of their box, and John came across and studded me down my face and chest, so you can understand why there were other reasons I was really hoping that we would beat Villa that day. Was I ever going to get even?

At the end of the game, he didn't shake hands on the field or anything like that, but he waited for me in the corridor and said well done. That was the only positive thing he had to say.

However, in the after match press conference, he said that "the scoreline flattered Darlington" but I responded by saying that "he should look at the reasons why his team only beat us 2-1, and why there were only 22,000 people in the ground, even though admission prices had been cut." I thought that John was bang out of order, and then he had the temerity to reply to a letter from one of our fans by saying that he "didn't know why your manager had a problem with me."

My next brush with authority was at Rotherham. We were winning comfortably 1-0, but then Leo Fortune-West elbowed Asp, who went down with a head injury. Our lads stopped playing, but Rotherham went on and scored, despite our protests. And late in the game, they scored another for a 2-1 win.

All hell broke loose after the game. I lost my temper with a couple of Rotherham fans that were very abusive to Benno, and then the referee reported me for my comments afterwards. I blasted him and to be honest, I thought we were fitted up. The referee told me that he didn't think that Asp had suffered a head injury, a very dubious decision.

My so-called misdemeanours meant that I was handed a touchline ban. We played at Northampton at Christmas, so I sat in the press box.

We won 3-0, but defensively we were shocking, with Asp and Steve Tutill having a nightmare. I gave Asp a real bollocking at half time, and I think I shocked him. We led 2-0 at half time with goals from Jesper and Gabbers, who got another in the second half.

Despite our dodgy defending, the win was total pleasure. After we tightened up at the back, we thumped them, and I would say that the victory was probably one of the best during any of my spells as manager.

One of our next away games was at Brighton's Withdean Stadium. I was still banned from the touchline because of my indiscretions, but the stewards wouldn't allow me into the stand, although Micky Adams, the Brighton manager, was sitting only ten yards away from the dugout. Eventually, after a heated argument, the stewards had no choice but to find me a seat, which was right in the middle of a noisy section of Brighton fans.

When Duff put us in front, I didn't dare stand up and celebrate. Unfortunately, "Tiny" Taylor, who we'd just signed on loan from Blackburn, made a mistake for their equaliser, when he headed a ball down to the feet of a Brighton player.

That was the last point we dropped for six matches, because suddenly we hit top gear. We won all six, three of them by scoring four goals, and it looked as if promotion was beckoning because we were in a breakaway group of three clubs, with Swansea and Rotherham.

We played Peterborough at Feethams in front of the Sky television cameras and beat them 2-0. I can remember that their striker Andy Clarke missed a sitter for them, and we went straight up the other end and took the lead, when Duff glanced the ball on for Gabbers to run through and score. Neil Wainwright, who we'd just signed on loan from Sunderland, scored the second, and we were comfortable winners.

The next stop was Exeter City, and we cruised to a 4-1 win. Gabbers, with whom we were talking about another contract, scored with his head for a change, while Wainy scored a superb goal, cleverly beating two men and cutting in to score.

The momentum continued, and confidence increased. Michael Oliver scored a late winner at home to Southend, and then Gabbers and Jesper scored for a 2-1 win at Mansfield.

We then thumped Rochdale 4-1 at our place, and on the Monday morning, I bumped into Steve Bould, who was then playing for Sunderland.

He took his daughter to Polam Hall School, where my daughters went, and when he saw me, he thanked me for spoiling his weekend, because Rochdale manager Steve Parkin, who was staying with him, was down in the dumps all weekend!

We hit top form again three days later against Barnet, thumping them 4-0, Wainy scoring a cracker with his left foot from the edge of the area.

The winning run unfortunately came to an end at Leyton Orient, who were then managed by Tommy Taylor, later to come to Darlington.

The players maintained for a long time afterwards that the game changed our future. After a goalless first half, Gabbers raced clear at the start of the second half to put us into the lead, and we seemed to be on the way to our seventh successive win.

But they equalised, and then I had to bring on Gary Himsworth for Hecky, who was injured. Unfortunately, as I learned later, Himmo didn't know our free kick defensive routines, which was a disaster, especially as Butts took great pride in drilling these routines into all our players. When Orient had a free kick near the end, everybody pushed out – apart from Himmo, who played their lad onside for the winner.

We then drew 1-1 against Swansea, one of the teams above us, but it still looked as if we'd finish in the automatic promotion slots, because we had a big lead over Northampton.

We then lost at Torquay in a midweek game, in which Lids was sent off, and he was so annoyed that he kicked a hole in the dressing room door, and we had to pay the repair bill. I locked the players in the changing room for over half an hour that night. Why had they suddenly stopped playing football? Moving the ball around was suddenly becoming a problem that had to be put right quickly.

By now, there was speculation about Gabbers and a possible move. Several clubs were rumoured to be interested in him, and Brian Talbot, the manager of Conference club Rushden, travelled to Torquay to watch us.

I contemplated taking the money for Gabbers. Talks about a new contract had dragged on and on, and several clubs were waiting in the wings. And the thought in the back of my mind was that Gabbers was going to be a free agent in the summer. Every meeting was cancelled by the chairman, who had uttered the words leading into one Gabbers discussion; "There's room for only one lead singer in the band." Did he want me to tell Gabbers that he was starting to steal his thunder?

Gabbers was missing for the Hull game because of injury, so Nogs came back into the starting line up and scored the winner, but he knew that he would be back on the bench the following week. Nogs and Gabbers just couldn't play together, even though we'd tried several times.

The Hull players were really fired up for the game. Their attitude was aggressive and they were making comments like "Let's stuff these big time Charlies" and "You're not going to get a f...ing grand a man out of us today." The players had heard these sorts of comments from the beginning of the season, because it didn't take long for other players to find out what bonus they were on, and they became hell-bent on stopping our players from winning a grand.

I remember one of their players being so determined early in the game, he put Neil Heaney into one of the advertising boards around the pitch. When Neil went off the pitch, strangely enough the boards were moved back a yard or two!

Then the season started to go wrong, and we couldn't buy a win when we needed it most. We drew 2-2 at home to Rotherham after leading 2-0, but they stormed back in the second half for a point, and maybe should have beaten us.

Rotherham manager Ronnie Moore complained to me about socks after the game and we had a heated row.

Their kit man, John Newey, whom I'd known from my days at Sheffield Wednesday, had forgotten to put the right colour socks into Rotherham's skip – their choice of socks clashed with ours.

The referee had no choice but to ask us to lend them our away socks. To us, the socks were perfectly normal, but Ronnie took the hump after the game, claiming that I'd given them socks that were too small and too tight and I'd done that deliberately to wind the Rotherham players up. (Sorry, Ronnie, I don't come from the John Beck school of football). I remember saying to Ronnie; "There's a war taking place right now and there are thousands of kids starving and losing their lives – all you can grumble about is some socks."

His response was; "Typical big time Charlie from Liverpool, put a sock in it."

We drew 2-2 with Shrewsbury three days later, in an amazing last few minutes. They led 2-0 with five minutes left, then Jesper charged upfield and smacked one in, and Glenn Naylor scored in stoppage time, prompting a pitch invasion. Shrewsbury even thought about asking for a replay, but the row blew over.

But it was starting to go wrong for us. We'd lost that ability to win matches, when we'd had it in bundles only a month before. Gabbers wasn't looking as sharp as he should be.

We went to York, another team who were fired up to play us. There was a feeling of nastiness in the game, and Neil Heaney got caught up in an exchange of words with one of their defenders.

When the game finished 0-0, York thought they'd won the cup, and with tempers frayed, there was a fracas in the tunnel, in which Neil was punched in the mouth. I also had to have a go at one of their directors because he was shouting abuse at Gabbers. I'd never known it as hostile as that at York before, or since.

The crunch game that season was against fourth placed Northampton.

People have often asked me if something was wrong with Gabbers over the last two months of that season. Some people thought his legs had gone, others thought that he'd already agreed to go to Northampton, who were managed by his old Derby teammate Kevin Wilson, when his contract ran out at the end of the season.

I actually said to my staff before the Northampton game that something wasn't quite right. I certainly had to work hard on him, and because he wasn't as sharp and not taking the chances he would usually have gobbled up, I thought about leaving him out for a couple of games.

On the other hand, there had been three cancelled meetings with the chairman over his contract, and maybe he had decided that his future lay elsewhere.

Or, he was going through a lean patch as strikers tend to do – but he'd never had a one like this, in which he hadn't scored, or wasn't as deeply involved in our build-ups.

He was missing anyway for the Northampton game because of an accumulation of bookings, and we were beaten by an early Steve Howard goal. Northampton sat back after that, pulled everybody back in defence, knowing that we couldn't break them down. That defeat was crucial, because it allowed Northampton to close the gap on us to three points when it could have been nine and all over.

But, and maybe I'm being over-sensitive here, I'm convinced something happened the day we lost to Northampton. Someone put the light out for me that day.

It was now imperative to win games again.

Four games left, and our next was at Cheltenham, who were pushing for the play offs.

I had to begin playing psychological games now with the players. Somehow I had to get the point across to them what was at stake financially. I took with me on the bus that day £30,000 in cash and a toilet bag full of medals. On the trip down, the coach stopped at Tamworth services and I had to ask Butts if he could bring a sandwich for me on to the bus. Nobody knew that there was thirty grand and a bagful of medals in my kitbag – in no way was I going to leave the coach!

On the final journey from the hotel to the ground, I deliberately asked Gabbers if he really knew how much was at stake on a game like this, and were the rest of the players also aware of what was at stake. His response was "I don't think they have an idea of what we can win." That was the perfect answer, which allowed me to hand over a brown bag containing £30,000, which even surprised Gabbers. I asked him to pass it down the bus and let the lads see exactly what £30,000 looked like in cash.

When we got to the changing rooms, I then put my toilet bag in the middle of the floor. I then said, "You've seen the £30,000 you're playing for. What's in that bag will be the other reward if you get automatic promotion."

The point I was trying to make was simple. The £30,000 could change some of their lives or certainly pay off the mortgage, while the medals if they got promotion would be theirs to keep forever, but unfortunately wouldn't pay off the mortgages. Winning promotion would allow them the opportunity to keep both.

I fielded a very attacking side, with Jesper, Gabbers and Nogs in the forward line.

But the hardest decision I had to make was to leave keeper Mark Samways out of the team.

He'd taken over from Andy Collett, who had been out for several months with a thigh injury and if he played one more game, then according to his contract, he would be entitled to another one-year deal. Andy was only seventy per cent fit, and it was only later I learned that he'd been going to a doctor for injections.

Plus, I wasn't happy with some aspects of Mark's character. To me, he was an untidy person, and I'd had a couple of rows with him about that. I decided to tell Mark on the morning of the game, and I must admit, it was one of the hardest things I'd had to do.

I spoke to Monty, Benno and Butts, and none of them – not too surprisingly I suppose given the circumstances – fancied being with me when I told Mark the bad news. They didn't agree wholeheartedly with me anyway.

Mark took it badly when I told him. He could have planted me, but how he didn't, I'll never know. I told the staff what had happened, and they didn't believe that I'd gone ahead and told Mark the bad news.

So you can imagine how I felt when Colly tripped their striker when he was running through on goal after a few minutes of the game. The referee went into his back pocket, and I feared a red card if he decided that Colly was the last man. How could I expect Mark to do a job for us considering what I'd told him just a few hours earlier?

Fortunately, the referee must have decided that there was some defensive cover, and showed Colly the yellow card instead. Mark, who had decided to go and warm up on the touchline when he saw the foul, quickly sat down again. Andy saved the penalty and we drew 0-0.

Three games left, and next was a local derby with Hartlepool on Easter Monday.

Unfortunately, we drew 1-1, Hecky popping up with the equaliser in the second half.

But one incident stands out in my memory about that day. Gabbers managed to work his way through the Hartlepool defence, but then put the ball over the top from six yards.

He never missed from that range, and I'd certainly never seen him put the ball over the top, because he always kept it low. Hartlepool manager Chris Turner said he couldn't believe it in a million years. Nor could I. This wasn't like Gabbers, but all strikers miss chances at times, and he had been brilliant for us for two years.

Two games left, and Northampton were one point behind us.

Our last away game was at Carlisle. I hardly slept the night before the game, because I couldn't make my mind up on which team I should put on the field.

Something was telling me not to play Gabbers, something else was telling me to play him.

I was completely lost in thought, so much so that I told the bus driver to go past our house on the Staindrop road and through Barnard Castle instead of going along the A66! It was the route I usually took when I drove over to Carlisle by car, but not the one by bus.

I changed the team constantly on the way over, and I suppose given my undecided state, none of my staff would commit themselves too strongly.

I left Michael Oliver out of the team altogether, which didn't go down too well, and he showed his displeasure by moping around the changing room.

I fielded an attacking team that included Gabbers, but we only drew 1-1, while Northampton won 1-0 against Mansfield to go above us. Gabbers had possibly the worst game I'd ever seen him play, and I took him off in the second half and put Nogs on instead.

The chairman arrived at half time straight from Newcastle Airport and he walked over to our fans and lifted them, but the extra noise didn't help us to victory.

The game changed when Nogs went on, and we took control of the game, but we couldn't score a second.

I knew it was all over for automatic promotion then. Our last game was at home to Lincoln, while Northampton were at Torquay. It was completely out of our hands. We were helpless, and had to rely on Torquay. It didn't matter how many we scored against Lincoln, if Northampton won, we'd miss out on automatic promotion.

So while we played Lincoln at Feethams, I listened to what was going on at Plainmoor. I knew word would filter through from the press box whenever something happened.

There was a huge cheer around the ground when Torquay scored, and it lifted our players. We went a goal up which meant if results stayed the same we'd be third.

But within ten or fifteen minutes, there was a silence around the ground, because Northampton had hit back to lead 2-1. It didn't matter how many goals we scored, as long as Northampton stayed in front, we were out of it. My hopeful glances towards the press box weren't returned. There were shakes of the head instead.

The final whistle sounded at Feethams. We beat Lincoln, but I knew that Torquay had lost because there was no reaction from our fans. Northampton had won their sixth game in a row to clinch the third promotion spot ahead of us.

In the minutes after the final whistle, the mood in the dressing room was sombre – we had blown automatic promotion. I couldn't help feeling that of our previous seven games, we didn't win any. We lost one, and drew six, and if we'd turned two of those draws into wins, that would have been enough. How were we going to raise ourselves for the play offs?

The play-offs and the aftermath; "Fish and chip paper."

I told the lads that we had blown our chance of automatic promotion and nobody disagreed. We had played all season – 46 games – and it was all down to a goal here and a goal there on the very last day.

We perked up and reflected on the fact that at least we had enjoyed a good result on the final day, winning 2-0. Then word came through that Hartlepool had won at Hull to reach the play-offs – and as they were the seventh placed club and we were fourth, they would play us.

That gave us an almighty lift. Instead of going a long distance down country to somewhere like Cheltenham, we had two games against our local rivals. It completely changed our outlook.

The dressing room erupted, which I must admit surprised me, I would have thought there could have been a fear factor. After all, what would be worse than blowing a promotion that seemed in the bag, only to have it rubbed in by losing to our arch rivals in the play off?

But that thought didn't seem to enter the head of anyone except our skipper Craig Liddle. However he's a worrier and any team will frighten him, until he gets out on the pitch against them. Then it's a different story as he is invariably in control.

Lids apart, it was a collective thing. Everybody was singing and dancing up and down, and to be fair to Lids I think he probably joined in.

I wondered if it was fate, and we were destined to go up through the play-offs. I was envious of Jim Platt when he became the first manager to go down Wembley Way with Darlington. Now my turn could be just around the corner.

The players had been on £30,000 each for automatic promotion. That was more than many of them were being paid in a year. To the likes of Phil Brumwell, Michael Oliver, Mark Samways, Glenn Naylor, Paul Campbell and Jesper Hjorth it was a fortune.

Not only had they missed out on promotion, but they had let a fortune slip through their fingers. Yet they were still jubilant to be facing Hartlepool.

I bet one or two of their wives had already worked out how to spend the £30,000! There were so many reasons to be devastated, but as soon as the word 'Hartlepool' was mentioned, they were all on cloud nine.

But again I couldn't help feeling that of our last eight games, we won only one.

Now, we needed to win over two legs against our old enemy to reach the play-off final at Wembley.

After the Lincoln game I went out to the Tontine restaurant with Beverley and some friends from our Sheffield days. England manager Kevin Keegan was there, no doubt relaxing before a big occasion just like me.

Only he faced a bigger challenge – Euro 2000 in Holland and Belgium. He sent a nice bottle of wine to our table, and I said to Beverley that I would go over and ask him to sign it to Brogan and Alessia. Beverley said I couldn't do that, as I was a manager just like he was.

I reminded her that I was building up to a game with Hartlepool, while he was trying to plot the downfall of the likes of Italy and France. We were miles apart.

I went over, and we wished each other well. He said we had done brilliantly to reach the play-offs.

We tried to keep our build up low key and focus on all the right things. The lads were back in training on the Monday after the Lincoln game. We used the Durham City pitch which was in excellent condition, and went to town on all the drills we had worked on all season: passing the ball crisply, keeping our shape and all the basics that made up our game.

Iain Leckie, our youth development officer, brought food up to us to make the preparations go as smoothly as possible. I didn't want to leave anything to chance. It was mainly pasta, and a lot of the professional approach was down to Ian Butterworth, the assistant manager, who was very much up to date with nutritional thinking.

He was also a rock solid coach, looking after the defenders, which was his position. The importance of clean sheets was drummed into them time and again. I was happy to win games 4-3. He wanted 1-0. He had a George Graham approach to football – you must not concede!

I had the utmost trust in Butts. He did the warm ups and was extremely methodical. That was a major factor in the squad having so few injuries. Everything he did, he did right.

The only time I can remember laying the law down was very early on in his time at the club, when we trained at Catterick army base.

When I arrived at the base at 10.50am, the lads were already jogging, ten minutes before we were due to start training. I asked what was going on. Butts told me that the lads had been keen to get going. I told him that we made the rules, not them. If the starting time was eleven o'clock, then that's when they should have started, and not a minute earlier.

But in the build up to the play-off Butts was at his very best. Even so, we took another step to make sure that everything was right. I took Kev Smith out with all the players to an Italian restaurant in Shildon. Smudger is Darlington through and through. I felt that to have his presence at such a crucial time for the club was very important.

He had already been out with the lads six or seven games before the end of the season, and at my request had taken on board the mood in the camp and brought it back to me. He had told me that Marco Gabbiadini was a natural leader and that all the lads were focussed and talked about the game.

Yet still we blew it. It just goes to show that talk means nothing and results mean everything.

I still had a nagging doubt that it was not going to happen for us against Hartlepool. What worried me was that all season we had been given all the headlines. There was the George Reynolds factor, the lucky losers draw in the FA Cup, the bonuses the players were getting, the crowds we had attracted. It was all about Darlington, and yet here were Hartlepool, also in the play-offs, starting off on level terms with us. They must have been sick at all the good publicity we had, and were determined to grab their chance to ram it down our throats.

They also had some old heads who had been there and done it, especially Gary Strodder and Paul Stephenson.

Yet despite that, I knew that over two legs if they played their best and so did we, they couldn't live with us. When you looked at our dressing room and theirs, man for man, there was no comparison. We were miles better.

We didn't stay in a hotel before the game because I wanted the players to have a normal build up and sleep in their own beds.

We met at Feethams before travelling to the game at Victoria Park. A lot of fans had gathered at Feethams to watch the game on the big screen. I went onto the pitch with John Foster of TFM Radio, and spoke to the fans.

I told them that I felt we had let them down by not winning automatic promotion, but would beat Pool. It was a risky thing to do, because if we had lost, they might have lost faith in me. At that time half a dozen of our players had arrived, and I wanted them to see how confident I was.

Then we set off, all in the right frame of mind. We picked up the York contingent – Steve Tutill, Neil Aspin and one or two others – at the Blue Bell hotel in Billingham. I remember that we had the club doctor Kamal Banupe on the coach, which was unusual, but pretty much everything else was normal – we even had Tommo, the groundsman, driving my car, so that I could make a quick getaway after the game.

The lads had the music on that they always blasted out at that time, and were singing and looking cheerful as we drove past the Pool fans on their way to the game. The fans were giving us stick and the lads were giving twice as much back.

The rivalry between the two camps was so intense that I half-expected the bus to be stoned. When we got to the ground we went out to look at the pitch, which was in good nick.

It suited them, because at the time they were trying to play the same passing game as us.

I saw Chris Turner, the Pool manager and an old mate of mine, before the game. He looked confident enough, but I was bordering on arrogance. It's not an attitude

The play-offs and the aftermath; "Fish and chip paper."

I liked to have, but I had been too relaxed before the league game there the previous autumn, and we had lost when I had been sure we were going to win. So this time I had really fired myself up.

I didn't have to say much to the players in the changing room, however. The lads were in the mood. There was no game plan to keep it tight then try and beat them at our place, which was the usual tactic over a two game tie.

We were there to win, and I could sense that the lads were right up for it. There was to be no holding back. We were going to apply everything we had worked on, even though we knew we were about to step out into the most hostile atmosphere.

But I must praise the Pool security staff, who were brilliant. The head of security was a Hartlepool lad, but he was professional, courteous, and very efficient.

Not so, those people in the executive boxes. Even from the so-called respectable element, came a shower of abuse as soon as we emerged from the tunnel. In fact they had started even earlier when we went out to look at the pitch.

The players went out before the staff. Butts, Tommo, Ian Darke the kit man, John Murray the physio, waited behind with me in the changing room. We all shook hands, said we had done what we could, and now it was up to the players.

The dugouts were at the far side of the pitch from the tunnel. Butts walked straight over the pitch, but I went along the touchline and behind the goal in front of our fans, to make sure that they knew we were up for it.

I always believe in trying to have a rapport with the fans. When you have people like big Dave Hardisty as fans, people who live and breathe Darlington Football Club, I like to show that I feel the same way.

I once did the same thing at a home game after a bad run of results. I said to the lads that there was no hiding place, and if they had to go out in front of the fans, then I could do the same.

Our fans at Pool that day appreciated it, but the Pool fans didn't. By the time I got to the dugout, walking in front of the Mill House stand, my coat was covered in saliva from the Pool fans spitting at me. The things they were shouting were vile, even bringing Beverley into it. It was a football match for goodness sake. Sure, both sides wanted very badly to win, but how can you have an ounce of respect for people like that – though I'm not branding all Pool fans like that. It made me even more determined to make sure that we had the last laugh.

But despite all that I was quite relaxed. I even made a few comments during the game, to Pool manager Chris Turner. But he blanked me.

When Craig Liddle struck our opening goal I jumped up, fist in the air. I was always confident we would win, but suddenly it was happening for real.

Neil Heaney had got away down the left and had been brought down. He took the free kick, which went beyond the far post, and either Steve Tutill or Marco Gabbiadini jumped to head it back across goal. I wasn't sure which of them did so, but there was no doubt who touched it next – Lids, and the ball flew into the net.

But it was far from all over, and was a tight game. Craig Midgley appeared to

201

have a tap in for an equaliser, but felt the ball was going in anyway, so left it, and it crept past the post after rolling virtually along the line.

But even if he had scored, I felt the lads had enough in the locker to go on and win. The atmosphere grew even more hostile as the game went on, but our fans, packed behind the goal, were magnificent. They seemed to share my confidence.

The second goal came when the Pool keeper, Martin Hollund, tripped Glenn Naylor inside the area. The home fans accused him of diving, but the keeper caught him. Glenn wouldn't know how to dive.

Hollund was sent off and was replaced by Andy Dibble. I always had confidence in Gabbers to score from anywhere, let along the penalty spot, but I wondered about his state of mind as he stood there waiting for Dibble to get between the posts.

But Gabbers struck it sweetly into the net in front of our fans. What a fantastic moment seeing the fans erupt. 2-0 was a fair reflection of the game.

But the Pool fans turned really nasty, showering me with objects including a fifty pence coin. The stewards came and stood behind the dugout, but even one of them was giving me abuse. But there was no way I was going to retreat to the dugout and sit down. I stood my ground. The lads were magnificent on the pitch, and I was going to stand there as close to them as I was allowed. They were not intimidated and neither was I. I remember once confronting our fans when one of them threw the ball at Mick Tait when he was Pool boss, and I thought Chris Turner might do the same thing to try and calm the Pool fans down. But I don't think it would have made much difference.

We were jubilant at the final whistle, then Gabbers was punched by a fan, and punched hard, as he left the pitch, but I didn't see the incident. The security people looked after me well, surrounding me to lead me back to the tunnel. I gave a salute to our fans, but was not allowed to walk back past them.

When I got back to the changing room, Gabbers was seething. He was hurt and wanted to go to the police. He was perfectly entitled to, but I asked him not to, because we had a second leg coming up, and I didn't want an unsavoury incident to be a talking point.

When I went to speak to the media, I needed escorting out again, because people were in the executive boxes and still having a go at me.

I remember saying to the media that the hatred in the game was similar to that when Celtic play Rangers. I would not have been happy if our fans behaved as badly as some of the Pools fans that day.

I walked back to the car with Tommo, and he was panicking because there were still a lot of Pool fans around. When we got to the car four of them walked towards us, and I threw a bunch of bananas at them. I had a bunch in the car, though I didn't bring them for that purpose, it just happened on the spur of the moment.

We drove off, but almost immediately came to a red light. The four lads were running towards the car, and Tommo was telling me to drive through the lights. I told him not to worry, but fortunately the lights changed anyway, and we were away.

The play-offs and the aftermath; "Fish and chip paper."

I was on cloud nine as I walked through the front door. Beverley and the girls had been watching the game at Feethams on the giant screen, and had loved it. I can't remember whether we went out that night. The adrenalin was still flowing and I really don't know what we did.

But I remember getting up on the Sunday morning thinking, "Pool won't score twice at Feethams. Or will they?" I was not at all complacent.

At training on Monday I stressed to the players that it was not all over, and they must keep their feet on the ground. I told them not to go out and have a drink, because we would do that on the Wednesday night after the game – if we won.

On the day of the second leg, I was nervous – more nervous than before the first game. I was worried that if Pool could get an early goal, we would be on the back foot.

But the lads were brilliant before the game. I could tell that they had not switched off. As far as they were concerned there was no way back for Pool. We wanted to nail them and show them for once and for all who was the better team.

The pitch was in poor condition, hard and bumpy, which suited us, because I knew Pool couldn't play on it. The shame was that we lost Jesper Hjorth to a pulled hamstring, and he would have done well at Wembley.

We warmed up for the match on the best area of turf, which was at the Polam Lane end in front of the Pool fans. Once again the stick came in my direction.

I gave them the Winston Churchill salute, meaning not only victory, but also 2-0 to us. I asked them why they had wasted their money coming to the game, then said: "Oh yes, you don't have a big screen."

Any thoughts of a Hartlepool comeback were killed off after just a few minutes, when Phil Brumwell whipped in a great cross, and Gary Strodder, Pool's central defender, turned the ball into his own net right in front of the Pool fans in the Polam End, and sank to his knees.

I felt for him, to score an own goal in such an important game must have been horrendous. But what mattered most of all to me was that it was game over. There was no way back for them, because if they had piled forward we would have hit them on the break.

The game was played out with no further incident. I shook hands with Chris, though I can't remember what he said. Though I can recall somebody telling me that when I went on the pitch after the game, George was right next to me hogging the limelight. I had no problem with that. He deserved it.

The club took a lot of money that night; probably record takings in the bar. In fact all season the drinks were flowing because we were doing well, and fans were stopping back for a few drinks.

We also got compensation for the Wembley play-off final being on a Friday night, to accommodate England's friendly against Brazil the following day, and the Sky television money. So financially we had a good season.

After beating Hartlepool I told the players to have a couple of days off and enjoy themselves.

On the Saturday we went to Richmond for a run, then went to Norton to train for the rest of the week. It was quiet and out of the way there, which is exactly what we wanted. Our chef Paul Cabourne prepared the food and Iain Leckie brought it to the training ground every day.

I let Sky television in, but tried not to turn the Wembley build-up into a circus. However, when Alpha Radio turned up, Gabbers and me were having a right ding-dong on the pitch. It was something to do with him not closing people down.

I told him that nobody was too big to be left out of the side at Wembley. Unfortunately the reporter put it out that Gabbers was being left out at Wembley. I then had to go to the media and tell them that it was a typical training ground bust up, and no more.

And that was true. It was. As I've said about Gabbers before, he could be difficult in training, but was a dream in matches. Give me that any day. It makes a change from all those players who were easy to deal with in training, but got it wrong on Saturday afternoons.

Overall the week went well, though all the time I was pondering on what the team would be on the day. And the other thing that was bugging me, was when to travel down to London.

Should we travel the day before, or on match day? The problem with the day before, as I saw it, was that we would have too much time to worry about the game. I decided that we should travel on the day, as we had done on all London trips during the season. This was even easier, with it being a night game.

Away from the training ground that week there were growing problems between the chairman and me. We were crossing swords all the time. He told me to get the Wembley suits, but take it out of the players' money.

And that was just one of the confrontations that week. I had set aside tickets for the match for everybody who had helped all season with things such as the pitch covers, and all those essential jobs that go unseen by the public. But then I had to put a load of money into the pot for tickets for the players' families. There were also disputes to do with the buses to take everybody to Wembley, and Lisa and I had a lot of work to do to sort everything out. The club offered no support at all. Lisa and I did all the preparations.

During the week I had to travel to Doncaster, to meet Barry Fry, the Peterborough manager for promotional photographs ahead of the game. I refused to touch the trophy for reasons of superstition.

Barry told me that all their players had got complimentary tickets. Yet I had to pay for all ours out of the play-off pool. It dawned on me that the Darlington players were being treated like second-class citizens, with everything being badly organised at our end.

All the players' wives had to travel down with the fans. It brought back memories of the trip to Wembley with Sunderland in 1986, when the wives were badly treated.

The play-offs and the aftermath; "Fish and chip paper."

Lisa worked very hard that week, but had too much to do, what with sorting buses, booking accommodation, and all manner of other jobs. Things were beginning to fall apart, but the full problems kicked in on the Friday, the day of the game.

I decided that we should get to the hotel in time for the players to have four or five hours in bed before the match. I sent the team bus to meet us when we got off the train.

Had we got off at Stevenage, we would have been at the hotel in a 45-minute drive. But we were told the best thing to do was go to King's Cross. We ended up being on the bus for two hours, and got to the hotel in time to have a quick meal but no sleep or relaxation. We took so many wrong turns before finding the hotel (which was just up the A1), that I couldn't believe it. I thought it was a set up.

Even so, I felt that it might not be a bad thing, because there was no time for nerves to build up.

Our wives arrived at the hotel just as we were leaving, but I didn't want the players to see their wives because we were all focussed on the game. Beverley said she was worried because she'd been told that Butts had been meeting the chairman behind my back, and she thought that he was getting my job if we lost. Audrey, Benno's wife, had filled Beverley's head with garbage. But I completely trusted Butts, and knew that this would never be the case.

I had another reason for knowing it to be wrong. The chairman did not like Butts, ever since the dispute over his expenses, the stamp duty clause when he moved house. It was typical of the sort of negative talk and rumours that were beginning to circulate in the club.

We travelled in tracksuits, which surprised the Peterborough lads when we got to Wembley, because they were all in suits. We looked like cheapskates, but even so, the spirit in the dressing room was good.

I went to the top of the tunnel and looked out at the torrential rain lashing down on the pitch. Water was lying on the surface and the ball wouldn't roll. The players felt the game would be called off.

I saw the referee talking to officials from Wembley and the Football Association. But he didn't consult the two managers. I don't think he had a choice. The game had to be played because I don't think that the FA or Wembley wanted anything to get in the way of the England v Brazil game the next day.

But my attitude was that if the game was on, it was on. We had to get on with it. But it began to affect the players. We had pitch problems at Feethams all season – surely not at Wembley. We should have been looking out at a perfect pitch on a mild May evening. Instead it was pouring down. Some of the players were clearly thinking that it was not going to be our night.

I had made my decision about the team. Gary Himsworth, Adam Reed and Phil Brumwell were to be left out. Himo was coming back from injury, but had played well in practice games in an attempt to prove his fitness. The other two were tricky decisions too. Phil had played well in both games against Hartlepool.

I didn't decide on the substitutes until we were on the way to Wembley, and I was later told that the chairman had said I picked Paul Holsgrove for the bench because I was trying to sell him.

That wasn't true. He was an excellent passer of the ball.

As every Darlo fans knows, we dominated the game, creating chance after chance, but missed ones we would normally have buried. Gabbers, Neal Heaney and Peter Duffield all missed, Duff hitting the post with one he would normally have scored without batting an eyelid.

Gabbers was struggling to run with the ball in his usual style because it was sticking in the water on the pitch. On a dry pitch he would have destroyed Peterborough.

It's no exaggeration to say that we could have been four goals up at half time, instead of it being 0-0. I remember looking at Barry Fry. He didn't have a clue what to do. As we walked off at half time he told me he couldn't believe that they had kept a clean sheet. He said he didn't know what he was going to say to his players.

I think the world of Barry, and I said to him before the game that if we were to be beaten at Wembley I would rather it was to him than anybody else.

I can't remember Peterborough having us on the back foot once in the first half.

In the second half Paul Heckingbottom, our left back, slipped on the wet surface and damaged his groin. He had battled all season with the problem, and missed only one game. Now his groin had gone, thanks to the conditions, at a crucial time.

While he was being treated it was decision time. Did I bring Glenn Naylor off the bench to put in that role, or drop Michael Oliver in there from midfield? I opted for Olly.

Peterborough were beginning to get a foothold in the game now, though their keeper needed to pull off a fabulous save to keep out a raking low shot from Gabbers after Heaney pulled the ball back to him. The ball seemed to be beyond the keeper and inside the post, but he somehow clawed it out.

Then Peterborough looked set to score when Andy Clarke went round our goalkeeper Andy Collett, only for Lids to make a sensational saving tackle.

We cleared the ball to the halfway line, and the defence all moved up, except Olly. Clarke nipped in, Olly playing him onside. Although Colly blocked his shot, Clarke knocked in the rebound.

Even after that we had chances, but couldn't force the ball in. When the final whistle went, I had never been more stunned in my life. My stomach just turned over and disappeared. I fell to the ground punching the drenched turf in disbelief, anguish and all the worst emotions you can name. I don't know where Butts or anybody else went, or what they did at that moment.

All I can remember is Barry Fry putting his hand on the back of my head and giving it a consoling shake as I lay on the ground.

When I picked myself up, Benno was having a meeting with the lads in the middle of the pitch, but by then Gabbers had walked off, handed his shirt to a fan, and gone up the tunnel.

Benno said that the players had done all they could, and at least they hadn't walked off like Gabbers. I wasn't pleased with Benno for saying that.

In the changing room I said to the players that everybody dealt with situations differently, and reminded them that if it wasn't for the goals that Gabbers had scored we wouldn't be at Wembley. He gave everything that night, and without him we would have been in mid-table.

I know how Marco must have felt. The way the ball stuck in puddles when any other night he would have waltzed around the keeper and scored, had left him distraught. I had a word with the lads who had not played, then did the media interviews and congratulated Barry.

Then I saw the chairman going up the tunnel. I told him to stay out of the changing room, because the lads wouldn't want to see him. He said not to worry; we had just had a great season, despite the defeat. He asked me which other club had no debt and was going to build a 25,000 all seater stadium.

At that moment I didn't care about that at all. The chairman's wife Sue said to me that George would know what to say. And in he went. But I knew that nobody could say anything to make them feel better.

The players were in despair, and many of our loyal fans felt the same. When I found big Dave Hardisty he was in tears. What could I say?

I dragged myself up to the Wembley function room, and saw Lennie Lawrence, the former Boro manager. There was even talk of him getting my job. Steve Cotterill, the Cheltenham manager, came over for a chat, and said he couldn't believe we had lost. He was very complimentary. He said we deserved to win by four or five goals.

Everybody said how well we had played. It was nice to hear, but it changed nothing, and was no consolation whatsoever.

Then the lack or organisation kicked in again. I had wanted the bus to take our wives and families back to the hotel, and then come back for the players who were by now having a drink. But in the end 80 or 90 people had to cram onto a 40-seater bus, which was dangerous.

I couldn't get on. It was a complete embarrassment, and I ended up getting a taxi to the hotel. No other manager in the country would have had to deal with a situation like that, and that was only part of it.

Beverley and Butts' wife did not even have tickets for the directors' box. It was full of the chairman's friends, and many people in there had never supported Darlington in their lives. They had their own coach, and there was me, packing people into ours like cattle.

I don't dispute that the chairman had put a lot of money into the club. It was his club, but the treatment of a lot of people was wrong that night.

When we got back to the hotel it was dead. We grabbed some food, and then went into the bar. I was then faced with the task of arranging how everybody would get home. I had to sort out buses and mini buses to get people to the station, and then see which of the players wanted to go back on the team coach.

It was almost 5am by the time things were sorted. At last I managed to grab an hour of restless sleep. I got up, packed my case and decided to go. My head was still buzzing, not so much from the frantic arrangements, but from the decisions I had made regarding the football.

If Mark Samways or Phil Brumwell had complained about being omitted, for the first time in my life I would have been speechless. I had made decisions and had to live with them.

I caught the 6.30am train from King's Cross, and travelled through Peterborough, looking out of the train at their London Road stadium that would be hosting second division football the following season.

I didn't hear from the chairman on the Sunday, and on Monday I took the family on holiday to Portugal. But there was no peace there.

I had Gabbers' agent on the mobile battering me to let him out of his contract, as we had a year's option on him. There was a dispute over whether he was entitled to a free transfer as he claimed he hadn't had a letter from us stating our intention to keep him.

Every other player had their letter, but, according to Lisa the club secretary, not Gabbers. I said that he should have it, because it should have been sent recorded delivery. I asked the agent which club he wanted to join, and was far from happy when I was told it was Northampton.

The chairman wanted money for him, which was a reasonable request. I then spoke to Gabbers and agreed to let him out of his contract in return for what he had done for the club over his two years. Other clubs wanted him too, and I understand that Doncaster offered him a fortune, even though they were in the Conference.

He could have gone there without having to move house, but he wanted to play at the higher level, which I can appreciate. However I told him I felt he had already made an agreement with Northampton, but he denied it.

I wasn't prepared to let the matter spoil our friendship. What he had done for the club was second to none, after all, over fifty goals in two years wasn't bad going by any standard. And he was doing what was right by his family, and you can't argue against that.

So one way and another it was not much of a holiday. However, despite all that had gone wrong over the preceding weeks, I was still up for it, and ready to give the job my best shot the following season, even without Gabbers.

But the chairman wore me down. There was a whole host of problems. Even the Gabbers affair was not resolved, because he was owed money by the club, though in the end he forfeited it so that he could leave.

Then I got a call from an agent asking me if I wanted the manager's job at either Bristol City or Notts County. Beverley said that I should leave Darlington. She said that I had given everything and more, and that it was time to go. Besides, I had no contract.

I was invited to meet the Bristol City board. Beverley persuaded me to go, if only to get an insight into another club.

I said I would go, but demanded that those involved in setting it up, kept it quiet. The flights were booked, when the story came out that I was going to Bristol. I rang Bristol City and told them I wasn't going down there to talk to people who could not conduct themselves professionally.

It needed to be kept quiet because I didn't want to be in the spotlight. Losing at Wembley was still an open wound, I felt a tremendous loyalty towards the Darlington players and fans, yet at the same time I had to do what was right for me, Beverley and my daughters.

Once the details became public, I said to Beverley: "It's not meant to be, so we don't have to agonise over it any more."

Derek Pavis, the Notts County chairman, then rang me to ask whether I wanted the job there. I told him it was not the right time for me to speak to him.

Then Benno rang me to say that he felt the chairman was being awkward, and that Steve Tutill was now not getting paid money he was owed. The amount was £10,000 from a signing on fee. I asked Tuts which club wanted him, and he told me Chesterfield. I told him that it was best that he went.

I had been tipped off by one of the players that Tuts had also spoken to Scunthorpe manager Brian Laws. I know that in the modern game loyalty does not exist. Players will speak to anybody who might give them a better deal.

Knowing Lawsy as I do, I couldn't hold anything against him, especially as I had earlier pinched Gabbers from under his nose.

I still retained my sense of humour, however, and made a call to Tuts pretending to be Brian Laws! I deepened my Geordie accent to sound like Lawsy, and it worked for I held Tuts in conversation for around 10 minutes.

Tuts said he had to get away from Darlington because he felt that the ship was sinking, and he was having problems with the chairman.

Luckily he didn't bad-mouth me once. If he had done, his move would never have happened.

There were two or three members of staff in the room when I made the call. I don't know how I kept a straight face, but eventually I felt that I had to tell him it was me, and not Lawsy.

His response was: "You're joking." There was a spell of silence, and then the phone went down. I called him back just to remind him that I was always one step ahead.

However, I did understand his circumstances. Not being paid £10,000 that you are owed is a lot of money to anybody, especially a player who has spent his career in the lower divisions.

He had done a good job for me. He played through injuries and never gave less than 100 per cent. I told him that he would definitely get his move, whether it was to Scunthorpe or to Chesterfield. In the event it was Chesterfield. What I didn't tell Tuts was that I had Alan Whyte lined up to replace him for around half of his salary.

I had not yet recovered from the longest season of my life and was still getting badgered about other people's problems.

As I saw it the chairman was trying to save money, though as far as I was aware we had made a profit in the season just ended. I spoke to Derek Pavis again, and told him to ring me later. He told me he would be upfront, and would tell George that they wanted me as manager.

That was the last I heard from him, so who knows what George said to him. I asked Luke Raine, our PR director, if the two chairmen had spoken. Luke said that if they had, George would not have said anything good about me.

My heart told me to ride through the storm with George, but my head said that it was a battle I couldn't win.

I felt that I had not been on holiday, but nevertheless, for the time being I was determined to battle on. I was pleased to have Alan Whyte lined up, as he was a good player, was from the area and would settle in well. Tuts got his £10,000 paid by Chesterfield when he joined them, so it looked as though everyone would be a winner.

When Alan went to Shildon to see George, the chairman said he would be paid £500 a week, less than I had agreed with the player. There was no logic in it. He would be on a lower wage than Tuts, and we had saved the £10,000.

And George had been given a tremendous profile through his involvement with the club. Yet here he was upsetting a potential signing who could have taken us forward. At this point we really crossed swords.

Beverley told me that I should move on, as there was no chance of me getting through the season with George at the helm. I knew she was right, but even though I was angry, I was still prepared to scrap it out.

It was supposed to be the quiet time of the year, but I was never off the phone. I couldn't even let the girls out to play because I was too busy to keep an eye on them. I managed to sign midfielder Stuart Elliott and wide left player Richard Hodgson, two youngsters who didn't command high salaries.

But bonuses we had been promised were not forthcoming, then the chairman put the block on us playing in a pre-season game at Scarborough, though in the end they paid us to play.

When I spoke to one of our fans, Neil Johnson, he was talking about what a disastrous season it would be, yet we had not even kicked a ball. I felt lower than a snake's belly.

The chairman then said that he would come to the training ground in Durham to speak to the players and sort out the issue of the bonuses. I said that I would do speak to them, but he insisted that he would.

The lads all sat down in a squash court. He marched up and down telling them how much he had put into the club, before asking them why they were not prepared to take a cut. They agreed to do so, but he still turned on them, and said they would not win much in bonuses without Gabbers.

He asked the players one by one whether they would put their house on the line for the club, and of course they each said "No." When it came to my turn I said, "Yes," and he was fuming.

He walked slowly around the court and eventually stopped in front of Brian Atkinson, a player never particularly forthcoming with words. Why he picked on Brian, I don't know. Maybe it was because he was local and never wanted to leave Darlington. This gave George the perfect opportunity to single him out for some very harsh words.

The chairman also grabbed him by the shirt, at which point Brian turned as white as a sheet.

By the time I got across the court to confront the chairman over such ridiculous behaviour, several of the players had jumped between Brian and George. Brian was not putting up a fight, but the lads didn't want one of their own to be bullied.

At this point I called an end to the meeting because it had become ridiculous.

George wanted to carry on, but when I told the players that I wanted them out there and then, I knew that they would listen to me, and go.

George then demanded that Butts, Benno, Monty and I went to meet him in his office at Shildon.

When we arrived, twenty minutes after leaving Durham, the atmosphere was still frosty. Something was bugging me. Normally when the chairman wanted to discuss anything, it was between him and me, but this time he demanded that the others be present.

His old rule of divide and conquer was coming into force. He was getting Monty and Benno, and even Butts to an extent, to agree to a bonus system that he had conjured up.

After an hour or so of getting nowhere, we all agreed on what George proposed, though I knew in the back of my mind that it was wrong.

By letting him have his way on bonuses, which should have been agreed by the players, I left the room feeling very uncomfortable.

Indeed, by 8am the next day I was back in front of him and Luke Raine, to tell George that I had changed my mind, and that the bonus system he had come up with would not be acceptable to the players or staff.

He pointed out that I had agreed to it the previous evening, and could not change my mind. I said that I could.

I had suddenly gone from being club manager to union leader, and we had another big bust up which ended without agreement.

That Sunday there was a small story in the News Of The World about his bust up with the players. The chairman phoned me at around 7.30am and asked whether I had seen it. Of course I hadn't, but when I did I told him that it would be tomorrow's fish and chip wrappings. But he told me that there would be a response to it.

I asked the players who had spoken to the News Of The World, then left them to discuss it. They then told me that none of them had, and I believed them. I also asked the chairman, and he was adamant that it wasn't him.

He said they had done him up, and he would show the world what they were like. I didn't know what he was going to do, but I soon found out.

He handed all their wage dealings over to the Northern Echo. They printed it, without even speaking to me.

I felt it was disgraceful, and caused untold problems. The players were all on different amounts from £75,000 a year downward. But they were all equally important to me.

Of course it caused resentment among wives, girlfriends and families.

I told George straight that I thought it was a scandal. But he was waiting with his answer: "Don't worry. It will be wrapping tomorrow's fish and chips."

I asked the Professional Footballers' Association to defend the players. I don't know whether they made more than one call to George.

I knew that I had to get Neil Heaney, our highest paid player, out of the club. It wasn't fair on him, because every time he made a mistake on the pitch – which wasn't very often – or was out injured, the fans would have used it against him now that they knew that he was top earner.

Dundee United manager Paul Sturrock wanted him, and while Neil desperately wanted to stay because he loved his season with us, he knew he had to move on. The fee was £150,000 that Neil ended up getting himself. His agent had rung to say that they would sue us if he suffered any stress because of his salary being disclosed and fans giving him a hard time.

By then we had started to lose key players, and not long afterwards Peter Duffield, Michael Oliver and Paul Holsgrove had all followed Heaney, Tuts and Gabbers through the exit door.

Throughout all this time I was trying to persuade star defender Craig Liddle to stay with the club, because he was thinking of moving on. It was an horrendous time.

We had a tournament in the Isle of Man lined up, and the organisers paid for twenty players to go over there. I wanted to take two or three more, but the chairman wouldn't sanction it. In the end we paid for them out of the players' pool money.

Whenever a club goes away on a pre-season tournament, especially like the Isle of Man where four British teams are to take part, you must always take some sort of pennant or souvenir to hand out before every game.

However Lisa, the club's football secretary forgot, and, I must admit, so did I.

So by the time the first game against Stoke City came along, we were in an embarrassing position. We had nothing to present to them.

At half time in the game I decided to write on the back of the pennant that Stoke had given us: "Sorry, we're skint. The money has dried up."

Even though they had an Icelandic manager, his English was quite good and found it funny, as did his assistant Nigel Pearson, a former Sheffield Wednesday teammate of mine.

Of course we had all sorts of club souvenirs back home that we could have taken, but had too many other problems to think about at the time we left.

But the occasional light-hearted moment didn't compensate for what was going on. I sat at Durham one day with a couple of our keenest fans, Dave Hardisty, and his mate Peter. They asked me what was going to happen, and I answered them honestly. I said I didn't know.

I had managed to sign only a couple of players, though I had Ton Kaak, a young Dutch striker, as a possibility. I had agreed with him and his agent that we would make a final decision about him after the pre-season tournament in Scarborough, and not before.

However the chairman had taken it upon himself to announce publicly that we were to sign a Dutch international. It was only because a radio station contacted me at Durham, where we were training, to say that George was signing a player, that I found out that he had made the announcement.

Within a minute I was in my car making my way to Shildon to block the signing of Ton. I made it quite clear in front of Ton, his agent, and the chairman – and there was a loud speaker in the background – that the only man to sign players was I.

As far as I was concerned the lad had to prove he was good enough to play for Darlington, and not just become part of a propaganda war.

We played the Isle of Man tournament, and then went to Norton to play a friendly – part of the deal for them letting us use their facilities before Wembley.

Bt the atmosphere was terrible, and Barrie Geldart, an old and trusted friend, said to me that something was not right.

Then I received a couple of messages from my mate George Spriggs urging me to ring him. Before I had the chance, the chairman, who was due to go on holiday, suggested we have a meeting at Feethams to clear the air and attempt to take things forward.

I told him that if it developed into a fiasco, I would leave. Monty, Benno and Butts were all there, with the players, as were Luke Raine and Bernard Lowery.

There were four chairs at the front of the room, but I didn't sit there. Instead I stood with the staff.

The chairman talked about this and that, then said: "All those under contract go to that side of the room. All out of contract, go to the other side."

I said: "Hold on, nobody is going to split them up," but George said he would find out who would accept the bonuses. I told the staff not to move. The chairman said that my problem was that I wanted to run with the fox and hunt with the hounds.

I told him that the problem he had with me was that I didn't have a George Reynolds head on my shoulders. I told him I would solve his problem there and then by resigning. I walked straight out of the door, leaving him talking to the players.

I got in my car and breathed the biggest sigh of relief ever.

I rang Beverley and she said: "That must have been a short meeting." I said it was for me, because I had resigned.

Almost immediately Butts rang me, but Monty and Benno didn't. Butts said: "Please tell me you're coming back." I told him there was no chance, so he said that he was coming with me.

Then Paul Heckingbottom rang and said that the players needed to see me. I said that we would meet in the usual place – Blackwell Grange Hotel.

Whenever I resigned from Darlington I went to Blackwell Grange. The players asked me to return, and I said that I couldn't and explained what had been going on. I then shook hands with all of them, and apologised to Stuart Elliott, whom I had just signed. However I had told him when he signed what might happen.

Hecky was particularly cut up, and it was lads like him that I felt for. He had never let me down, and he clearly thought the same about me. Leaving the players is always the hardest part, because they are what football is all about. Working with players is why you become a manager.

Butts told me that within thirty minutes of me leaving, Benno and Monty were sorting out salaries with the players. I'm led to believe that Benno had wanted to walk out with me, but Monty had persuaded him to stay, pointing out that bust ups and resignations were common place in football. But I will never know whether that was the case.

Ton Kaak and Mark Angel were given deals straight away, as was Andy Collett, who had been told that I didn't want him, which was totally untrue.

Then George Spriggs rang me and I immediately apologised, telling him I had forgotten to return his call after receiving his messages.

He had urgently wanted to get in touch with me to find out what was happening because he had heard on Five Live radio that I had resigned. He said that he had been trying to get hold of me for four or five days to inform me that the chairman had spoken about the issue to Mark Meynell's father, who had a thriving pet shop business in Shropshire.

Mark was a season ticket holder, and at the time, I believe, an associate director. I'm led to believe that the conversation between George and Mr Meynell went something like: "Hodgy won't be in charge for the first game of the season (at Rochdale). Benno and Monty will be in charge of football affairs (though he didn't say whether I would still be at the club in any capacity)

George Spriggs couldn't get his head round this, and was trying to tip me off. That made me more convinced that the meeting before George's holiday was part of a stitch up.

I had told George that if he split the players, I would leave, so I think he did it deliberately.

I was angry with Benno, and wasn't too chuffed a little later when he said that no team of his would lie down and die, implying that mine had. But he was part of my team, and when he was coming to the end of his playing career, was paid for the best part of a year without kicking a ball. But it's water under the bridge. I get on fine with him now. Monty was right in a way. Football is a volatile business and when people leave a job, others must take it if it is offered to them.

I wrote an official letter of resignation, a nice letter saying that George and I were no longer compatible, but thanking him for certain things. When I took it to him, he threw it on the table, and told Luke to read it. Luke did, and George said: "Fine."

I'm told he later told people that I had begged to stay, which was nonsense. I believe that he greatly increased some of the wages to persuade players to stay, but I don't think that the public was told about that.

It was propaganda to make the fans think that the players were happy to stay without me. But it backfired because when the team struggled, the crowds dropped and there was less income for the club.

That said, George saved on the win bonuses!

The propaganda war; "Come into the studio and have your say"

I felt a huge weight lift off my shoulders when I left Feethams for the last time. So many meetings, so many arguments, so many disagreements, so many phone calls had taken their toll on me. I was mentally exhausted. Martin and Jackie Corney, good friends of Beverley and me, had told me that my character had changed incredibly, while Beverley and the girls had also said that I was bad tempered too often.

There was a piece in the Northern Echo the day after I resigned, which referred to a quote by the chairman at a fans' forum. "He who has the gold rules," he had said. At that point, I knew exactly what it meant.

I had got to the end. It was clear that I was never going to win the battle against the chairman, because when I thought we'd reached an agreement, he would come back with something else, or move the goalposts.

I felt that I couldn't get him to see common sense about how to run a football club. He seemed absolutely determined to do things his way, and his way only. So for the first time ever, I put my own interests before Darlington Football Club's. The chairman had said that I would never be sacked, but one of us had to give in the end.

Shortly after I arrived home, and feeling relaxed for the first time in ages, I looked out my window and saw Ian Kenyon from BBC Radio Cleveland wandering up and down outside my gates, trying to work out, presumably, where my house was.

So I grabbed the kitchen intercom, which was connected to a speaker next to the front gate. "Are you looking for me, Ian?" I called in a deep voice.

He didn't know where the voice was coming from until I walked into our front garden.

Radio Cleveland's interview was the first since my departure, but I resisted the temptation to criticise the chairman. I told Ian that my resignation was because I wanted to spend more time with my family, and that I was mentally tired.

A few days later, it was my 40th birthday, and Beverley treated me to a fantastic weekend in New York, which we had previously agreed. It was a certainly a case of getting away from it all.

I understand afterwards that George told people that I'd asked for my job back. Typical George. There is no way I would have gone back under the circumstances. When I left the office after handing in my letter of resignation, Luke Raine pulled me aside and said: "Do you realise what you have done?"

I replied: "Yes. I've escaped. This isn't a normal life. This isn't the way that football should be run. No manager should have to go through this."

Luke replied: "Your troubles have only just begun. He hates rejection. Nobody walks away from him."

I was accused of walking out deliberately to sabotage the club before the season started, but that was ridiculous. There were so many arguments, discussions, and long meetings that I just couldn't take any more. Even if the season was one week away, or it was three months old, I would still have walked out.

The chairman also increased the wages of some of the players, and even doubled Craig Liddle's. But in my opinion that was just to convince the fans that the players had stayed because I'd left.

My personal life then became horrendous for over a year. Every time I spoke to somebody, it appeared that I'd been bad-mouthed about one thing or another.

The chairman blamed me for the players' contracts, but that was incorrect. I didn't do anybody's contracts, either the management team or the players. The chairman did all that within a budget, and signed them. Yes, I talked figures with the players involved, but that was always with the chairman's knowledge and backing. He always met the person concerned to finalise the deal in writing, as well as talking to them about the plans he had for the future. Neil Heaney was a particular bone of contention, but more of that later.

It seemed that no matter which game I went to see, somebody there had spoken to the chairman.

Barry Fry at Peterborough did a piece in a Sunday newspaper article, during the Isle of Man tour, about the chairman, but after I spoke to Barry, he retracted it the following week.

The chairman said that we had the biggest budget in the Third Division, but that was incorrect. To my knowledge at least five clubs had bigger budgets than us that season. I believe that they were Northampton, Peterborough, Hull, Swansea and Carlisle.

The first phone calls started a week or so after my official resignation. One in particular, was about Neil Heaney's car. The chairman maintained that I was responsible for paying AMEC for the car, but I pointed out that it was a personal deal between Neil and AMEC, nothing at all to do with me. Needless to say, I refused to pay.

The war intensified when I decided to go back to being an agent.

I joined a company called Pro Active, which was run by Paul Stretford. It was a Manchester-based company, and Paul had come a long way since our meeting six years earlier.

When the chairman heard about it, I'm led to believe that he phoned Pro Active, and made an allegation, which was not correct, in reference to the deal in which Paul Robinson and Jamie Coppinger were transferred to Newcastle.

The transfer money had all been dealt with quite legitimately through the FA, who had handled all the payments for the deal. Kenny Dalglish didn't even get involved at the Newcastle end; he left it all to club official Russell Cushing, once he decided that he wanted the pair of them. It was, after all, Russell Cushing's job to look after transfers.

I went to the League Managers' Association for their help in recovering the considerable sum of money I was owed by the club from the sale of players and training equipment that I had bought out of my own pocket.

The chairman of the LMA, John Barnwell, called me for some information, and a day later, after speaking to the chairman, came back to me and said: "Do you know what we're dealing with here?" Obviously, he'd had an eventful call, and eventually the LMA said that it didn't want to take the case on. They felt that because there was a possibility the matter could lead to court action, they didn't have the funds to represent me.

People from inside the club kept in touch with me. They told me that on match days the chairman was making every effort when talking to visiting directors, to turn the conversation to me. He talked to them about the amount of money I had spent, bonuses, cars, and all manner of expense. I must admit, I was very concerned.

I felt that, if I wanted to go back into management, I had a decent record to present to other clubs, considering that I'd built teams at Darlington with hardly any cash outlay and they'd climbed up the league.

The possibility of taking over at Halifax cropped up. I spoke to Ian Butterworth, who told me that he was interested as well because he was out still out of work, so I applied for the job, with Butts as my assistant.

I arrived early at Halifax, and waited outside in my car to see who else was in for the job. Three people, who were just ordinary fans on the board, interviewed me and I ended up virtually interviewing them!

At the end of my interview, they said that the job would be mine if I let them know my intention the next day, but I asked for time to consider. I wasn't too sure whether it was the right step, with all due respect to them and to the Halifax club. I was worried that I was going into the same sort of situation I had found myself in first time round at Darlington in 1995.

I set off home, and later in the evening I discovered that the chairman of Halifax had met George at a game against Bradford the same night of my interview.

I spoke to Butts, and told him that if we went to Halifax, we'd be making a big mistake.

So I faxed a letter to Halifax, withdrawing my application.

The Plymouth job came up. I received calls from journalists at Plymouth newspapers about it, and I must admit that I was interested.

But suddenly Plymouth's interest in me faded, and I discovered that had happened after the Plymouth chairman, Dan McAuley, had called George.

It seemed as if people were prepared to ignore the positives, and listen to the so-called negatives.

The propaganda war; "Come into the studio and have your say"

Some time later, I helped take a player called Jason Bent to Plymouth, and I had cause to meet Paul Stapleton, the new Plymouth chairman, over the terms of the player's contract.

He admitted that he wasn't looking forward to meeting me because he had heard bad things about me, but after a few minutes he said: "You're exactly the opposite. None of what I've been told is true."

But the war continued.

I had a meeting with my accountant, Andrew Green in Sheffield, one day, and I phoned him from the car asking for directions to his office.

I arrived there a few minutes later, and his secretary told me to go straight in.

No sooner had I walked in, then his phone rung. "Hello, it's George Reynolds," said a familiar voice. "Is that Hodgson's money man?"

Talk about coincidence, it was really spooky.

I grabbed the phone, and asked George: "Who are you to ring my accountant?"

"Dodgy dealings," he said.

I slammed the phone down, and carried on with the meeting.

A couple of hours later, while I was on the motorway, Beverley called me, and I could tell she was upset. "You must ring Andrew Green," she said.

So I did, and Andrew was very upset. "I'm sorry for what I've done, but George Reynolds threatened me, so I had to fax up all your details."

I couldn't believe it, although I could understand Andrew's position.

I drove home quickly, charged straight into the house, grabbed a bin liner, argued briefly with Beverley, put all my paperwork inside – cheque stubs, files, the lot – and drove straight to George's office in Shildon.

I charged up the steps, stormed into his office, and flung the bin liner into his lap. "You can keep this lot, it's all in there," I shouted.

We had a huge argument, probably the worst we ever had, lasting half an hour.

Eventually he said: "We must put an end to this. Let's shake hands, it's all over." I took that as a genuine gesture, and walked out, taking the bin liner with me.

But later that day, Luke phoned me and said: "It isn't all over yet."

You can bet it wasn't.

Something else sinister happened. I took my daughters to school one day, and was met by Stuart Gibson in the car park. I thought he'd broken down, and wanted a lift somewhere.

I took the girls into school, and then Stuart and I sat in the car.

"Your house could be bugged," he said, and he proceeded to tell me the details of a telephone conversation I'd had the night before with Darlington player Paul Heckingbottom over a stomach strain he had. I believe that it may have been possible for anyone listening in to hear only what I said and not what the person at the other end of the line was saying. But Stuart had been told, by the chairman, some details of the call.

This was scary. I contacted a friend, who made a private call to the police, and in no time officers arrived at my house, with equipment to check the house. They swept it from top to bottom, and checked the telegraph pole opposite, looking for any device that could record conversations. The police used sophisticated equipment, and while this was going on there had to be complete silence in the house. Everyone held their breath. You could have heard a pin drop. As it turned out, they found nothing suspicious.

Neil Aspin and Stuart signed letters to the FA and the police that they had heard details of the telephone conversation in the presence of the chairman.

The police advised me to be careful who I talked to and what I said. But I must stress that I had no physical evidence that anyone bugged the house – though it's worrying when you hear that people have repeated conversations you thought were private.

And to make the situation more mysterious, there were several occasions that Luke and I were dragged into conversations with George about his boast that he had the advantage over his rivals, by being able to listen into their conversations.

Some of his tales were fascinating, especially in the early days of his reign at the club, and I lost count of the number of times he said he would show us the latest devices, which he claimed were tucked away in boxes at Shildon.

But he always seemed to come out with the story that somebody had moved them, or say 'can you see onto that top shelf?' knowing fine well that we couldn't.

So in all the times the conversation came up I never saw any of the devices, so have no idea whether they existed at all. So I could not point the finger at him.

But whatever the truth of it, one good thing did come out of the saga at my house. The house became a whispering zone – and I made the most of it. In a house like ours with two noisy little girls, it was heaven!

The war, for want of a better word, hit new heights on Century Radio.

One day, again on the school run, I stopped in the school car park, and one of the mothers, Anna Noble, came up to me and asked if I was listening to Century. I was also getting a couple of strange looks from some of the other parents. Obviously, something was wrong.

So I quickly dashed into school with the girls, dashed back out again, jumped into the car, and turned on the radio in time to hear George on Goffy's programme.

He was on the programme regularly, apparently, but on this occasion he ripped into the players, and a few minutes later, started on me. I was told later, by Hartlepool manager Chris Turner who was also in the studio, that they were supposed to be talking about the derby match that was coming up a few days later.

He ranted on about bonuses, about contracts, about signings, about everything.

I stopped the car – I think I was in Staindrop Road – and phoned Goffy's studio.

His producer put me straight through to Goffy, who asked me if I was sure I wanted to go on air.

I'm told that George thought that this was a set up, because I'd reacted so quickly to what he'd said, but bearing in mind what had been going on in the previous few months, I wouldn't set him up in a million years.

Goffy put me live on air, and there was an exchange of words between George and me.

I must admit that I was angry, and not as composed as I should have been, but I told George that he was talking a load of rubbish, twisting everything to make it sound as if he had been cheated.

Goffy suggested, "Come into the studio and have your say," and George said "Yes, let's have a head to head."

I didn't want it to become a circus, so I said to Goffy, "I'll come on the radio by myself if I get the same airtime as George. It's impossible for me to reply in a 30 second radio show to what George is coming out with."

George tried to make a point about the contracts he'd spoken about being right or wrong and I said: "The contracts are right because you are reading the figures out, but why have the public not been told the salaries these players were on at their previous clubs."

George replied that a lot of them were First Division, to which I responded: "You wanted to go to the Premier Division."

He retorted: "Yes, but with first division wages we got no result", and again I replied: "Excuse me, aren't you the chap who actually said you wanted this type of player at the football club, to increase the hype of your arrival at the club, and raise your profile?"

Some people told me at the time that I was being set up by Goffy and George, but I didn't think that was the case. Goffy was brilliant with me at the time, making private calls to me to reassure me before the final interview.

He promised me that all we would talk about would be within the context of the interview between him and George.

He admitted he was milking the situation, because his ratings were going through the roof. I had no problem with that, because that was his job.

I know that people had previously changed stations when George went on his programme, but when a date was set for my response, the listening figures indeed rocketed.

I could have pulled out, but I was adamant to go through with it. I got a flood of calls from friends, the LMA, the FA, family, and even the police, suggesting that I didn't do it, but this was a perfect opportunity to respond to the allegations. I wanted to tell my side of the story of my relationship with George.

George wanted to come in at the same time, but Goffy refused, saying that a deal's a deal. It was just Goffy and me in the studio, no calls from listeners.

In the days before the interview, I even stopped listening to Century because of all the plugging that was going on – there seemed to be a trail every few minutes! Goffy even played the record "Two Tribes" on some occasions for a bit of mischief.

A couple of days before the show, I received a call from a withheld number. The voice of a woman said. "Don't do the radio show, because George Reynolds is plotting your downfall."

I told Beverley, and she insisted that I shouldn't do the programme, but the call had made me more determined than ever.

An hour later, Luke Raine rang. He always said that if he knew something was going to happen, he would let me know. He said I must either pull out, or I was stupid, then he quickly put the phone down.

Maybe it was a ploy to get into my head, I don't know.

I sat in a room for two nights, studying every piece of paper. I drove up to the studios in Gateshead really early, listening to Goffy's programme on the way.

I told the whole story as it was. I was asked if I could turn the clock back, would I do anything different?

"No, I wouldn't," I replied. "Without doubt, it was the best year I've ever had. Put aside all the fighting, both professional and personal, I wouldn't change it for the world."

I explained about the bonuses, how they were calculated, who calculated them, and who agreed them.

I explained about the salary of Neil Heaney, whose wages were top of the list when the Northern Echo had published them the previous summer. Neil had been on £154,000 per year at Manchester City.

He came for a £72,708.33 basic salary, less than half his salary at Manchester City, but the lure of playing for the club in the direction the chairman wanted to take us in was a big attraction.

The bonus system was made up by achievement only. Nobody got a bonus unless they played; nobody got a win bonus unless we were in the top three, or unless the team was in fourth to seventh position. Nobody got appearance money unless they entered the field.

Neil Heaney achieved some aspects of the bonus system, others he didn't. In the end, he made £139,251.33 at Feethams.

It sounds a lot, but remember the chairman, who wanted to climb straight into the Premiership agreed everything before he signed — and he had everything explained to him by Mark Hayton, his accountant, and myself.

I explained about players' cars, and why they weren't part of their contracts. No player had a car written into his contract because it was a taxable problem. Instead, our players had a deal set up through motor dealer Reg Vardy, with the help of Ian Parker, and they paid for their own vehicles.

I talked about my relationship with George. I said that he was a genius with money, and that never in my lifetime had I known anyone who was so good at money.

He was also a genius with hype — he sold a product at the football club better than anyone else, and I was delighted to be a part of it.

It was an amazing experience to work with George to start with. The unfortunate thing was, football was no longer the issue towards the end of my days at the club. I learned one hell of a lot of business sense from George, and I put that in writing to him, but at the end the football club was no longer going in the direction a football club should have been going in, considering that we were supposed to have been going from the Third Division to the Premier League.

The interview was broadcast live at about 8.30 in the morning. I was on for about thirty minutes, and I'm told George listened to the whole interview, turned to the staff and said: "I'll take my hat off to him, not once has he bad-mouthed me."

I had no intention of bad mouthing him, because it wouldn't have solved anything, probably only created more problems for other people and me. Two wrongs didn't make a right in my view.

The propaganda war took another twist on 8th April 2001 – the date is etched in my mind.

We had been on holiday, and when we touched down at Teesside Airport, Beverley phoned her mother. "Whatever you do, don't read the News of the World," she said.

Well, what would you do? Curiosity obviously got the better of me. In it, there was a big headline "FA probe £84,000 fees" and a piece by reporter Ray Ryan alleging that I wrongfully took a slice of the Jason DeVos transfer fee when he moved to Dundee United. He tried to substantiate his piece with a copy of a document, which had my address on it.

To say that we were distraught on reading this was an understatement.

Two weeks earlier Tony Henry had called me to say that a national newspaper was chasing up the relationship between Tony and me, and whether there was still a connection between us. So I was aware that something was going on, but didn't expect this.

The Northern Echo phoned, and asked to see me because they'd been given certain documentation by George regarding the Jason DeVos transfer. One document in particular was a so-called invoice from my old company, European Sports Promotion, which showed Beverley as a director.

They came to see me with these particular documents, and I told them that if they were used, I would sue. Instead, I showed them copies of letters from the FA, which showed that the transfer was completely in order.

Tony Henry, who was now running the agency, said that he'd received a call from the News of the World whilst I was away, but didn't comment at the time.

And also while I was on holiday, I'd received a simple text message, "please ring Ray Ryan at the News of the World." However, no phone number was left. That was all; nothing to say what he was ringing about, no indication of what was to come. That was how in the piece he'd managed to write that I was unavailable for comment. I was on holiday, after all, so I just ignored it. I didn't even know who Ray Ryan was – and he only tried once to contact me.

The story was completely untrue, but there was a lot of damage done. I knew people were talking about it and making reference to it.

I phoned the News of the World, and managed to speak to the Sports Editor demanding a retraction, and if one wasn't printed, then I'd sue.

But I got nowhere, instead the person concerned spoke to me as if I was nobody, and it was clear he wasn't going to back down.

I rang the Football Association, and they confirmed that they had no intention of carrying out an investigation, because I'd done everything properly and legally regarding Jason's transfer – after all, they'd approved all the documents. They had been asked a question in the original piece about managers acting as agents, and a spokesman had said that it was against the rules – but it was only a general question, not one specific to me.

Once I heard those words, then I breathed a sigh of relief, and I knew I was going to win the libel case I was putting into motion.

I felt as if my credibility had gone, whenever I went into town shopping or to pick my children up from school. I felt that everyone knew about the article, and that they were judging me. It even got to the point where Beverley said we should move away, but that wouldn't have made any difference. If we moved away, then George would have achieved what he may have sought to do all along – get me out of the area.

Loads of people rang me to talk about the situation and offer me support. But because my full address had been printed in the News Of the World — which should not have been allowed to happen — people used to drive along the lane outside our house, just to see where we lived – and then we laughed as they realised that they were driving up a cul-de-sac, and had to reverse into the farmer's field at the end to turn around. I even used to pop out of the house and help them do three point turns when I was feeling mischievous.

At the time, I was working for Pro Active, and they were about to float the company on the stock exchange. I was really concerned that the article would cause them damage because of my association with them.

Paul Stretford asked if the story was true, and I put him straight. He said that they would stand by me, but I would have to understand that the company would come first. I could see where he was coming from, and I decided that it was in everyone's best interests that I resign from the company. I was out of work.

The story affected my family. Beverley was distraught, because she'd been named in the News of the World article, and that's when the effects started to kick in.

I phoned George, and told him what he had done was disgusting. He said that Beverley was a director of the agency, and was still operating as an agent. I told him that she wasn't. When he had come to the club, I had Beverley removed as a director by Companies House – and I had the paperwork to prove it. And she had never acted as an agent. In fact she didn't even know our players, let alone any other club's players.

Meanwhile, George was apparently saying that he was going to bankrupt me, that Beverley wouldn't be going to Saks to have her hair done, and the kids wouldn't have shoes to wear. That's how bad it was. That really hurt.

It was a huge change in attitude by George towards Beverley. When Beverley found she had skin cancer – which she has now happily beaten – he sent her a card, with the verse "We will love you until the desert turns to ice, and the camels come sliding home." What a lovely, profound thought that was, an incredible comment. The same man was now going to great lengths, for no reason, to destroy me. I hadn't even criticised him since I'd left. This was the George Reynolds that people had earlier told me about.

I contacted the News of the World, and set up a meeting with Ray Ryan and my lawyer Bill O'Hanlon, from Crutes, in Middlesbrough.

I showed him all the documentation from the Jason DeVos transfer, explained it all in depth, and asked him to run an apology and a retraction. He said that he would, but nothing came of it.

In the light of that decision, I decided to sue. After all, I was in the right, they were in the wrong. They had libelled me, printed untruths.

Terry Venables, who wrote a weekly column, told me that the newspaper would deny it all, until the story no longer existed in people's minds, and they would hope it would be quietly swept under the carpet. He should know, for he has had his fair share of libel cases.

That was no good to me, I had been wronged. Unless I got them to accept my innocence, I was always going to be tainted in the eyes of other people. I wouldn't have been able to walk around Darlington without somebody nudging someone else.

I knew that if I was going to take it all to court, I would have to spend a considerable amount of money in barristers' fees, so Beverley and I put aside a lump sum. My solicitor warned me that there was a possibility that people might try and find skeletons in the cupboard, but there weren't any to find. Everything was above board. I had always kept records, and had them approved by the authorities. I had plenty of paperwork.

The News of the World came back with two proposals, and I rejected them. The article had cost me a living from football. I had to resign from Pro Active, plus no management offers had come along. For a good six months after the article was published, I'd been forced to live on savings.

I was adamant, and stood my ground, and two days before the case was due to be heard, the News of the World contacted my solicitors and we agreed a settlement – five figure compensation, my legal costs and an apology. I was vindicated.

There was a really funny incident one day in the Imperial Express restaurant in Darlington when the propaganda war was its height. Can you remember the western films, in which the villain walks into the saloon bar wanting to shoot the sheriff and the whole place stops, partly in fright, partly in expectation, and people put their heads down?

One day, Beverley and I were finishing a meal in the Imperial Express, and across the road, we saw George and his wife Sue, buying some flowers.

We thought that he wouldn't come in, but he turned around and walked across the street into the restaurant.

There's quite a good atmosphere in there, especially when there are a lot of people inside, just like this particular day.

But the whole place stopped, and fell silent. People stopped drinking, eating and talking, and instead just watched as George walked slowly across the room.

If looks could kill, Beverley would have been tried for murder.

George then had the nerve to hold his arms out, and said: "David, my friend. How are you?"

"I would be a lot better if I didn't have to put up with all this hassle," I replied, through gritted teeth.

I think he expected a further reaction, but Beverley and I kept our dignity, and walked out. I think he got the point. People then restarted their meals and conversations!

Maybe the war eased after the News of the World piece, although there were still occasions when my name resurfaced. It certainly did at the fans' forum a year later in Susan Reynolds' speech before the players walked out.

I considered seeking legal advice on suing her for comments made about me, but I decided not to.

But none of the unsavoury incidents around this time affected my love for the club. For ages, I listened to the match commentaries on the radio. There was one occasion I was listening to Radio Cleveland when we played Hartlepool, and goalkeeper Andy Collett was keeping Hartlepool out on his own. It was so one-sided, I couldn't believe it, so I switched radio stations, and Century was saying exactly the same.

Beverley would go berserk with me while I sat in the house listening to what was going on, and making comments.

No matter what part of the world I was in, I would receive a score alert on my mobile – the Bradford City game in the Worthington Cup cost me a fortune because the lads lost 7-2!

The fact that I still wanted to know every one of Darlington's results, and the detail, proved that my love of the club had not diminished even though I had been through such an ordeal with the chairman.

And even when the next episode of my career took me thousands of miles away, the football club was never far from my thoughts.

16

Don't cry for me Darlo; Life in Argentina

After leaving Darlington, I had a total break from football for three months, which coincided with my daughters' school holidays and so the situation was perfect for Beverley.

Kenny Dalglish contacted me on three occasions, wanting to talk to me about a project he wanted me to join, but I told him that I would only speak to him on November 1st.

As good as his word, he rang at about 8pm on October 31st.

I was led to believe that he wanted to talk to me about soccer coaching schools, but instead he wanted to talk to me about an agency, Pro Active, of which he was a director.

Paul Stretford, who was also a director of the agency, wanted me to link up with them.

I had only one slight concern, which was that I had to travel once or twice a week to Pro Active's office in Manchester. I didn't mind travelling up and down the country once a fortnight with Darlo, but going to Manchester twice a week somehow didn't appeal to me.

I decided to give it six months, but because my name found itself in that News of the World article, the decision about my future with them was virtually made for me. The story couldn't have come at a worse time because Pro Active was floating on the Stock Exchange, so in order to save any embarrassment, I resigned and formed my own company.

I believed that I could still make a success of being an agent again because I felt that my record of being able to buy and sell players was as good as anybody in the business.

No more than a couple of months had passed when I got a call from Leon Angel, who was Neil Heaney's representative when he signed for Darlo, from the Base Soccer agency in London.

I liked Leon enormously so I didn't really want to turn down the offer of becoming a consultant for all overseas affairs.

By then I was back in the business at full flow. Trips to France, Scandinavia and Austria were becoming frequent, and I was talking to many players and clubs as well as watching games. It was during one of those overseas trips, to the Czech Republic, that I bumped into an old friend of mine who was working on a move to bring Diego

Three times a Quaker

Forlan from Independiente to England.

I brought back three videos of Forlan, which I studied very closely over the following few days. I was convinced that he could play at Premiership level, so my first port of call was Peter Reid at Sunderland. I put together a CV of Forlan, re-recorded the video to make it look more presentable, and took it to Sunderland.

Peter's response was immediate – he wanted me to bring Forlan to Sunderland for three days' training, with a view to signing him permanently.

Unfortunately, Independiente weren't prepared to accept the type of deal that Sunderland proposed, and the move broke down.

I kept looking at the videos over and over again, and it was during this time that I realised a player alongside Forlan, Matias Vicente Vuoso, also looked very good.

I then called an agent in Cadiz, Marcello Betnaza, who was very knowledgeable of the South American market, and had been recommended to Base by Terry Venables a couple of years earlier.

Marcello knew the player immediately and within hours of my request had all the facts and figures that I required, should I want to pass them on to any interested club in England.

Within days of speaking to Marcelo about Vuoso, Forlan's name appeared in the national sports headlines about a move to Middlesbrough, which appeared to be done, even Middlesbrough manager Steve McClaren thought so as well when he spoke to me.

Steve was convinced that he was going to sign Forlan as well as Dwight Yorke from Manchester United, two players who would have been excellent signings. But right out of the blue came Manchester United, and stole Forlan from underneath Boro's noses, and Yorke went to Blackburn instead.

The alarm bells started to ring in my head immediately. I knew that Kevin Keegan at Manchester City was looking for a young striker at that moment, and I was quickly on the phone to Arthur Cox, whom I'd known for many years. He was a straight talking, no nonsense type of bloke and would give me a straight yes or no if I asked him if City were interested.

I explained to Arthur about this young player and it was only by sheer luck that Dean Saunders of Blackburn, a good friend of Arthur's, had only been speaking to him a day or two earlier.

Dean had just spent a fortnight in Argentina looking at Forlan, but Vuoso had also caught his eye. Apparently he even told his boss at Blackburn, Graeme Souness, to forget about Forlan and go for Vuoso, but for some reason the deal never took place. Dean then phoned Arthur, his old manager from Derby, and he pointed out that Vuoso reminded him of Peter Beardsley, which as you can imagine from Arthur's days with Peter at Newcastle, went down very well. All this coincided with my information to Arthur.

I told Arthur that I was confident of getting Vuoso, so he asked me to go over there, and have a look at him, with a view of then persuading him to come to City for a week's trial.

It was to become one of the longest drawn out transfers from start to finish that I'd ever been involved in. The deal took ten months to complete.

Independiente had been approached, but after selling Forlan, they weren't keen on losing Vuoso until the end of their season.

I went with Frank Sibley, the ex QPR keeper, and a real gentleman who was in charge of City's overseas affairs. The fourteen-hour flight zoomed past as we talked about our many experiences with football.

We stayed in the Hilton hotel, which overlooks the Rio Plata in Buenos Aires and has an awesome view of the city.

Accompanied by the player's representatives, one of whom came from Herez in Spain, an area I was familiar with from my playing days, we went to see Independiente play River Plate.

Manchester City deliberately hadn't told Frank why he'd been asked to go to Argentina but after twenty minutes he knew who he was supposed to be looking at. Vuoso was very influential, his movement was outstanding and Frank turned to me and asked, "Who's that number ten?"

We went to a training session, in which Vuoso played in goal for some reason, and was the life and soul of the training session. Frank wanted to see the player at every opportunity.

We watched another game, Independiente versus Estudiantes that was more like a civil war! It took me back to my days of watching Newcastle against Sunderland. But again, even in that hostile environment, Vuoso shone.

On the way back to England, Frank told me he was going to recommend to Kevin Keegan that he should sign Vuoso. When I got back, we started the ball rolling, but there were a lot of negotiations with his club.

However, interest intensified from other clubs in the Premiership, but Kevin was determined to get his man and asked me to keep working on the deal.

I spent weeks and weeks on the deal, speaking to his Argentinean agent and his club.

Eventually, we cracked it. A £3.5 million fee was agreed with Independiente and the player, with a view to coming to City on £10,000 per week, when his wages in Argentina were just £500 per week.

He brought quite an entourage with him, ten in all, when he came to sign. His agent, his agent's agent, friends and the kitchen sink. We informed his hotel that only three of his entourage were there at our expense, but that didn't stop the seven from putting their expenses on to the bills of the other three, and our company copped a massive bill.

Agreeing the player's wages and the transfer fee was easy, but Independiente demanded bank guarantees from City to complete the deal, which was pretty rare.

Vuoso came back for the start of the 2002-03 season, and Arthur Cox was quite happy with his pre-season form in the friendlies. But then he nose-dived, and lots of things went wrong.

However to me, there was certainly an opening in Argentina. After all, I'd been a pioneer if you like in Europe when I'd originally started working as an agent, and I felt that I could use that experience to establish a supply line of players from Argentina to Europe. There was a demand for players who could turn games in the European leagues, players who had that little extra something that could swing a game.

So after talking to Beverley and the girls, I was able to convince them to uproot and head for Argentina. I was determined to make it work, but I was still in touch with what was happening over here. After all, it's easy to access the Internet from South America!

I had several deals lined up to Sunderland, Leeds and Birmingham, but they kept breaking down because of the excessive transfer fee demands of the clubs in Argentina.

I was quoted six million dollars by Estudiantes for an 18 year old who hadn't even played in their first team, so you can imagine the obstacles I was dealing with.

I picked out six players who I thought were capable of playing in the Premiership, but the problem was, they were all owned by agents, and not by the clubs. So in effect, I had to agree two transfer deals, one with the agent and the other with the club, as well as sorting out personal terms. The job was impossible at times, especially when disharmony crept in between the English company I was working for, and the Argentinean company we were partnering over there.

During the nine months we were out there, I watched 118 matches in Argentina and neighbouring Uruguay, which was just a short flight away.

Life was certainly different over there. There were kidnappings, shootings and murders, with a few political and social scandals thrown in for good measure as well.

We arrived at the wrong time of year, because it was their winter. We were dressed in light summer clothes at the airport; the locals were wearing something suitable for the wet weather. Beverley went crazy, but 70 degrees seemed like summer to me.

Home for the first three weeks was the Hilton Hotel in Buenos Aires, but we were advised not to go into the city centre because of anti-government demonstrations.

It was all right for me, because I went to football matches at weekends, leaving Beverley and the girls to fend for themselves. I must admit, the surroundings were a little sinister; there were security guards and policemen on every corner.

The cost of living was very cheap; the pound was worth ten pesos, which was worth a fortune to some people.

There was such a contrast between the haves and the have-nots. Obviously, we lived in a hotel, and later in a rented house, but some Argentineans lived in shantytowns, less than 100 yards away from us.

We looked at a compound that made Wynyard look like a minor housing estate.

It was full of magnificent houses, and was extremely well guarded with incredible facilities, such as restaurants, schools and every sports facility possible.

Unfortunately, some of the houses we looked at weren't furnished, which would have meant extra expense for only three months to begin with.

One day we looked at five different homes, and we finally settled for a house that wasn't even on the market.

It was only by chance that the lady who owned the house discovered that some English people – us – were looking for a house to rent directly opposite where she lived.

As we turned the corner into a cul-de-sac to look at the house that had been suggested to us, on the left hand side we saw a big blue house, which the girls took an instant dislike to, and they prayed that we wouldn't go and look at it.

We told the girls that we weren't, but we ended up viewing it when the lady concerned invited us in. It was certainly well furnished and the owners clearly came from a wealthy background. And the girls' views quickly changed when they realised that it had a magnificent swimming pool! The colour of the house no longer seemed important.

A three metre high wall surrounded the whole compound – it was a different part of the world in there, compared to the squalor and poverty on the other side.

There was a school on site, but the problem for the girls was that even though it was English-speaking, the curriculum was Spanish and Argentinean. Fortunately, we continued to pay the fees for Polam Hall, who generously agreed to keep their places open in the circumstances, and when we eventually came back to England, they were re-admitted there.

Football-wise, I kept my eyes on twenty teams, fifteen of whom played in Buenos Aires. I watched games, at various levels, all over the place.

I went to an Independiente game once with Antonio, my escort. A huge brawl broke out around us, and people were laying into each other. Then I lost Antonio in the mayhem, until I realised that he was standing a few rows of seats away, frantically waving at me to join him, while I was calmly watching the game.

I could see four games in one day, and fortunately I had a driver who took me to matches.

Good job, really, because driving was a nightmare. The main road from the city to St Georg, where we lived, consisted of eight lanes of madness, with neither slow lanes nor fast lanes. There were always pile-ups and there just didn't seem to be any rules of the road.

Police cars had no lights because there wasn't the money to repair them, car windscreens smashed because of the intense heat that was well over a hundred degrees. When I drove myself, I always made sure that I gave the kids who came up to the car outside the compound some coins – protection money I suppose!

The cost of living was cheap, so eating out became regular, just £10 for the four of us.

We went to one restaurant that had closed circuit television at the tables, so we could keep an eye on the kids in the play zone. We got on really well with the owner there, but I suppose we were regulars. One night though, we arrived and there was a long queue – and we discovered that he'd shot somebody and had escaped by jumping into a helicopter!

But even though it was a great lifestyle, it didn't suit Beverley and the girls. To be fair, they knew how much it meant to me to make the trip a success, but they were homesick.

There were growing problems with the Argentinean company we were working with, and it all came to a head when the transfer window was introduced in England.

Base suggested that I could stay, but they wouldn't pay all the bills. They would pay for a house, but not for the kids' schooling.

So one night I walked into the house and announced that we were going home. The place erupted! Beverley told me how much she and the girls had tried to make it work, but they were unhappy.

When I woke up the following morning, it really hit home how much the three of them had gone through. I thought they were loving it, but they weren't. Beverley, for example, couldn't go out of the compound without an escort; I suppose it was like a prison to them.

We were back home within ten days. Now what was I going to do?

17

Fighting the drop; "Never again, please."

Within a few months of returning from Argentina, I was back in the Darlington hot seat. How that came about is described in the next chapter – but you know me by now – football comes first and the priority was having a successful end to another incredible season.

I returned as manager again just two days before the away game at Oxford United – the only problem was, I couldn't go to Oxford because I had a long-standing family commitment. I was hoping that the chairman would delay announcing my return until the following week.

I knew some of the players, but not all of them. Some people spoke to me about them, and one comment was that two or three were no better than UniBond League standard. Mick Tait and Martin Gray also filled me in. But I had to see the players in action of some sort before I could make a real judgement.

I knew Craig Liddle and Neil Wainwright from my previous spell and what to expect from them but I didn't have a clue who some of the others were.

Lids actually thought before I arrived that we were Conference bound. The team had a good September, and Mick nearly won the manager of the month award, but some of the results in October were poor. Lids is a bit negative sometimes, but it's that very negativity which drives him on – he doesn't want what he's worried about to happen, if you see what I mean.

One of my first acts was to take the captain's armband off Lids and give it to Neil Maddison, because I thought with the problems Lids had off the field – his father was fighting cancer at the time – he had enough to contend with, rather than worrying about the team captaincy as well.

I received six letters from fans complaining about Lids losing the captaincy, one of which said that Maddo would lead us to the Conference, but I like to think that I made the right decision there, although Lids got the captaincy back for his 300th game for the club against Swansea later in the season.

Of the others, I knew David McGurk and Chris Hughes from before, because they were apprentices, but that was it, nobody else. I didn't have a clue.

I hardly knew Maddo. I met him briefly once in a health club in Darlington and we hardly spoke to each other, mainly because we hardly knew each other.

My impression then was that he was a bit arrogant, but since then I've come to like him immensely, and I haven't heard anybody say anything negative about him.

The Oxford game was an opportunity for Martin Gray to take charge of the team against his old club. He was a crowd favourite there during his playing days, and I think he relished the challenge.

I spoke to the players the day before the game, and told them what I expected from them. Plenty of hard work and a good attitude, and then afterwards we'd work on what I wanted in training.

However, to keep the players on their toes in the dressing room before the game, Martin told them that I was in the stand watching how they performed, how they reacted in certain situations, what their attitude was.

I wasn't at the game really, but I kept in touch with what was going on through the press lads on my mobile. My main concern was that the players worked hard, and apparently they did, losing 3-1 after taking the lead through David McGurk, who was later sent off along with Danny Mellanby.

I classed my first real game back away to Essex club Hornchurch in the FA Cup, one that we desperately needed to win for financial reasons. The club badly needed some cash from a Cup run.

But even though they played in the Rymans League, one step below the Conference, Hornchurch would be difficult opponents. Their weekly wage bill was higher than ours, because they had full time players, even at non-league level!

Martin marked my card about our players, and I made my mind up that Ryan Valentine should play on the right, and not the left, in order to give the team better balance.

And I also made my mind up that in most games we would play with three central defenders and two wing backs, which unfortunately meant that David McGurk, who I understand was one of the best players of the season until that point, would lose his place at the back.

The first training session must have made the players wonder what was going on. It was a real crash course in the way I wanted them to play, I had to analyse them, work out strengths and weaknesses. I also had to educate them to pass the ball better and move more off the ball. It was a case of them changing as quickly as possible.

From what I was told, in the past, there were too many fancy flicks and chips that gave away possession too cheaply. I drilled it into the players that I wanted them to pass the ball, and I almost lost my voice by the day of the game.

Barry Conlon earned my respect for playing at Hornchurch. He wasn't fit enough, but we didn't have any forwards apart from him. He was nowhere near fit, but he made the effort to play, and we were grateful for that. I'd heard rumours about his socialising, but he's lost his three chins now!

I must confess that I didn't know Danny Mellanby by sight. I'd heard plenty of good things about him, but I also knew about his injuries.

On the Monday after the Oxford game, I went to the training ground, speaking into my mobile on the way. I bumped into a lad with a shaven head, who said he wanted a word with me.

I didn't have a clue who he was, so I took him into the changing room, where one of the other players said "Hello, Danny." I knew who he was then! One of my first jobs was to lift him, because he was feeling down after being sent off the previous Saturday.

Ian Clark was worried about my attitude towards him, after what he'd said to me in the dressing room after the Hartlepool play-off game at Feethams. I'd gone into their dressing room after that game, and genuinely wished them all the best, only for Clarky to tell me where to go. It was a reaction I could understand after a play-off semi-final defeat.

The lads wound him up something terrible, saying that he would be the first out of the door, but I reassured him that I wasn't bearing any grudges. Twenty years ago in the same situation I would probably have thrown a boot if someone had said that to me.

I knew Gary Pearson, funnily enough from a friendly we'd had in the summer of 2000 at Durham, when we had a little dust up near the end of the game. I took exception to something Gary had done, and confronted him on the pitch, but at the final whistle I went into Durham's dressing room and apologised straight away, saying that I'd had a bad day with one thing and another. The year should give you a clue!

I addressed all the team, and while I was doing that, I was watching who was making eye contact and who wasn't. Wainy and Maddo looked at me, some of the others looked at the floor.

I explained what I wanted from them as players, and then said: "The chairman has promised that he will never be aggressive or abusive towards you. There'll be no more phone calls." And to this day, the chairman has kept his word. He has never contacted any of the players.

In that first training session, Ashley Nicholls stood out, with the way he powerfully ran with the ball, but I couldn't see the strengths of Joey Hutchinson and Ryan Valentine. Early days.

I had a horrible feeling of fate before the Hornchurch game. The day didn't seem quite right, maybe because we were playing on a Sunday, maybe because it was an unfamiliar ground, maybe because we were playing non-league opposition.

When I came back for my second spell, my first game was an away Cup tie, at Runcorn, and we were second bottom of the table.

There wasn't much difference this time round. For various reasons, the club was deep in the doldrums. A win at Hornchurch would give everybody a lift; provide some much needed prize money and hope of a lucrative cup run.

Some fans thought I gave Matt Clarke a rollicking before the game, but that was incorrect. All I asked of him was that he passed the ball correctly. To be fair to him, Matt had lost his confidence and was wary of me. But he improved as the season went on, and he won three player of the year awards at the end of the season.

Unfortunately, we lost 2-0 to a goal in each half, one of the goals a penalty awarded when Clark Keltie dived into a tackle and caught the man. There was no doubt about the task ahead on that display; the honeymoon was well and truly over after those ninety minutes. We didn't create many chances, confidence was low and our passing wasn't very good. I played Clarky up front with Baz, because Clarky had been very industrious in training, and Baz wasn't fully fit. But Clarky isn't a recognised striker; he's more suited to a wing back role.

I also emphasised to Clark Keltie that instead of diving into tackles, he should close players down instead, and force them into mistakes.

The next game was at home to Lincoln, my second homecoming.

I was given a warm reception as I walked across the field to the far side. I can't say that I walked across to the dugouts, because there weren't any – they had been repossessed – so instead we sat in the front row of the stand on the far side. There was no atmosphere at all, just thousands of empty seats.

It wasn't long before I had arranged for dugouts to be constructed in front of the main stand. I much prefer to have the public behind me so then they can keep me on my toes with their comments, and besides that, they might spot something nobody on the bench has. It's funny how an innocuous comment can turn out to be so important.

I didn't even have any kit, so I had to dig my kit from 2000 out of the cupboard and use that for training, and on matchday I went to TY McGurks and bought some. Since then, Peter Cook has been superb for the club with his Adidas connections, although we did have some kit stolen from a storeroom at Feethams.

I decided to use three strikers against Lincoln, because I didn't want to start the first home game with a defensive formation. Ross Turnbull, who we'd got on loan from Middlesbrough, had plenty of height and presence in goal, while I knew that Joey was quick and read the game well. Lids was his usual self, while Matt was good at heading the ball.

Maddo was essential in midfield, but I still wasn't sure of some players.

We drew the game 0-0, which wasn't a bad point against a team chasing promotion, and it ended a run of defeats for the team.

The next game was away to Swansea, one of my old clubs. We travelled down the night before, and stayed in a hotel which showed the Rugby World Cup final on television between England and Australia – and boy were the locals supporting Australia! They booed everything England did.

Mind you, I had an embarrassing moment beforehand. I knew of somewhere in Swansea where we could train beforehand, and I decided to have a light session the night before the game.

When we got there on the bus, the pitch was no more – there was a new housing estate on it. I had to turn round and apologise to the players, some of whom were doing their best to stifle the giggles. Instead, we improvised on some spare land at the hotel, and I was encouraged by what I saw.

We lost the game to a Lee Trundle goal, but we played some good football, although we never really looked like scoring because we still had a makeshift forward line. At least afterwards I didn't have to climb up the rusty ladder to the BBC press box as I did on my previous visit, because it had been moved.

Our next home game against Scunthorpe saw us throw away a two goal lead, and draw 2-2.

But afterwards, I truly felt a part of the club again, because I was annoyed with the manner in which we'd had two men sent off – Baz and Ryan – and thrown away victory in the last twenty minutes. It sparked off some negative comments, such as "Has this game cost Darlington their place in the league?" I wasn't very pleased at all about that, and I used those comments on the next occasion I spoke to the players. It was far too early for comments like that. I wasn't very happy either with the manner in which the players had cost themselves victory.

Neil Wainwright set a superb example to the rest of the players, to the point that I was worried he was going to burn himself out. He was all over the place, closing people down, making runs, tackling back – he was unbelievable – but on the plus side his efforts were rubbing off onto the other players.

From the first day right up to the end of the season, the players trained to their maximum. We had to be careful with them on the training ground. A full session lasted seventy five minutes, of which forty five minutes was the maximum for work. After that, I feel that players lose their concentration, they become sloppy and their enthusiasm disappears.

The fitness level was very good, and I would like to think that because we kept the sessions short, we avoided injuries that we couldn't really afford when we were very restricted to what we could do in terms of bringing players in. I can't recall a hamstring injury since I returned, nor can I recall many training ground injuries that kept players out of the team. I think our really good injury-free record was a big factor in us staying up at the end of the season. We would have been in deep trouble if, for example, we had four players missing for long spells.

Because we'd lost in the first round of the FA Cup, we brought forward our home game with York from later in the season, as they had also gone out of the competition. We needed the gate money badly, and it wasn't a bad three points either from a 3-0 win against a team in the top half of the table. That victory made a difference at the end of the season, because York slipped dramatically down the table after the turn of the year and were relegated. Baz, Wainy and Craig James, who was on loan from Sunderland, scored for us.

Lee Nogan, who was assistant manager at York, thought his team played poorly, but I thought we made them look poor with some very good football.

Unfortunately after that, the suspensions of Baz and Ryan kicked in, and they were costly. We lost our next three matches 1-0, and it was clear that without Baz in particular, our link-up play in the last third of the field disappeared.

We missed some good chances for a point at Cambridge, and we outplayed both

237

Macclesfield and Huddersfield at home, but just couldn't score.

We broke the sequence at Carlisle just after Christmas, when we drew 1-1, Lee Matthews, who I'd got on loan from Bristol City, scored for us, although he could have scored a winner.

Only Baz knows how he managed to miss so many chances at Leyton Orient, where again we lost 1-0, and then we lost 1-0 at home to Hull, even though we played the better football.

So you can imagine the mood that was beginning to descend over the club. Five out of our previous six were 1-0 defeats, only one point gained from a possible eighteen. Were the doom-mongers right? Were we heading for the Conference?

I never thought so, because I had belief in the players. They never gave up, never showed signs of buckling. Despite being paid late sometimes, the place was buzzing and the atmosphere was terrific.

I kept the players informed about what was happening with the administration every step of the way, so then they had no surprises from the media. I tried to keep the players happy, and they responded. Any player could have walked out, as they were entitled to, or ask for a transfer – but none of them did, and that speaks volumes for them.

Maybe I will upset the players of 2000 when I say that the 2004 players were a better squad, but that was because the 2004 team went through a lot more. There was pressure of a different kind in 2004, one that had the club's existence at stake.

It looked as if the sequence of 1-0 defeats was going to continue at Kidderminster as we trailed going into stoppage time. And then, sub Mark Sheeran raced to the byeline, crossed left footed to the far post, and there was David McGurk to force the ball home.

Talk about delight and relief! The players' celebrations at the final whistle showed that we had turned the corner, and there was a great atmosphere on the trip home. TY will never score a more important goal than that, no matter how long he plays football.

Everybody started to believe that we could get out of trouble. I knew it, the players knew it, and the fans knew it. TY's goal was the turning point of the season.

I still had to strengthen the squad to get us through the remaining games and cover us for any injuries or suspensions that might crop up. I had already let Glen Robson go to Durham City, and then I released Mark Sheeran and Fabien Bossy. Unfortunately, Craig James decided that he wanted to go back to Sunderland and that gave us a problem at left wing back, but Clarky solved that problem for us.

I'd heard that Sunderland chairman Bob Murray wouldn't deal with Darlington, but I rang him up and he said he would help us in any way he could – so at the start of February, with the blessing of manager Mick McCarthy, striker Neil Teggart joined us. I knew Bob a little from my days at Sunderland, and he became chairman instead of Tom Cowie just as I left the club. He was a gentleman to deal with.

I rang Boro about striker Danny Graham, but I couldn't sign him when I wanted to in December because he was still a YTS, and I had to wait until March, when he became a professional, before I could. They had also let us have keeper Ross Turnbull, but then he was called up for England Under 19s. We made our circumstances known to England, but they insisted, even though I loaned them videos of games involving opposition players from Mexico, Brazil, Uruguay and Chile. When Ross came back from Qatar, Michael Price had done a very good job, and I couldn't really leave him out, even though Boro wanted me to take Ross back.

Again, we have to thank the Boro for their help.

My problem was that because we had no money, I had to rely on local players. Yes, in my previous spells we'd brought players in from abroad, but we couldn't afford to pay air fares and put them in hotels this time. We don't even know any bed and breakfast places now.

We started to pick up the wins and close the gap on the other clubs. Chris Hughes scored a late winner at home to Rochdale on a dreadfully wet day in which all the other games in the north east were postponed, except ours. It was the only time in nine years I gave Tommo the groundsman a pat on the back! Other people were also to thank, like Richie Tennick, Dave Hardisty and the security people who helped with covers. If we had more people with Richie's workrate, we'd win the Champions League!

Two tough away games followed. The first was at Huddersfield, who were in the promotion places, and had just sold striker Jon Stead to Blackburn Rovers.

I was very confident that we'd win, and I even went on Five Live to say so!

There was a howling gale blowing down the pitch, and I told the lads to keep the ball on the floor. Neil Teggart had just signed on loan from Sunderland, and he played a big part.

Clarky scored from the penalty spot to deservedly put us in the lead in the first half, then Maddo scored one of the luckiest goals you will ever see, a volley from the edge of the box which must have gone a hundred feet in the air, and dropped behind the bemused keeper. It was our first away win of the season.

The atmosphere during the game was fantastic, but if the fans thought Huddersfield was a great day, then Bristol Rovers the following week was even better, probably helped indirectly by the comments and actions of Roddy Collins, which I talk about in the next chapter.

We travelled down the day before, and trained at Bristol City, courtesy of their manager Danny Wilson. The lads were buzzing, and former Darlo player Alan Walsh, who is on the coaching staff at Ashton Gate, said: "That's the best training session I've ever seen." Lee Matthews, who was on loan at Bristol Rovers now, couldn't believe it either.

We had an excellent win at Rovers, all the goals coming in the second half. Lids opened the scoring with a volley from the corner of the box that many people called the goal of the season, and we carved them open after that, with Teggs again doing well.

When Baz scored his second goal and our third of the game to complete a 3-0 win, we were actually out of the bottom two on goal difference.

The backroom staff at Rovers were excellent, and were very helpful. However, when they were in our dressing room before the game, they fell for the team and set pieces I'd left on our notice board, because I knew they would report back. The team and tactics were completely different.

When Lee Matthews went into the Rovers team meeting, he knew that we'd done them after seeing us train the night before.

So that was three successive wins, and a midweek home game against Northampton coming up.

However, we just couldn't get the ball in the back of the net in the first half, and we missed chance after chance. We took the lead with a fluke own goal just after half time, when their keeper drove the ball into his own net off the backside of one of his own defenders. But we couldn't hold on to it, and we had Clarky sent off for deliberate handball giving away a penalty, and Northampton eventually won 2-1.

The other results on the night went against us, and we were back in the bottom two again, with Carlisle showing plenty of signs of life below us. It was going to be close.

We had another home game the following Saturday, refereed by Premiership official Dermot Gallagher, against Yeovil. Gallagher dismissed a man from each side, one of their defenders for a dubious professional foul in the first half, and Teggs in the second half for his second bookable offence. It was a cracking game, we led 2-0 at half time, with goals by Baz and Wainy, but we needed a second goal from Wainy, a lovely dribble down the left finishing with a low shot, to finish it.

That sparked off another good run. We drew 1-1 at Bury the following week on a partly frozen pitch, which didn't suit us at all. Baz scored from a few yards to give us the lead and they equalised in the second half through a player who wasn't on the teamsheet at the start of the match! I'd agreed that he could replace another player who was injured in the warm up. Somebody asked me if I'd regretted my decision, but I didn't in the slightest – I would expect other managers to do the same for me.

We were annoyed at the end of the match for a different reason, because Baz had a goal disallowed for a foul on the word of an assistant, even though the referee didn't see anything wrong. Even Bury manager Graham Barrow said there wasn't a foul.

Our next game was at Macclesfield, who were below us in the table, and a big opportunity to open some daylight between us and the bottom two. The administrators gave us permission to travel the night before, and stay in a hotel, because the game was so important for us.

Macclesfield annoyed us when we got there; maybe they were trying to upset us. They wouldn't allow us any complimentary tickets and their manager was disrespectful towards Martin Gray before the game. It got our backs up, and I made a point about it towards the players in our pre-match team talk.

We never looked in any danger of losing, and Craig Russell struck a marvellous winner, a sweet left foot shot, early in the second half. Craig had looked phenomenal in training, and he was hitting the ball with tremendous pace, which he did for the winner. It was another big turning point.

We kept the momentum going in the re-arranged midweek game against Cheltenham, beating them 2-1 with first half goals from TY and Baz, putting us up to fourteenth in the table. We were nearly on the previous page on the Teletext league table!

However, we blew it in the next home game, against Cambridge the following Saturday. Maybe some of the players had also looked at the league table, and thought we were safe. There was a touch of complacency in the air that day, and we let ourselves down badly with some awful mistakes, losing 4-3. We scored two goals in the last ten minutes and nearly equalised, but we wouldn't have deserved it.

Michael Price took the blame for our defeat, but to his credit, tried to put it right the following day by having a session with our goalkeeping coach, Mark Prudhoe, but Hartlepool, who paid Prud, wouldn't allow it to happen. Nevertheless, Pricey picked himself up for our game at top of the table Doncaster.

Now, we were starting to wonder exactly how many points we needed to be safe. When I arrived at the club back in November I hoped that around 43 would be enough, but that was wrong, and then 46 was banded about. But with Carlisle improving all the time, then maybe 50 would be safety. In that case, we would need at least two wins, maybe three, from our last eight matches.

I thought we were on the verge of the first win at Doncaster on a very windy day. It was so windy, that our dugout had to be removed because of safety reasons, although someone suggested that Doncaster had removed it because they didn't have one at our place back in September!

We defended well against the wind, and Pricey only had to save a couple of long range shots. We took the lead when we had the wind at our backs with a shot by Mark Convery, and looked as if we would win the game as we pinned them into their half. But they equalised five minutes from the end.

However, I was delighted with the lads' performance, as I'm sure George Reynolds was – he had made the journey down to watch the game from the directors' box.

Another tough game followed against Torquay, another team chasing promotion, and we drew 1-1 thanks to an early goal from Baz.

But we'd slipped down to 20th, and we would stay in that position after losing on a tight pitch at Boston.

We had plenty of chances to win that game, especially in the opening half. It was just a bad day all round. We had to make a detour to get there because the A1 was blocked slightly upsetting our preparations, and we couldn't put the ball in the net. And to cap it all, the following day I decided to stay at home while my family went on holiday, which, not surprisingly, didn't go down too well.

I'd heard some nasty things about Boston manager Steve Evans, but I had no problems with him. He was as good as gold. When one of his players got injured – he had a nasty gash down his leg – I cradled him because he was in shock.

I was in shock at the end of the game too. The pressure was on again, because we had blown our chances of climbing away from trouble. Carlisle were winning games, and to make matters worse, Macclesfield won at York the following day.

I went to see that game, because I was totally immersed in our relegation fight. I had to be there to see it. Macclesfield deservedly won 2-0, leaving York without a win since January.

Just two more wins, that was all, but we had some tough games coming up against teams chasing promotion.

Mansfield, who I'd also watched against Oxford in midweek, came to our place in a real ding-dong game, decided by a header by Matt from close range. Our lads battled all the way to put us on 43 points.

That was on Easter Saturday, and forty eight hours later, we were at Southend, a good six hour bus journey away. Fortunately, we arranged a deal thanks to Bradley Woods, a big fan of the club, through Easyjet, which enabled us to fly down on the Sunday, and relax before the game.

I thought we were safe at half time. We led 2-0, thanks to a rebound from Danny Graham, and a penalty by Ryan Valentine, although to be fair we were ahead against the run of play.

I told the players at half time not to give away an early goal in the second half, to kill the game. So what happened? We conceded a 46th minute goal, then we had Joey red-carded for a penalty that they scored from, and then they got a late winner.

I really thought we were over the finishing line at half time, and I was very upset afterwards, especially when I heard the other scores. I didn't speak to the players all the way home.

It was now crucial to beat Oxford in our next home game; otherwise we would be dragged back into the middle of the fight. Carlisle kept winning matches and York would surely win another game sometime, although they failed again in midweek.

I explained to the players about the importance of listening and keeping what we were telling them on board, and that they had five days to become men against Oxford United.

Our visitors badly needed the points, because at one point they were top of the table, and they were in the play-off positions, without an away win for three months.

The lads rose to the occasion, and we won 2-0. Ryan scored with a low right foot shot, and Baz got a second after half time. We were now on 49 points, just one short of the safety target.

Our next away game was at Lincoln City, where we had another great following of fans for a tough match against a play-off chasing team. The players were really determined to collect at least one point to guarantee safety, because York and Carlisle would be unable to overtake us.

We slightly changed our formation, and the switch worked well. We hardly allowed Lincoln any chances, and we took the lead from a free kick routine, the same one from which Mark Barnard scored at Middlesbrough against Burnley in the FA Cup way back in 1998. This time, Wainy peeled away from the wall, picked the ball up from Ryan, and scored with a diagonal right foot shot.

Lincoln equalised in the second half, but we held on for a point to spark off celebrations, both on and off the pitch. There were plenty of tears, both of joy and relief, and it was an unbelievable feeling to pick up a point. Carlisle could still level with us on points, but their goal difference was much worse than ours, and we were well out of York's reach. In fact, it was such a massive relief, that I bought all the players a drink on the way home! The journey home was brilliant, with the celebrations in full swing – but I insisted on having my favourite artist, Chris Rea, as the music.

Even though we were mathematically safe, I wanted to finish the home season with a flourish. There was a feel good factor amongst the fans since the signs on the side of the arena had come down, and I wanted the players to put on a show to remember, and give the fans an insight into what they could expect next season.

So what happened? We lost 2-1, and I was so annoyed that I didn't join in the celebrations on the pitch afterwards. In my view, it was another let down for the supporters, another occasion in which the team needed to produce a good performance, but didn't.

But maybe that is too harsh on the players. They had achieved safety with two games to spare, something which appeared well out of reach to some people way back in November.

But you know me. I set high standards, and I hate losing matches, especially in front of our own fans.

The defeat by Swansea allowed several clubs to overtake us, and we went to our last game at Scunthorpe in 21st place, just one above our opponents.

Scunthorpe, managed by my old friend Brian Laws, had avoided relegation the previous week when Carlisle were held at home by Cheltenham, so the losers in our game would be third bottom.

But roared on by over 800 fans from Darlington, we won 1-0, thanks to a header by Baz in the opening minutes. We could have scored more, but we were happy enough with victory. There were some emotional scenes at the end, and I must take this opportunity to thank everybody for the ovation at the end of that game. There was certainly a lump in my throat, because the support of the fans was invaluable both home and away.

Let's face it; it would have been a disaster if the club had gone down. It would have been difficult for everybody concerned to face life in the Nationwide Conference. What would the fans have done? Would the players have stayed? Would I have stayed? Would the club have managed to continue? There was so much uncertainty over the future, but all the time while I was in charge, I felt that we had to keep believing that our problems would be over by the end of May.

The players were magnificent. When you consider that because we were in administration, there was automatically an embargo on the club signing players, plus there was a limit placed by the Football League on the number of players we could have in the squad, which eventually wasn't lifted until the 2004-05 season had started.

And every week in the media there was always a story about the club's finances or the latest happenings off the pitch. To rise above all that and save the club was magnificent.

In fact, the off-the-pitch story needs a chapter of its own. Many managers don't have to worry about the whole club. They have no concerns beyond dealing with the players. No such luxury at Darlington!

18

Blame Brogan; "You love the club, and if you don't go back, you're stupid, daddy."

WHEN I returned from Argentina in April 2003 I was beginning to get frustrated with the company I was working for, and was considering resigning and setting up on my own again.

I had spent months identifying players of potential and reporting back, but was not convinced that those I was working for were matching the standards that I was setting. I felt that they were not using my efforts as effectively as they could have done.

I trust my work ethics and judgement, and when others don't meet them, I get disgruntled. When that happens I'm the worst person in the world to be with. It's perhaps a fault of mine, and I recognise it, but you can't help the way you feel.

But it's funny how destiny takes over. I believe in fate – I always have done.

When I was watching one of my daughters in athletics at Polam School, overlooking Feethams, some chap said to me: "What a pity Feethams is no longer being used."

He was right. The East Stand cost around £2.2m to build and was being left to rack and ruin. And it was even sadder to think that the stadium had been the soul of the town for over a hundred years, yet was turning derelict and had lost its role of bringing people together to enjoy sport.

It was a situation I wanted to address for the sake of the town, and as a challenge for myself. As I left the athletics that day my brain started to whirr.

I made a call to George Reynolds' right hand man Luke Raine, and asked him what the chairman was doing with the stadium. Luke told me he would sell it tomorrow should the opportunity arise.

I spoke to people involved in sport to bounce ideas off them. There was no indoor hockey facility in the town, no full five a side football venue, except to an extent the Dolphin Centre. Yet at Feethams the opportunity was there to provide and develop these things.

I went to meet Brian Johnston from the Cricket Club, which runs the land through a Trust. We had five meetings before he even offered me a cup of tea. When he did, I took it as a sign that I was finally getting somewhere.

The cricket club is in a good setting, and the last thing they wanted was an eyesore on the doorstep.

I decided to grasp the nettle, go and see George and tell him why I wanted

Feethams and develop a sporting set up to include tennis. He asked for £200,000. I told him to forget it, adding that it would cost a fortune to put right, so the figure was far too high.

I said I would give him a six-figure sum – subject to planning permission, and assessing the cost of development. "Deal." he said.

By now it was August and my plans were developing all the time. Indoor cricket was another idea, as it would complement the cricket club.

I consulted Kenny Dalglish, and he liked the idea, and wanted to become involved, though he had bigger ideas, and wanted to develop the facilities beyond the standard I had envisaged.

One possibility was to knock down the West Stand and have a much bigger area. I sought further advice from a mate of mine who was head of sport at Norton School.

Throughout all this it was never on the agenda for me to return to Darlington Football Club, even though I was still in touch with Lisa, the football secretary at the club, and Martin Gray. We chatted, but not in depth. It was simply a case of keeping in touch with old friends.

But perhaps it was already on George's agenda for me to return. Richie Tennick, his cousin, and a tireless worker at the club, has often said to me that George wanted me back. George and I are both strong and determined characters, and while we sometimes didn't see eye to eye, we perhaps had a mutual respect for each other. I certainly didn't always agree with his methods, but even when we were at loggerheads I could see logic in the way he thought.

I had to go to the new stadium a couple of times to check over with George matters to do with the transfer of Feethams to me. It wasn't plain sailing because there was still a feeling of dispute between George and the cricket club.

He felt that the cricket club should not dominate Feethams in the way that it did, and he wasn't the first football club chairman down the years to feel that. My aim was to agree everything with the cricket club then tie up the details with George.

At one point, when he rang me about Feethams, he made a fleeting comment about me coming back to the football club.

I said to him that I had heard that he was interviewing people about taking over from Mick Tait as manager. I said to him that he really ought to tell Mick that he might be on borrowed time.

I pointed out that as we spoke, Mick was on his way with the team for an away game, and it wasn't right that any mention should be made of the possibility of me taking over. In a way a similar situation was developing to that which occurred years earlier before I took over from Jim Platt. It's not my way of doing things, and I was uncomfortable with it.

But things had started to go wrong for Mick, despite three wins and three draws in September that had taken him to within a whisker of the Manager of the Month award.

"You love the club, and if you don't go back, you're stupid, daddy."

Shortly afterwards Lisa rang me and said that George was again going to speak to me about the job. I told her that he would get no response from me while he still had a manager.

Lisa asked me if I would come back. I refused to answer because if what I said had got back to George, it would have influenced the situation. I still felt that as the team had won games earlier in the season, it would go on another winning run, and the matter would drop.

But the chairman didn't ring again. I thought he was up to something by being quiet, and I was worried that there might be a hitch in the Feethams deal.

However, I knew that eventually the call would come, because various people had rung me to tell me that he had mentioned to them the possibility of me returning.

The situation at the club was the cause of much speculation in the local newspapers. All aspects of the club were making news, including the possibility of car boot sales being permitted at the new stadium, the views of George, the views of the council, the business side of the club.

In fact, everything except football. That worried me.

Eventually the Feethams deal was concluded in all detail but the handshake. George invited me to the Reynolds Arena to shake hands on it. He showed me round the ground. I was looking, and at the same time not looking in any detail. I felt very uncomfortable. He showed me everything I had heard about. The carpets (£67,000 worth I had been led to believe), the escalators, solid oak doors, marble floors, catering facilities, the automatic flushing toilets.

I was worried that people might think that he was showing me round because I was going to be the next manager. I just wanted to get out of there. But me being me I couldn't help but point out to him that the changing rooms were not good enough for the players.

When we had done the plans four years earlier, they were going to be a lot better. But to be fair to him, I'm sure that had the money not become tight, the changing rooms would have been the very best. I will stick up for George on that.

I had heard that the finances were very stretched, but ever the raconteur, George had the ability to make everything sound hunky dory.

When I left, I told Lisa to put Mick straight. I was not there to take his job. Throughout my visit I had refused to talk to George about the team or football.

After the team lost 3-1 at home to Bury, a game where some of the fans turned on George, he rang me to say how badly the team had played.

He then turned to the real reason he had rung, and it was George at his persuasive best.

He said he didn't know if he wanted to sell me the stand at Feethams. I pointed out that we had put together a deal and shaken hands on it. He asked me what I wanted it for, and I replied that he knew, because I had already told him.

He said: "But what do you want it for if you are coming back into football?" I said that I wasn't going back into football.

At that point he said that he wanted me to return as manager. I said "No," so he said that he would not sell me the stand. I told him that I wouldn't discuss it further until he told Mick.

Then he said: "So you do want to come back." It was more of a statement than a question.

By then my daughter Brogan had turned the speaker on and was listening in. "I'll make him come back," she said. George heard what she said.

She added: "You love the club and if you don't go back, you're stupid Daddy. You tell me about it every time we go past Feethams." Children see things in black and white. While adults argue and try to make a point, children's minds are not cluttered like that. They say it as it is.

George said that he would tell Mick, and I said that that was his prerogative. I added that if he was not the man for the job, in George's opinion, then fair enough, irrespective of whether I returned.

I put the phone down. Beverley said nothing, but Brogan piped up: "You and your pride," she said. That, from a girl not yet ten years old!

I went to bed with everything whirring round in my head. I was excited about the prospect of going back to the club, but also remembered the bad times. However, the year when we reached Wembley was my best year in football.

The phone went again on the Sunday, and George asked me whether I had been subjected to any more grief from Brogan. I told him that there had been plenty of it.

He stressed that he would tell Mick, and that he must leave the club altogether if a new man came in. But I said that I didn't want him to leave, and would like a role found for him.

George said he didn't feel that Mick had enough discipline to be manager, but then again, he had also said the same about me at one point. George rang me back fifteen minutes later and told me that he had broken the news to Mick, and told him that I was to be asked to replace him.

Still I refused to give a decision. I phoned Mick, told him that I had not made my mind up, but added that if I took the job, he could have the role of running the youth academy.

Dave Cowling, who had that role, was already on his way out of the club anyway. Mick was embarrassed because it looked as if he had made the job available for himself, by getting rid of Dave just the day before. That was not the case.

I decided to go back under certain conditions, which were put in writing. Among the terms was that Mick was to stay, the Feethams deal was to go through. We disagreed about one of two aspects of the deal, some items having been removed that I felt should have been included among the fixtures and fittings. But they were minor details.

Another of the terms was that George was either to stay away from matches, or stay behind the scenes and not go in the directors' box at matches. To his credit he accepted that. His relationship with the town was, for various reasons, at an all time low. Whatever the rights or wrongs of that situation, it was a fact.

But suddenly I was shoulder to shoulder with George again. That was hard for me, and it must have been hard for him too, because he had spent the previous three years hammering me, and I guess I had not been too full of praise for him either!

My dad wasn't too pleased that I had gone back, and mates like Kevin Ratcliffe and Jan Molby were shocked that he had asked me back. After all, they were managers, who had been in directors' rooms after games and had heard what George said about me.

Yet Richie Tennick, a Darlington director as well as George's cousin, told me that George always wanted me to come back. He said that even if the team had been successful without me, George would have wanted me back. Maybe he respected me, because I'm as forthright as he is. We can both be pretty stubborn.

Perhaps he knew how much the club meant to me. George admires loyalty, and knows I am loyal to the club. It was hard to have my photo taken with him when I returned. We held aloft the Darlo scarf, but there was a tension between us, because we were not as close as the smiling picture made us look. There was more than a little hypocrisy about the whole thing. That's why we didn't have a press conference. We both agreed on that.

I was giving up a lot of money to go back, for I was earning far more than I would be paid as manager of the team.

But that didn't matter. All I wanted was for the town to be talking about football again, instead of car boot sales, computer fairs, concerts and councils.

For the first couple of months it was not easy for me. I felt awkward being back at the club, though it felt very different going to work at the arena rather than Feethams.

I was inundated with calls from friends who could not believe that I had gone back considering the circumstances under which I had left a few years beforehand.

I tried to explain that it was to unite the club and the town, but somehow it didn't seem to be a valid reason.

I was lost in body as well as mind. The new surroundings were so strange to me that one day I walked into the broom cupboard!

When we let a 2-0 lead at home to Scunthorpe slip, I was furious that night, but it did me a favour, because that was the point when it really hit me that I was back in the job. I read Scott Thornberry's comments on the Darlo Uncovered website, that those two points could come back to haunt us. That was the sort of Darlington negativity that infuriated me, but for a long time it looked as though it might have been a valid comment, because we were to face an almighty battle before climbing out of the bottom two.

However before then, came the financial problems that we had to face. I knew that they were bad before I returned to the club, but I didn't know how bad.

To George's credit he told me around a fortnight before we went into administration that it was going to happen. He came clean and told me that the Inland Revenue would do it if he didn't do it voluntarily.

I assumed that George had expected crowds at the stadium to be at last the break-even figure of 6,000. He maybe expected the team to have been a lot more successful, perhaps thinking they would be inspired by the stadium.

When he told me how deep the problems were, I didn't deal with it as if I were in shock. That's not the way to respond. I felt that if we could get everything running in as professional a way as possible, then we might come through.

It always takes a while to implement things the way you want. That's why there's never any point in a club in trouble appointing me as manager in March. I don't do the shock treatment thing whereby managers get instantaneous results, but the same problems surface a few weeks later.

Teamwise, I build things gradually, and responded to the administration crisis in the same way.

Just after Christmas the administrator paid us partial wages. Credit to administrator David Field. He explained the situation very clearly, and in return I promised I would do everything in my power to help the club survive.

I said I would cut costs if I had to, but they must leave footballing matters to me. They agreed and never went back on that agreement until the day the Sterling Consortium took over, and the administrator walked out of the door.

One of the reasons we survived was that everybody trusted everybody else to do their job. Throughout that troubled spell the players rallied round magnificently, while David Field quietly went about doing what he had to do. And to be fair to George, he did what he could as well.

I took the decision to offload players, despite not being asked to do so. Mark Sheeran, Fabien Bossy, Glen Robson and Mark Kilty left, while Alan Morgan returned to Blackburn following his loan spell. We were paying for his accommodation, and couldn't afford to.

The same administration team were in place at Carlisle the previous season, and I was told that whatever they asked manager Roddy Collins to do, he did the opposite. There were no such problems with me.

I checked on the rules of administration with my accountant and solicitor, so knew what I was dealing with. They told me that the administrator must pay the wages.

When the Northampton game was postponed, David Field came to me and said that we were in a bad way and needed income. But I had promised the players they would be paid. We were living game to game, and with a game called off (because Northampton were still in the FA Cup), the money had dried up.

But it was a blessing in disguise that Northampton had beaten first division Rotherham, because otherwise we could not have held the fundraising game that proved so important in saving the club.

But there was something I needed to do before preparations were put into full swing. I decided to have the stadium blessed by the church. An unusual step, I know, but the stadium was hollow and soulless.

I have a picture – a caricature drawing of all the Liverpool lads taken from Phil Neal's testimonial – which I hang in my office wherever I go. It adds character and heart to my office. And I felt the stadium needed something similar.

George phoned the church, and they said they would come the following Thursday.

When the vicar arrived I told her that I was embarrassed, because I was not sure that it was the right thing to do. I asked if she could do or say something to make the stadium come alive.

We walked out onto the pitch, and she asked me all sorts of questions. Then she said a prayer and blessed the stadium, saying a wonderful piece about the club and giving us strength. I was quite choked by it – and it's not often that I'm speechless.

When almost 15,000 fans turned up for the charity match, I thought to myself: "Now the place has a soul."

Virtually all the stars came to the charity game, and we had the most amazing day. I didn't know some of the celebrities, like Lee Sharpe for example. But he still came. Even those who couldn't come along for genuine reasons, among them Ally McCoist, apologised. I thanked every one of them.

You hear people say that top football stars are overpaid prima donnas, who don't care about the game. Yet these people played a vital role in saving Darlington Football Club.

I made a point of telling our players that these big names from the game had not come for me, but to keep the Darlington players in a job. I said to them that from that day they must give 100 per cent for the club, in training and matches. If they didn't I said I would forever ram it down their throats that they had failed to respond to the biggest stars in the game.

To be fair to the players, from then until the end of the season their commitment was total.

I expected around 6,000 fans to turn up for the fundraiser, maybe 7,000 tops. But the whole thing snowballed. We sold around 10,000 tickets in advance, and the queues on the day were unbelievable. And they were not all Darlington fans. They had come from everywhere. When I walked around, a lot of them didn't know who I was.

The media were brilliant in promoting it. Chris Kamara built up the game on Sky television, while the Northern Echo, Evening Gazette, Sunday Sun, Radio Cleveland, Magic and TFM were fabulous.

In total, we probably made around £180,000. The administration people were blown away. It solved all our immediate problems. My only regret was that I couldn't field our play-off finals teams of 1996 and 2000 against each other. It wasn't possible for insurance reasons, though some of them did play.

I had a two sets of shirts, one blue and one white, but the problem was that everybody wanted to be on the same team as Kenny Dalglish and Bryan Robson.

All the local businessmen who had paid to play, were given the same treatment as the stars.

I had to tell our lads not to try and make fools out of Kenny or Robbo. I warned them that those two didn't know the meaning of friendly games, and if anybody took the piss, they would get them.

I didn't know whether I was coming or going. The whole day went in a blur. Looking back there are maybe one or two things that I would have done a little differently, but overall it was a wonderful occasion.

Kev Smith was a huge help in sorting things out on the day. As a former Darlington captain he has always been a hero to the fans. That day he was a hero to me too.

What I do remember is Gazza. He stole the show, whether he was standing there with a can of Red Bull and a cigarette, or out on the pitch showing off all his skills. He was high on adrenalin – but not drunk despite rumours to the contrary. Some of the children, mine included, came down to the tunnel and said that Gazza was drinking beer before the game. The word spread like wildfire, but it wasn't true.

He slipped in the tunnel, but anybody could have done that. I was giving the lads a teamtalk, when Gazza burst in, turned to our skipper Neil Maddison, and said: "You, you bastard. You're the one who got me into gambling." Gazza had the broadest grin imaginable on his face, and all the lads started laughing. I gave up, and said to Gazza: "You finish the team talk."

Straight after the game I went home. I was shattered. With all the organisation and my head spinning, it had been the hardest week of my life.

One of the problems we had was that although the pitch was covered in the run up to the event, the covers had become frozen solid. But the stewards, youth team players, and even St John's Ambulance people had helped get the game on by removing the covers. If the covers hadn't been on, there's no way the pitch would have been playable.

Dave Hardisty led the effort. He's a super fan, who will do anything for the club. He'll moan when the team plays badly, and thinks nothing of having a go at directors. But the effort he makes for the club is phenomenal. And whenever the team wins, I'm delighted for him.

In the end we made so much money from the fund-raiser that maybe some fans felt that the club was safe and didn't come to more matches. That didn't wash with me.

I had come back to work with George despite the problems we had in my first spell under him. If I was prepared to do that, then I could expect the fans to turn up in numbers for every game.

After the fundraiser, some of the crowds in the remainder of the season disappointed me. But the day galvanised the players and made them respect the public.

"You love the club, and if you don't go back, you're stupid, daddy."

Amidst it all I respected George for staying away. It must have hurt him to do that because he would have loved it that day. Being with stars such as Gazza and appearing on television was right up George's street. But he was as good as his word. He even congratulated me on attracting a bigger crowd than had come for the opening game at the stadium.

That was typical of the way he had been since I returned to the club. He didn't object to me giving Neil Madison or Craig Liddle new deals, even though he didn't see eye to eye with Maddo. Nor had he minded me lifting the bans that he had imposed on fans.

He did have a go at Lisa once, reducing her to tears. But he later admitted he was wrong and apologised to her. You can't say fairer than that.

By this time the fund raising game had taken place, several clubs were interested in our top scorer Barry Conlon. I was disappointed in both Rushden and Hartlepool, because they made an approach to the administrator. But going by the back door didn't work, because the administrator directed them to me.

Swansea, Northampton, Sheffield Wednesday and Macclesfield came to me first. Macclesfield offered £45,000, Swansea £60,000.

A lot of administrators would have snapped off the hand of the highest bidder, but not ours. They trusted my judgement, and also realised that £60,000 was peanuts if it cost us our league status.

In the end Baz's goals did help keep us in the league, and when he left in the summer on a free transfer to Barnsley, he left with the blessing of everybody at the club.

David Elliott was the tougher of the two administrators, David Field being a more gentle, easygoing person. They made a good double act, and with Sterling in the background willing to take on the club if necessary, I had the feeling that all would be well off the field, as long as we avoided relegation on it.

But I tried not to get too involved with the media, and the council and the host of concerns regarding the future of the club. I did what I could to help raise money and get the team winning, but I avoided the propaganda.

There were a lot of unfavourable headlines about the club's survival chances, and while I knew that the picture was not as bleak as that being painted, I have been in the business long enough to know the power of headlines, even if the story itself is not that bad.

I like people who are happy, upbeat and optimistic, and in that respect I could leave England tomorrow, because this country is so negative in so many ways.

I enjoy seeing people succeed. I want everybody in the world to be a winner. So why is this country so negative?

I always tried to keep the players fully informed, but there was so much doom and gloom in the papers that I began to wonder if the players believed me.

As I have said, in terms of boosting the fund raising game, the media were fabulous. But while the sports pages were upbeat, the news pages began to be filled with doubts about the club's survival prospects. But we did survive. I was right all along.

I always felt that Sterling would step in, because I could see the value of the stadium. I knew that the Sterling people were shrewd businessmen, and wouldn't let such an asset go to the wall.

The land that the stadium is built on is worth a fortune. That was the bigger picture, and commonsense told me that we would be all right.

From a visual point of view the stadium is striking, and you have to give George credit for that. The entrance is visible from air, road and rail. As soon as you come over the brow of the hill of the A66, or pull into Darlington station you can see the entrance to the stadium. It was too impressive to have all been built for nothing.

Somebody was going to claim it, and I always fancied that somebody to be Sterling. I didn't believe the Ted Forster thing. In fact I didn't believe he even existed, though it turned out that he did, though without the money he appeared to have. His claims, mainly on the Internet, that he would fly over from his home in Greece and take over the club, turned out to be empty promises.

His supposed bid was a distraction we could have done without. So was talk of the Irish takeover with Roddy Collins, the former Carlisle manager, getting my job.

The Irish had real money and came over to see the administrator.

It always struck me as strange that when the asking price was £12 million they seemed interested, then when it dropped to £6 million they pulled out.

While the whole circus was going on, the prospect of me losing my job did not worry me, but the prospect of the distraction costing us games did.

What really annoyed me was that Roddy said that within a fortnight he would be manager. When the club was in crisis, that was out of order. Kenny Dalglish, Sir Alex Ferguson, or Gerard Houllier would not have said a thing like that. When Sir Bobby Robson got the Newcastle job he didn't shout if from the rooftops. He just went in quietly and got on with it.

From when I arrived at the club the previous October, not one player had asked for a transfer. When news broke of the possibility of Roddy Collins taking my job, all the players said that they were leaving. Roddy turned up at our game at Bristol Rovers, but the lads stayed focussed and won 3-0.

When he was at Carlisle, Roddy, so I'm led to believe, was interested in signing Baz. Because of that and the Irish connection Roddy phoned Baz to say he might be coming to Darlington.

Baz could have kept that to himself, but he didn't. He came and told me. That was the point when I knew for certain that I was working with good, honest lads.

I had always been honest with Baz, telling him when clubs were interested in him. And he repaid me by being truthful with me. The club and his teammates mattered to Baz and he earned my full respect for that.

Had Roddy come in, Baz would probably have been handed a big contract, but he did right by everybody else rather than himself. That's priceless.

But while I was fully aware of the situation, I never took it home with me. Even so, Brogan got wind of it.

"Who's Roddy Collins?" she said dismissively. "He doesn't love Darlo. He can't have Daddy's job." It was the definitive answer. You can't argue with Brogan.

In the whole of this troubled time, the fans' forum we held was as uplifting as the fundraising game. When that hardcore of fans gather in a room, you can tell they care.

There were questions of genuine concern only, no stupid comments. And these people listen to the answers because they care.

I was as honest as I could be with them. And I asked them questions too. I will always try and involve them. I wanted them to choose which strip we would wear the following season.

It is their club, and they deserve their say on how it is run. A say that had been denied them for too long under the previous regime.

It was at this forum that I told the supporters that I was owed a lot of money by the club, and therefore, in theory, had a say in its destiny. I would not call the debt in, but it would give me voting power.

One fan asked, in the question and answer session, whether I knew anything that was not common knowledge about whether the club could be saved.

I felt I had to reveal that I had documents that were, as far as I had been told, legally binding, and if I pursued it through the right channels I would, in theory, be the biggest creditor.

That was the £118,000 previously mentioned, a figure that had escalated hugely because of the compound interest. Knowing the subject might arise, I had checked with my solicitor Bill O'Hanlon, that the documents were legal and correct. He assured me that they were.

I knew that it was critical that the morale of the fans stayed high. They cared passionately about the club. I've sometimes criticised the local community for the lack of support at matches. Sometimes the crowd figures get me down.

But what has always filled me with admiration, and determination to succeed, is the tremendous support of the hard core of fans. They are magnificent. I revealed the facts because I wanted the fans to have something to hang onto, an assurance that the club would survive.

But no sooner were the words about being owed a fortune out of my mouth, than young Northern Echo reporter Sam Strangeways was making her way out of the room, mobile phone in hand, and a smile as wide as the Tyne Tunnel, across her face.

She had an exclusive. She never thought for a second before the meeting that she would get a headline like that the following day.

Within seconds of her leaving, I too was making a call to her editor, Peter Barron, informing him that he would be getting a call from Sam.

He was not available, but I left a clear message, saying that while the story was true, I had divulged it for the benefit of the loyal fans who were fighting to save the club, and didn't want a headline making me look ridiculous.

But the editor put his newspaper first and the headline read: "Hodgson owed millions."

Sam returned to the forum, and spoke to me afterwards.

She said to me that she had to use the story, because if she didn't, the Evening Gazette would, as Gazette sportswriter Andrew Wilkinson was present at the meeting.

Sam didn't see that Andrew was standing just a few feet away, and heard what she said. I turned to him, and asked tongue in cheek: "Is that right, would you use it?" He said: "Not if you didn't want me to, Hodgy." That probably made Sam feel rather small.

The truth is that he – and Ray Simpson – had known about it for some time, because we had discussed it when writing this book. I suppose that all sorts of 'exclusives' were revealed in meetings between the three of us. But I trust them, and know they wouldn't reveal anything in the Gazette or Radio Cleveland, that was specifically for this book.

But I think my revelation in the forum did galvanise the fans. There was a feelgood factor about the club again, and it was evident in the way that the collection buckets rattled in the ensuing weeks, and in the enthusiasm with which the players, fans and myself engaged in the bag packing sessions at Marks and Spencer and events in the Cornmill Centre in Darlington.

I was happy to attend these fund raising sessions, because I wanted to be in the thick of things.

It's as if your house in burning down, and you stand there thanking others for throwing buckets of water on it. I wanted to be active in saving the club, and not just be the figure that handed out the plaudits to others.

The players felt the same, and it was at that time that it was so obvious that Neil Maddison was a genuine fan of the club, as well as a key member of the squad – and at that time team captain.

Out of all the players, Maddo came to the forefront. The affection he held for the club was obvious.

With him living in the town rumours sometimes circulated of him not being committed to the club. Stories of which pubs and bookmakers he had visited were forever doing the rounds.

But I can reveal that nobody wears the Darlington shirt with more pride. He was at the cutting edge of the efforts to save the club.

As regards me having any other inside knowledge, I can assure you that I didn't. I had worked out for myself that the Sterling Consortium, in the event of them not being paid what they were owed, would take on the stadium.

That's what happened. They wanted to stamp their own identity on it, and that meant the name 'Reynolds Arena' would have to change.

I followed George into the ground the day the lettering was being removed from the side of the stadium.

When he built it, I never imagined that I would be invited in. Yet here I was driving in behind him. Despite all the problems and worry he had put me through, and despite us having a different outlook on life, I felt for him enormously that day.

He had put so much into the stadium, in time and energy as well as finance, that it was impossible not to feel for him as the lettering came down. It must have hurt him, but he didn't bat an eyelid.

Yet while the stadium had changed hands, and tangible signs of George Reynolds were being removed, nobody can erase him from the history of the club. He is probably the biggest talking point in the club's history, all 121 years of it. Nobody will ever surpass the amount of publicity he generated, good and bad.

Just like Jack Walker at Blackburn, and Sir John Hall at Newcastle, George Reynolds changed the face of Darlington Football Club.

For all the admirable owners and chairmen of the club down the years, such as Ken Warne, Alan Noble and John Brockbank, who also put time, money and enthusiasm into the club, George is the one who will leave the biggest mark in history.

Just about everyone involved in football throughout the country knows about him, and talks about him. And what's more they will continue to do so, when we are both long gone. He had a massive impact on the club.

But life went on – and unfortunately so did administration. Some of the players we had earmarked to come in slipped through our fingers, among them Dean Windass, Craig Ireland and Allan Smart.

I had no real idea what the budget would be, which made my job difficult. The fans expected a new dawn, and we were determined to deliver it, but our hands were tied while the financial situation was unravelling.

We thought that we would be out of administration on July 27. But the date came and went. Then I was told it would probably be August. The month slipped by without the problems being resolved, and we had started the new campaign without all the players I wanted. Rob Friend, Greg Pearson, Tom Brighton and Lee Matthews were others who slipped through the net. I understood the circumstances and had to get on with it.

But one thing I'd learned from my experience at the club, was that the defence must be strong so that we were hard to beat. In that respect the arrival of Curtis Fleming was a huge bonus. The way that he speaks, trains and lifts those around him, made him exactly the sort of player I wanted.

Like Ian Clark, Neil Maddison, Craig Liddle and Craig Russell, he is an example I can use to the younger players.

Off the field however, progress was good. I was pleased to see Bob Gorrill, an old friend from Sheffield Wednesday, come in as commercial manager. He has a wealth of experience in the role, from his time at several clubs.

I wanted to have someone established in the commercial world of football, and he is just such a person. I knew how vital commercial income would be, as the new regime, led by chief executive Andy Battison, began the business of transforming the image of the club.

The whole club had to be structured with the right personnel in the right posts. After all, there was no point in saving the club for it to fall back into the same rut.

These people will get better and better as time passes and they gain experience in the ways of football. They come from all walks of life, and are quickly adapting to their roles in football – which is very different from other businesses.

A happy public makes for a happy club. We must serve the public right, on and off the pitch. That's one of the reasons we agreed to have hooped shirts – it was by public demand. I talked to four companies and was delighted to choose Xara.

I'm now very pleased with the off the field standards being set. Now I have to make the football side match it.

But while this hectic life, with new challenges every day – sometimes several a day – continues, I occasionally take a glance back to remind myself of where we came from.

I never thought for a second, when I first walked into Feethams, that I would now come to work each day by driving into a huge car park, walk into a plush foyer, and look out over a green, even pitch.

I remember when I first arrived at Feethams with Jim Platt in the summer of 1995. We had a tiny car park, with the directors names' written on a piece of fencing a few inches high, in front of cramped parking spaces.

We had two atrocious changing rooms, even by the standards of the day. I walked down the tunnel with Jim, and there was Tommo the groundsman.

He was standing holding a hosepipe about one inch wide, from which splashed a hopelessly inadequate trickle of water onto a pitch that was yellow and uneven.

Now he has state of the art equipment and works on a green sward that would be the envy of the fussiest of groundsmen, gardeners and greenkeepers. Yet still he moans.

Sometimes I find that reassuring. It's good to know that after nine and a half years of bewildering change at this amazing club, that there is one constant factor.